Y0-BCY-759

Varieties of Activist Experience

Series Note

Governance, Conflict, and Civic Action Series

Series Editors: David N. Gellner, Krishna Hachhethu, Siri Hettige, Joanna Pfaff-Czarnecka

Volume 1: *Local Democracy in South Asia: Microprocesses of Democratization in Nepal and its Neighbours*, eds David N. Gellner and Krishna Hachhethu

Volume 2: *Ethnic Activism and Civil Society in South Asia*, ed. David N. Gellner

Volume 3: *Varieties of Activist Experience: Civil Society in South Asia*, ed. David N. Gellner

Volumes in Preparation and Planned

Volume 4: *The Politics of Belonging in the Himalayas: Local Attachments and Boundary Dynamics*, eds J. Pfaff-Czarnecka and G. Toffin

Volume 5: *Governance and Development: The Postcolonial State and the Development Process in Sri Lanka and its Neighbours*, ed. Siri Hettige

This volume has been produced with the financial assistance of the European Union (EU). The contents of the book are the sole responsibility of the respective authors and can under no circumstances be regarded as reflecting the position of the EU.

The Asia-Link Programme was launched at the beginning of 2002 as an initiative by the EU to foster regional and multilateral networking between higher education institutions in EU Member States and South Asia, South-East Asia and China. This five-year programme, which has a total budget of €42.8 million, aims to provide support to European and Asian higher education institutions in the areas of human resource development, curriculum development, and institutional and systems development.

Varieties of Activist Experience: Civil Society in South Asia

GOVERNANCE, CONFLICT, AND CIVIC ACTION: VOLUME 3

Edited by
David N. Gellner

www.sagepublications.com
Los Angeles • London • New Delhi • Singapore • Washington DC

First published in 2010 by

SAGE Publications India Pvt Ltd
B1/I-1 Mohan Cooperative Industrial Area
Mathura Road, New Delhi 110 044, India
www.sagepub.in

SAGE Publications Inc
2455 Teller Road
Thousand Oaks, California 91320, USA

SAGE Publications Ltd
1 Oliver's Yard, 55 City Road
London EC1Y 1SP, United Kingdom

SAGE Publications Asia-Pacific Pte Ltd
33 Pekin Street
#02-01 Far East Square
Singapore 048763

Published by Vivek Mehra for SAGE Publications India Pvt Ltd, Phototypeset in 10/12pt Sabon by Star Compugraphics Private Limited, Delhi and printed at Chaman Enterprises, New Delhi.

Library of Congress Cataloging-in-Publication Data

Varieties of activist experience : civil society in South Asia/edited by David N. Gellner
p. cm.—(Governance, conflict, and civic action; v. 3)
Includes bibliographical references and index.
1. Political participation—South Asia. 2. Civil society—South Asia. 3. Political activists—South Asia. 4. South Asia—Politics and government.I. Gellner, David N.
JQ98. A91V37 322.40954—dc22 2010 2010017019

ISBN: 978-81-321-0450-6 (HB)

The SAGE Team: Rekha Natarajan, Shweta Tewari, Nand Kumar Jha and Trinankur Banerjee

Cover caption: Sit-in programme (dharna) held on 11 June 2008 in Naya Baneshwor Chowk by the Citizens' Movement for Democracy and Peace (CMDP) two weeks after the Constituent Assembly had voted for the abolition of the monarchy in Nepal. The sit-in called for a federal democratic republic and protested against the government's decision to allow former king Gyanendra Shah to continue to live in Nagarjun palace after leaving the main palace at Narayan Hiti.

Photo courtesy of Celayne Heaton Shrestha.

Contents

Development

Preface

This book is the third in a series on governance, conflict, and civic action in South Asia. The series grows out of the collaborations—and in particular the international workshops—made possible by the European Commission's support, 2004–07, under its Asia-Link Programme, for the MIDEA project (see www.uni-bielefeld.de/midea). Originally conceptualized and subsequently led by Joanna Pfaff-Czarnecka, MIDEA stands for 'The (Micro)Politics of Democratisation: European-South Asian Exchanges on Governance, Conflict and Civic Action'. Based in four institutions—*(a)* Institute for World Society Studies (IW), Bielefeld University, Germany, *(b)* the Centre for Nepal and Asian Studies (CNAS), Tribhuvan University, Kathmandu, Nepal, *(c)* the Social Policy Analysis and Research Centre (SPARC), University of Colombo, Sri Lanka, and *(d)* the Institute for Social and Cultural Anthropology (ISCA), University of Oxford, UK—the project brought together anthropologists, sociologists, political scientists, development specialists, and others from South Asia and Europe (not merely from the four participating institutions and countries) for a series of workshops, training sessions, and conferences.

A conference held at the Maison Française Oxford in June 2005 addressed in particular the 'civic action' part of MIDEA's brief. It grew from my long-standing interest and several years' research on activism in Nepal, and sought to draw in a wide variety of scholars from different countries to address similar questions and focus on types of activists and their relations to civil society in diverse South Asian countries (mainly Nepal and Sri Lanka, but with several contributions on India, and one on Bangladesh). There were a large number of papers on variants of ethnic activism, and these comprised the second volume of the series. There were also papers on social, developmental, political, and feminist activists, some of which are collected here. Apart from the paper sessions, those attending had the opportunity to view Helene Klodawsky's film *No More Tears Sister*, about the life and assassination of Dr Rajani Thiranagama, followed by a discussion with Sharika Thiranagama, who portrays her mother in the film. There was also a session in which Bela Bhatia and Om Gurung, both of whom combine activism and research, presented their reactions to the papers. In addition to the core EU Asia-Link funding, the conference benefitted from the support of the British Academy, the Leverhulme Trust, the Sub-Faculty of South and Inner Asian Studies (University of Oxford), and the British Embassy in Kathmandu; all these bodies have my belated but nonetheless heartfelt gratitude. I have an additional and substantial debt to record to the Leverhulme Trust, which entrusted me with one of their three-year Senior Research Fellowships, 2002–05, on the subject of activism in Nepal. I would also like to thank Nadine Beckmann and Anastasia Norton-Piliavsky, both doctoral students at ISCA, as well as Uma Pradhan and Kate Atherton for help in editing the contributions to this volume.

August 2009

David N. Gellner
Oxford

Chapter 1

Introduction

Making Civil Society in South Asia

DAVID N. GELLNER

WHAT IS THE THIRD SECTOR?

Civil society and the 'Third Sector' are conceptualizations that rather suddenly achieved prominence at the end of the 1980s and in the early 1990s—as political slogans, as ideals, and as descriptions of a particular kind of non-state action and associationalism.[1,2] The empirical realities that these terms attempted to capture were not completely new, of course. Associations for change did exist in previous eras: one thinks of E.P. Thompson's eighteenth-century working men's corresponding societies or the anti-slavery movement of the nineteenth century (Keck and Sikkink, 1998: 41–51). However, despite such antecedents, it cannot be doubted that an efflorescence of the 'Third Sector' has occurred in recent decades—an increase in its scope, depth, intensity, and international reach. In 2006 the British government recognized this trend by creating, for the first time, an Office of the Third Sector within the Cabinet Office with a junior minister at its head. Similar steps were taken in other countries. The increasing importance of the Third Sector has been measured in various ways, most notably by the Johns Hopkins' study that purports to show that it accounts for the following proportions of total paid employment: in the Netherlands 12.6 per cent, Ireland 11.5 per cent, Belgium 10.5 per cent, the USA 7.8 per cent, the UK 6.2 per cent, France and Germany 4.9 per cent, and so on.[3]

The Third Sector is defined negatively, that is, through its relation to what it is not: Third Sector institutions belong neither to the state nor to the market. In North America this kind of activity is often referred to as the not-for-profit sector, in Britain as the 'voluntary' sector. Those countries with particularly large Third Sectors tend to be those where the state sub-contracts many parts of the health service to voluntary (often, at least nominally, religious) organizations.

For key players in the Third Sector today, global links are crucial, as many scholars have emphasized. For example, Keck and Sikkink (1998: Chapter 3) show how international links enabled human rights activists in Latin America to withstand the pressure of authoritarian regimes and to apply pressure themselves that forced these regimes to liberalize, a process they diagram as a "boomerang pattern" (Keck and Sikkink, 1998: 13). In their words, "international contacts amplify voices to which domestic governments are deaf, while the local work of target country activists legitimizes efforts of activists abroad" (ibid.: 200). Through these links a kind of global civil society has emerged. Despite some who are sceptical of the terminology used,[4] there is a nascent reality—a form of social organization—across the world that social scientists should recognize and attempt to understand. As Fisher writes in Chapter 10, this emergent global reality should be thought of, and is thought of by those who are creating it, as a kind of 'imagined community'.

This volume brings together studies of activists working in the fields of politics, development, and environmental protection. An already published companion volume (Gellner, 2009a, the second in this series) collects the papers on various forms of ethnic activism in South Asia. In the invitation to the conference on which these two volumes were based, contributors were asked to consider whether activists were beginning to form a new class, whether there are particular patterns of recruitment to activist circles, and whether there were recognizable types of activists or stages of activist development. Some conclusions from my own research on these topics in Nepal, carried out in collaboration with Mrigendra Karki and Krishna Hachhethu, are given in Chapter 6.

An immediate question this approach must face is: Do 'civil society' and 'activism' in fact designate the same social reality? This is a crucial issue facing both scholars and practitioners (and perhaps particularly those who aspire to combine scholarship with practice), though each group may phrase the question differently. Radical activists often claim that the terms 'civil society' and 'the Third Sector' are the language of activists who have abandoned social movements, and that non-governmental organizations (NGOs) are just denatured political movements. From this point of view, the assumption that there are three sectors of society—politics, the market, and voluntary action defined by different goals and different motivations—is an excuse to remove radical alternatives. In this connection one thinks of Medha Patkar, the leader of opposition to the Narmada dam, and her mistrust of international funding.[5] The common accusation, as described by Heaton Shrestha in Chapter 8, is that well-paid employees of internationally funded NGOs are just 'doing a job' and cannot be considered activists. Indeed, 'activist' is a highly appraisive term, so that one person's activist is another's self-interested glory-hunter: some claims to be an activist are scornfully regarded by others working in the same field as transparent attempts to dignify self-enrichment.[6]

The charge that NGOs are—to use the language of social science—a routinized form of social movement certainly has some traction. This is especially so where Third Sector organizations are well established and do represent a career, and especially when there are evident links (through kinship, patron–client networks, and so on) with politics and making money, as in Bangladesh. Lewis (Chapter 7) describes how certain other Bangladeshi NGOs seek to position themselves as *not* routinized, as still maintaining social movement ideals of commitment and personal austerity that have been abandoned by their larger and better-known colleagues. As Shneiderman's account of leftist parties in Nepal shows (Chapter 3), the same kind of routinization, and the same kinds of contest over the embodiment of radical values, occur between and within straightforwardly political movements as well.

From an observer's point of view, civil society and activism do belong to the same social field, despite the fact that those who are happy with one kind of terminology may reject the other. The evaluative load and essentially contested nature of many of the key terms is part of what constitutes the field (as Fisher also argues in Chapter 10), with the result that many activists actively deny that they have anything in common with some other practitioners.

Standing back from these debates, however, there is also a deeper response to these charges, and especially to the charge that those working in NGOs, that is, in the Third Sector, have somehow 'sold out'. This more sociological response is that *(a)* working in the Third Sector does not suddenly transform people into saints: in other words, the *ideals* of the Third Sector are not shown to be false by the *practice* of NGOs, any more than the ideals of democracy are invalidated by corrupt politicians; and *(b)* the rise of the Third Sector is precisely connected to disillusionment with politics: disillusionment both with the promises of radical leftist movements to bring about an end to poverty and inequality, *and* with the promise that a system of political parties competing at the ballot box and alternating in power will do better. Standing—at least in principle—beyond the politics of capturing votes and powerful positions, while simultaneously not working purely for profit, Third Sector organizations are at the top of their own hierarchy of values. Disillusionment with conventional political parties also generates movements and activists who attempt to stand against or outside normal politics, while yet competing in elections, as described for Sri Lanka by Hettige (Chapter 4).

Comparison with a more 'classic' topic of anthropological discussion may make this clash of values clear. Some years ago Richard Burghart wrote an insightful paper on approaches to the caste system. He pointed out that it was a mistake to think that there must be a single dominant scale of values within caste societies, an assumption at work most obviously in Dumont's theory, but also shared by most of his critics. Burghart outlined historical and ethnographic evidence suggesting that there were at least three competing and coexisting models of Hindu hierarchy, each based on different and to some degree incommensurable criteria. In one the Brahman was indeed top, as Dumont had assumed; in the next the King was the first in the prestige ranking of the kingdom, as in theories taking their inspiration from Hocart; and in a third, which he was able to appreciate thanks to his own ethnographic research with them, ascetics have the highest position (Burghart, 1978). In exactly the same way, it is possible for politicians, businessmen, and those working in the Third Sector each to imagine that *they* best embody shared modern values of development, equality, and working for the common good, whereas the *others* are corrupt and self-interested.

These mutual evaluations are part and parcel both of relations between actors in different sectors and of the meaning of terms like 'activist', as noted earlier. Contests over ownership of key symbolic events of past historical struggle are shot through with claims to be the true activists and the true heirs to the activists of the past. The term 'activist' often has an oppositional semantic load, whether in English or in the terms used to translate it in various South Asian languages. These contests of value deserve to be studied in as impartial a manner as possible. The definitions adopted at the start of the study should not be skewed by the in-built evaluations of one or other point of view, but rather should seek to be as inclusive as possible (Gellner and Karki, Chapter 6).

Tackling these questions about the Third Sector through a focus on activists has certain advantages. It is true that 'activist' suffers from the same definitional instability as 'NGO'. There are many types of activists, following a wide variety of agendas. Looking directly at the activists who enact them enables one to appreciate the extent to which Third Sector organizations are processes, transforming over time and adapting to new circumstances, as Fisher emphasizes in Chapter 10.

STATES, THE THIRD SECTOR, AND THE MESSINESS OF EVERYDAY LIFE

The notion of 'three sectors' is, thus, an ideal type, but this does not mean it is 'just a model'. The distinction between the sectors is built into the institutions and practices of 'modernity'. It both structures much activity and, as a crucial organizing idea to be found everywhere in today's interconnected world, is subject to negotiation and contestation. The ways in which state law and institutional relationships are understood and develop vary considerably by country. As Lewis notes, in a recent publication,

> As an 'ideal type', the three sector model is at odds with the messy realities of political, personal organisational life, where neat separations across the boundary are impossible, and where context and history create very different sets of structures and incentives from place to place. But, at another level, people may experience the boundary as very real, where the 'rules of the game'—in terms of cultures, norms and laws—vary between sectors. (Lewis, 2008: 138–9)

It is the job of anthropologists to study just how these boundaries work in practice and where, when, and in whose interests different definitions are mobilized; one important way, advocated by many of the contributors here, is to look at the way particular individuals move across these boundaries, from state to Third Sector or from parties to Third Sector and back again. It should go without saying that scholars of these processes will be aware that in a broader sense politics are everywhere—in offices, homes, everyday interactions, etc.—and not just in 'the political' narrowly defined.[7]

States have a strong interest in regulating how civil society operates. More authoritarian regimes control who gets registration, and they limit the numbers and kinds of organizations that can operate openly and freely. The coming of more liberal regimes is marked by greater freedom to organize and greater freedom to protest, as well by more indirect methods of regulation. One should avoid the assumption that the state is always 'the enemy', that its role is always merely to resist the changes fought for by activists. In some cases, it is the state that is the agent of change, as described by Strulik in Chapter 5. She records men regretting the weakness of the state and wishing it had the power to force them to send their womenfolk into the public sphere, so that no blame would fall on them for allowing this shocking breach of the norms of appropriate female behaviour.

A strong developmentalist ideology is common to all the contexts examined in this book. This comes out most clearly in de Sales' description in Chapter 2 of the rural communist, Barman Budha, and his discovery of Rahul Sankrityayan's book *From Volga to Ganga.* Its simple evolutionist view of history is mapped directly on to his personal experience of backwardness and the communist promise of a better future. Even today the Nepali Maoists' vision of development is expressed in urban styles of living: for example, in the name of the martyrs of the People's War, memorial parks and flower gardens are incongruously plonked down in the middle of the Nepalese hills where associations are more easily made with the wandering spirits of dead souls and animal sacrifices to ancient mountain gods (de Sales, 2003: 352). Whether an explicitly Marxist framework is accepted or not, the evolutionary schema that makes rural places exemplary of backwardness and superstition, and seeks to transform them with literacy, self-improvement, urbanism, and science, appears to activists and intellectuals as self-evident and clearly warranted by the facts of history and their own experience.[8]

Activists hold the state to account, forcing it to live up to its own commitments (Guneratne, Chapter 9). They maintain the links between urban centres and rural flashpoints, and keep issues in the international eye. As such, activists and their organizations take on some of the mediating functions that have been seen by some as the key role of political parties (Lawson, 1980). They also, perforce, must adapt to the particular legal and state regime within which they work.

In analysing flows of activist ideas in South Asia, it is as well to bear in mind the distinction outlined by Fisher (Chapter 10) between transnational and global links. Both kinds of activist links are also in competition and (sometimes) in dialogue with the international links maintained by states. All the different countries of South Asia have links with each other and particularly with India; but these transnational links and flows of ideas are not always the same as, or 'in synch with', global trends. To some degree, India, being so large and relatively less dependent on outside funding, is more able to resist global trends (with regard to indigenous rights, for example). The fact that no effective all-India tribal organization has yet been created reflects not only the great size of the country, but its relative disengagement from the global indigenous rights movement.[9]

State schemes, different as they are, share in common the fact that they can never capture the full complexity, ambiguity, and nuance of everyday life and social interaction. James Scott (1998) has analysed this influentially as the state's inability to capture local knowledge systems, which he names *metis*. Tania Li (2005), in a thoughtful and appreciative critique, points out that his state-centric vision has failed to capture the diverse ways in which state schemes may be adapted; nor does Scott appreciate the way in which NGOs and other denizens of the Third Sector share the improving agenda of the state, while complicating its delivery. State or NGO attempts to incorporate 'indigenous knowledge' invariably end up systematizing it, creating something new that still has to be 'worked around' by those involved in implementing it. In the Indonesian cases cited by Li, peasants were not interested in supposedly traditional biodiversity heavily pushed by NGOs, and preferred monoculture oriented to the market combined with wage labour.

In a very different context a similar distinction—this time between the categories in which politics are conducted and, on the other hand, the language of the street or the pub—has been advocated by Gerd Baumann, when he distinguishes the *official discourse* from the *demotic discourse* in the London suburb of Southall (Baumann, 1996). Southall possesses five 'communities' (Baumann keeps the term in italics throughout the book to make the point that it is both a problematic and a 'native' term of art): Hindu, Muslim, Sikh, White, and Afro-Caribbean. Local politics and resource allocation are carried out on the presumption of equity between these five. But 'everyone knows' that many Southall people do not fit easily or unambiguously within one of these five. Moreover, 'everyone knows' that there are numerous cross-cutting links (of language, culture, kinship, origin, and so on) that tie people to members of other 'communities'. Thus, everyone in Southall is bilingual in both discourses, the official discourse, which takes just these five communities as constituting the borough, and the demotic discourse, which recognizes that things are a lot more complicated. It is not a question of one discourse being right and the other wrong. Both are necessary. Government and politics must act through simplified schemes and can never capture the full complexity of 'ordinary life'. Much activist campaigning centres on the attempt to have the state recognize some new category within the official discourse. Very often, NGOs operate as mediators between ordinary people and the state—both in terms of enabling this bilingualism to operate and in terms of negotiating how the official discourse will operate.

Activists, in short, play an important role in moulding the conceptual framework of modernity, in enacting and creating the new world their plans describe.[10] Latour (1991) refers to the conceptual distinctions presupposed by modernity (between subject and object, between self and other, between religion, politics, economy, and so on) as 'the modern constitution' and calls the process by which society is shaped to fit these distinctions as 'the work of purification'. He himself does not believe that we actually live according to this 'modern constitution'—hence the claim encapsulated in the title of his book. But his process of 'purification' can actually be observed in the ethnographic accounts presented here. Modernity may indeed never be achieved, so that modernization as a slogan must be reworked in every generation. But that modernity, however conceived, was and is a real goal for the activists described in this book, that they are willing to devote their lives, and sometimes to sacrifice their lives, to achieve it, cannot be doubted.

VARIETIES OF ACTIVISM IN SOUTH ASIA

As noted in the preface, this volume grew from a network that linked primarily Nepal, Sri Lanka, Germany, and the UK, though scholars working on and in other South Asian countries were also included in all the international workshops held as part of the project. As a consequence of this history, we have the temerity to publish here a collection of case studies about South Asia with only a single chapter based on India. (In the companion volume on ethnic forms of activism there are four and a half chapters out of 10 on India.) Disrupting the easy equivalence too often made between India and South Asia was indeed a subsidiary aim of the MIDEA project. That the great diversity of South Asia is somehow more properly captured by focusing on India alone is an unspoken assumption of too many otherwise excellent publications. Willem van Schendel has rightly criticized the 'methodological nationalism' of much South Asianist scholarship and the "partitioned academy" that is its consequence, and he recommends a focus on borderlands as an antidote (van Schendel, 2005: 366). This volume attempts to overcome South Asia's partitioned academy by including diverse examples mostly from what are often considered marginal South Asian states, but which, in their own way, are just as exemplary of important contemporary processes.

It is true, as already noted, that the state context, and particularly the legal and political regimes under which activists operate, makes a significant difference to what is possible and to the forms and ideals that animate particular activist organizations and movements. At the same time, there are sufficient cultural and historical commonalities for processes apparent in one South Asian country to have their counterparts in others. The relationship between communism and ethnic (and particularly 'tribal') identity, for example, is common ground between India and Nepal: the Naxalites and the Nepali Maoists have both established their 'base areas' in tribal districts.[11] Dalit movements face similar obstacles throughout the region, though it may well be that there are even greater difficulties having the discrimination they face recognized in Pakistan and Sri Lanka than in other parts of the subcontinent.

There are further commonalities which have their origin in the fact that, as discussed earlier, all the countries of South Asia are grappling with the gradual institutionalization of 'modernity'. The work of modernization is indeed never finished. But all the societies of South Asia have attempted, to different degrees, to institutionalize a separation between political, economic, and other (whether religious, cultural, or otherwise) organizations. Many of the organizations that have appeared have built upon pre-modern ascriptive identities; many have in effect created new identities as they have done so. The case studies focusing on these specific kinds of activism were placed in a different volume, simply for ease of consultation. Political activism should, I believe, be seen as a contribution to civil society, for all that the political sphere—insofar as it concerns the state—is separate from it. There is, inevitably, an overlap of political activists and other kinds. Arbitrarily excluding members of political parties from a consideration of the activist field would (as discussed in Chapter 6) leave a curious gap in any account that starts from people and processes on the ground, and it would ignore the extent to which people frequently cross and re-cross the modernist boundaries between politics and, say, social work.

In short, for the sake of exposition, modernist and official discourse distinctions between political, ethnic, and developmental types of activism have been accepted and used. But they are to be understood in a provisional and 'bracketed' way.[12] Our case studies show how, at the everyday, 'demotic', or unofficial level, such formal distinctions are, and indeed must be, breached. Holding on to both sides of this dichotomy between the formal and the everyday, both as students of the phenomenon, and for practitioners—living with the tension—is imperative, both for life and for understanding. Activists translate, mediate, and create the links that bind the unofficial and official levels together. They may set out to mould society in line with one framework, in line with one version of official classifications, but they often end up being moulded themselves in the process.

NOTES

1. I would like to thank D.P. Martinez, J. Pfaff-Czarnecka, and A. de Sales for helpful comments on drafts of this introduction.
2. Anthony Giddens' book *The Third Way* was a characteristic position statement by someone who was influential in the attempt to create a 'third way' in politics: "The fostering of an active civil society is a basic part of the politics of the third way... State and civil society should act in partnership..." (Giddens, 1998: 78–9).
3. Salamon et al. (1999: 14). The Global Civil Society Yearbooks (available at lse.ac.uk/Depts/global) likewise attempt to describe, theorize, and measure the growth of global civil society. Compare Keck and Sikkink's table (1998: 11) showing the increase of international social change organizations between 1953 and 1993. For attempts simultaneously to theorize about and to carry out the empirical and ethnographic study of civil society, see Hann (1996), Glasius et al. (2004), and the references in note 4. For a sample of theoretical statements, see Habermas (1989), Cohen and Arato (1992), Hall (1995), Kaldor (2003), and Walzer (1995). Hall and Trentmann (2005) is a useful collection of key texts.
4. I have examined the statements of the sceptics, the history of the concept of civil society, and some of the South Asian critics of the term (Neera Chandoke, Partha Chatterjee) in the introduction to the second volume in this series (Gellner, 2009b).

For a lucid introduction to the whole field, see Lewis (2007); for a survey of anthropological contributions, see Fisher (1997).

5. On the Narmada dam issue, see Baviskar (1995), Fisher (1995), Khagram (2004), and Pfaff-Czarnecka (2007).
6. The contested, appraisive, and shifting use of the term 'activist' is very clear in Riles' (2000: 148–51) discussion of the use of the term among women NGO workers attending the United Nations Fourth World Conference on Women in Beijing in 1995.
7. In addition to the studies in this volume, on specific civil society contexts in South Asia, see, on India, Chandhoke (2003), Elliott (2003), Mio (2007), Oomen (2004), Tandon and Mohanty (2003), and Varshney (2002); on Bangladesh, Lewis (2004, 2008); on Nepal, Bhattachan et al. (2001), Hachhethu (2006), Heaton Shrestha (2002, 2006), and Tamang (2003); on Sri Lanka, Wickremasinghe (2001); and on Pakistan, Mohmand (2008) and Weiss and Gilani (2001).
8. Pigg's (1992) article was an early and much-cited description of how Nepal's Panchayat-era (1960 to 1990) education system encouraged and embodied this view. See also Ahearn (2003) for an excellent ethnography of the consequences of literacy under this educational system.
9. Attempts have been made to respond to these global trends, for example, by the All-India Coordinating Forum of Adivasis/Indigenous Peoples and the Indian Confederation of Indigenous and Tribal Peoples. But neither appears to be, as yet, an effective representative body for all Indian tribals.
10. See Heaton Shrestha (2002, 2006), Gellner (forthcoming). Or as Riles puts it, "By the 'Network' I mean to refer to a set of institutions, knowledge practices, and artifacts thereof that internally generate the effects of their own reality by reflecting on themselves" (Riles, 2000: 3).
11. See Shah and Pettigrew (2009) for a collection bringing together studies of Maoism in both India and Nepal.
12. For a sophisticated survey of anthropological approaches to 'the political' in South Asia, which quite deliberately does not take the categories 'political', 'cultural', etc. for granted, see Spencer (2007).

REFERENCES

Ahearn, L. 2003. *Invitations to Love: Literacy, Love Letters, and Social Change in Nepal*. Ann Arbor: The Michigan University Press.

Baumann, G. 1996. *Contesting Culture: Discourses of Identity in Multi-ethnic London*. Cambridge: Cambridge University Press.

Baviskar, A. 1995. *In the Belly of the River: Tribal Conflicts over Development in the Narmada Valley*. Delhi: Oxford University Press.

Bhattachan, K.B., S. Rana, J. Gyawali, M.B. Basnet, K.R. Bhushal, and R.R. Pokharel (eds). 2001. *NGO, Civil Society and Government in Nepal*. Kathmandu: Central Department of Sociology and Anthropology, Tribhuvan University.

Burghart, R. 1978. 'Hierarchical Models of the Hindu Social System', *Man* (N.S.), 13: 519–36. (reissued 1996 in his *The Conditions of Listening: Essays on Religion, History and Politics in South Asia*, C.J. Fuller and J. Spencer (eds). Delhi: OUP.)

Chandhoke, N. 2003. 'A Critique of the Notion of Civil Society and the "Third Sphere"', in R. Tandon and R. Mohanty (eds), *Does Civil Society Matter? Governance in Contemporary India*, pp. 27–58. New Delhi: SAGE Publications.

Cohen, J. and A. Arato. 1992. *Political Theory and Civil Society*. Cambridge: MIT Press.

de Sales, A. 2003. 'The Kham Magar Country: Between Ethnic Claims and Maoism', in D.N. Gellner (ed.), *Resistance and the State: Nepalese Experiences*, pp. 326–57. New Delhi: Social Science Press. (Also published in 2000 in *European Bulletin of Himalayan Research*, 19: 41–71, and D. Thapa (ed.) (2003), *Understanding the Maoist Movement of Nepal*. Kathmandu: Martin Chautari.)

Elliott, C.M. (ed.). 2003. *Civil Society and Democracy: A Reader*. New Delhi: Oxford University Press.

Fisher, W.F. (ed.). 1995. *Towards Sustainable Development? Struggling over India's Narmada River*. Armonk: M.E. Sharpe.

———. 1997. 'Doing Good? The Politics and Antipolitics of NGO Practices', *Annual Review of Anthropology*, 26: 439–64.

Gellner, D.N. (ed.). 2009a. *Ethnic Activism and Civil Society in South Asia*. New Delhi: SAGE Publications.

———. 2009b. 'Introduction: How Civil are "Communal" and Ethno-nationalist Movements?' in D.N. Gellner (ed.), *Ethnic Activism and Civil Society in South Asia*, pp. 1–24. New Delhi: SAGE Publications.

Gellner, D.N. forthcoming. 'Rituals of Democracy and Development', in S. Hettige (ed.), *Governance and Development: The Postcolonial State and the Development Process in Sri Lanka and its Neighbours*. New Delhi: SAGE Publications.

Giddens, A. 1998. *The Third Way: The Renewal of Social Democracy*. Cambridge: Polity.

Glasius, M., D. Lewis, and H. Seckinelgin (eds). 2004. *Exploring Civil Society: Political and Cultural Contexts*. London and New York: Routledge.

Habermas, J. 1989 (1962). *The Structural Transformation of the Public Sphere: An Enquiry into a Category of Bourgeois Society*, translated by T. Burger and F. Lawrence. Cambridge: Polity.

Hachhethu, K. 2006. 'Civil Society and Political Participation', in L.R. Baral (ed.), *Nepal: Quest for Participatory Democracy*, pp. 111–32. New Delhi: Adroit.

Hall, J.A. 1995. *Civil Society: Theory, History, Comparison*. Cambridge: Polity.

Hall, J.A. and F. Trentmann (eds). 2005. *Civil Society: A Reader in History, Theory and Global Politics*. Basingstoke: Palgrave Macmillan.

Hann, C. (ed.). 1996. *Civil Society: Challenging Western Models*. London and New York: Routledge.

Heaton Shrestha, C. 2002. 'NGOs as *Thekadar* or *Sevak*: Identity Crisis in Nepal's Non-governmental Sector', *European Bulletin of Himalayan Research*, 22: 5–36.

———. 2006. '"They Can't Mix Like We Can": Bracketing Differences and the Professionalization of NGOs in Nepal', in D. Lewis and D. Mosse (eds), *Development Brokers and Translators: The Ethnography of Aid and Agencies*, pp. 195–216. Bloomfield, CT: Kumarian.

Kaldor, M. 2003. *Global Civil Society: An Answer to War*. Cambridge: Polity.

Keck, M.E. and K. Sikkink. 1998. *Activists beyond Borders: Activist Networks in International Politics*. Ithaca: Cornell University Press.

Khagram, S. 2004. *Dams and Development: Transnational Struggles for Water and Power*. New Delhi: Oxford University Press.
Latour, B. 1991. *We Have Never Been Modern*, translated by C. Porter. Hemel Hempstead, Hertfordshire: Harvester Wheatsheaf.
Lawson, K. (ed.). 1980. *Political Parties and Linkages: A Comparative Perspective*. New Haven: Yale University Press.
Lewis, D. 2004. 'On the Difficulty of the Studying "Civil Society": Reflections on NGOs, State and Democracy in Bangladesh', *Contributions to Indian Sociology*, (n.s.) 38(3): 299–322.
———. 2007 (2001). *The Management of Non-governmental Development Organizations* (2nd edition). London and New York: Routledge.
———. 2008. 'Crossing the Boundaries between "Third Sector" and State: Life-Work Histories from the Philippines, Bangladesh and the UK', *Third World Quarterly*, 29(1): 125–41.
Li, T. Murray. 2005. 'Beyond "the State" and Failed Schemes', *American Anthropologist*, 107(3): 383–94.
Mio, M. 2007. 'Public Space, Voluntary Associations, and Hindu Nationalism: Changing Urban Festivals in Udaipur, Rajasthan', in H. Ishii, D.N. Gellner, and K. Nawa (eds), *Political and Social Transformations in North India and Nepal (Social Dynamics in Northern South Asia, Vol. 2)*, pp. 239–62. New Delhi: Manohar.
Mohmand, S.K. 2008. 'Local Government Reforms in Pakistan: Strengthening Social Capital or Rolling Back the State?' in D.N. Gellner and K. Hachhethu (eds), *Local Democracy in South Asia: The Micropolitics of Democratization in Nepal and its Neighbours*, pp. 380–415. New Delhi: SAGE Publications.
Oomen, T.K. 2004. 'State, Civil Society and Market in India: Gradual Autonomisation', in T.K. Oomen (ed.), *Nation, Civil Society and its Social Movements: Essays in Political Sociology*, pp. 107–27. New Delhi: SAGE Publications.
Pfaff-Czarnecka, J. 2007. 'Challenging Goliath: People, Dams, and the Paradoxes of Transnational Critical Movements', in H. Ishii, D.N. Gellner, and K. Nawa (eds), *Political and Social Transformations in North India and Nepal*, pp. 399–433. New Delhi: Manohar.
Pigg, S.L. 1992. 'Inventing Social Categories through Place: Social Representations and Development in Nepal', *Comparative Studies in Society and History*, 34(3): 491–513.
Riles, A. 2000. *The Network Inside Out*. Ann Arbor: University of Michigan Press.
Salamon, L.M., H.K. Anheier, R. List, S. Toepler, S.W. Sokolowski, and associates. 1999. *Global Civil Society: Dimensions of the Nonprofit Sector*. Baltimore: Johns Hopkins Center for Civil Society Studies.
Scott, J.C. 1998. *Seeing Like a State: How Certain Schemes to Improve the Human Condition have Failed*. New Haven: Yale University Press.
Shah, A. and J. Pettigrew (eds). 2009. *Windows to the Revolution: Maoism in India and Nepal*. Double Issue of *Dialectical Anthropology* 33(3/4).
Spencer, J. 2007. *Anthropology, Politics, and the State: Democracy and Violence in South Asia*. Cambridge: Cambridge University Press.
Tamang, S. 2003. 'Civilising Civil Society: Donors and Democratic Space in Nepal', *Himal South Asia*, 16(7): 14–24. Available at www.himalmag.com. (accessed on 2 August 2006).

Tandon, R. and R. Mohanty (eds). 2003. *Does Civil Society Matter? Governance in Contemporary India*. New Delhi: SAGE Publications.
van Schendel, W. 2005. *The Bengal Borderland: Beyond State and Nation in South Asia*. London: Anthem.
Varshney, A. 2002. *Ethnic Conflict and Civic Life: Hindus and Muslims in India*. New Haven and London: Yale University Press.
Walzer, M. 1995. 'The Concept of Civil Society', in M. Walzer (ed.), *Toward a Global Civil Society*, pp. 7–27. Providence: Berghahn.
Weiss, A.M. and S.Z. Gilani (eds). 2001. *Power and Civil Society in Pakistan*. Oxford and New York: Oxford University Press.
Wickremasinghe, N. 2001. *Civil Society in Sri Lanka: New Circles of Power*. New Delhi: SAGE Publications.

POLITICS

Chapter 2

The Biography of a Magar Communist

ANNE DE SALES

Let us begin with the end of the story: Barman Budha Magar was elected as Member of Parliament (MP) in 1991, one year after the People's Movement (*jan andolan*) that put an end to 30 years of the Partyless Panchayat 'democracy' in Nepal. He had stood for the Samyukta Jana Morcha or United People's Front (UPF), the political wing of the revolutionary faction of the Communist Party of Nepal, or CPN (Unity Centre).[1] To the surprise of the nation, the UPF won nine seats and the status of third-largest party with more than 3 per cent of the national vote. However, following the directives of his party,[2] Barman, despite being an MP, soon went underground until he retired from political life at the time of the People's War in 1996.

He does not question the guerrilla war launched by the CPN (Maoist), to which he claims a moral attachment.[3] He gives his age (he was 66 years old at the time—no longer appropriate to a clandestine lifestyle) as the reason why he stopped being politically active. Now in his late seventies, he lives in his daughter's house near Kathmandu. Seated cross-leggèd on a carpet, invariably wearing the short home-woven kilt characteristic of Magar dress or wrapped in a blanket when it is cold, he looks like any elderly villager, taking care of his grandchildren and walking his dogs. However, the numerous visits that he receives from journalists and politicians bear witness to the fact that he was a key character in establishing communism in Rolpa and Rukum, the rebels' base.[4] As preparation for elections to the Constituent Assembly gradually got under way following the Second People's Movement of 2006, his presence as an honoured guest at Maoist meetings in what had become known as the Magarant Autonomous Region illustrates the iconic quality he has retained over the years as a local leader. (See Image 2.1, p. 20)

Unlike most political activists, who received a formal education and who developed their careers by remaining close to urban centres, most of Barman's political life remained anchored in his rural homeland. Apart from brief trips to India, he never wished to leave Nepal and indeed remained in his home territory. Nepal offered a large enough playground to satisfy his insatiable curiosity, and his ambition was to change his own society. How did it all begin? The growing politicization of the country over the previous 50 years, and an early communist presence in the area, helped Barman to find new expression for his opposition to what he initially conceptualized simply as unjust situations that demanded to be redressed. This study aims to retrace the process by which Barman's political awareness emerged from local conflicts and how he helped in turn to adapt communist propaganda to local realities. The following account, focusing on Barman's political awakening, will concentrate on the period preceding the People's War. The question that underlies it concerns the extent to which he became a modern activist or remained a traditional local leader.

As a Communist and a Magar, Barman stands at the crossroads of two different, even potentially antagonistic, movements that have dominated Nepalese political life since 1990: the Communists, including the Maoists, aim at the ideal of a nation of equal citizens through the 'class struggle', irrespective of all distinctions of caste and ethnic group. By contrast, ethnic movements fight for the recognition of the various *jati*s, or nationalities, and the eventual establishment of autonomous regions. This debate between the class- and ethnicity-based principles of political struggle will be discussed further towards the end of this chapter. Barman's biography, as recounted by him, should help us to understand how the potential contradiction between such principles are not only conceived but also experienced by a political actor in a rural area, which has been at the forefront of the media over the past 15 years.

The fact that Barman belongs to the Kham-Magar-speaking minority is not insignificant in this respect. The 50,000 speakers of this Tibeto-Burman language have long been considered 'poor relatives' of the Magar proper, the largest ethnic group in Nepal (1.62 million). Post-1990 publications concerned with the reconstruction of the history of the Magars present their original homeland as the medieval Magarant, covering the mountainous area between the Kali Gandaki and Bheri rivers.[5] The western region, Athara Magarant ('the Magar country of the Eighteen [Clans]'), is distinguished from the eastern region or Bahra Magarant ('the Magar country of the Twelve [Clans]'). The inhabitants of Bahra Magarant have been generally more exposed to national politics; they have lived for generations in multi-caste villages and provided soldiers to the British Army's Brigade of Gurkhas, whereas the Kham speakers, inhabitants of the Athara Magarant, remained further away from communication centres.[6] The Kham speakers are grouped together in 14 Village Development Committees on the upper hills of Rukum and Rolpa districts in Rapti zone. With the sole exception of two service castes, Blacksmiths (Kami) and Tailor-Musicians (Damai), who have been attached to their Magar masters (*bista*) for generations, this enclave has not attracted any other castes in search of land. Kham speakers are also found with other groups in 11 further VDCs. On the chequerboard of ethnic politics they represent a minority within the Magar group and a backward minority in the eyes of the Magar elite.

Due to the constraints of this chapter, I will simply mention two striking features of Barman's narrative. Barman and I initially chose to proceed chronologically rather than topically, but this approach soon had to be abandoned. Barman's memories moved naturally along the paths he had walked all his life. His biography would therefore more accurately be organized along routes: routes of transhumance when he was a shepherd; routes to the district headquarters for his many trials; to Kathmandu in search of a hospital for his wife; to the bazaar in the south where he sold hashish; and finally to the villages he visited during his political campaigns. The needs of exposition require the information to be reorganized along more chronological lines, but we should bear in mind that Barman's narrative is structured as a journey. Another remarkable feature is Barman's oratorical skill. He paces the telling of his stories with proverbs—or what sound like proverbs, although they may have been invented on the spot—and with quotations from local songs that encapsulate the moral of his story and stress its point.[7] Born in a society of oral tradition, Barman excels in storytelling and this talent no doubt contributed to his success as a leader. He is able to draw from a shared folklore and speaks to people in a language with which they are familiar.

These remarks about Barman's account do not take us away from the main theme of this volume: that is, activism. The notion of

Image 2.1
Barman attending the first national convention of the Maoist-aligned Magar Liberation Front in Tansen in June 2006 (photo: Kiyoko Ogura).

activism is concerned with the ambition to transform the world and mobilize people around new ideals. One characteristic of this notion, as a sociological phenomenon, is that it stands at the interface of the subjective and the social: it combines the transformation of the world or society with the transformation of the activist as a person, of his or her self. Activists venture on to a frontier between the world that they strive to leave behind and their vision of a new world. It is not irrelevant to the subject that, apart from hagiographies, the few modern biographies available in Nepal concern political activists.[8] They see themselves as part of history in the making and their trajectories acquire a reflexive dimension.[9] Given that such activities developed in Nepal relatively recently—hardly three generations ago—this transformation affected activists of Barman's generation even more radically.

In the following section a sketch of Barman's life in Rana times will show the ground that he has covered. The second section will give an account of Barman's political awakening following the first Nepalese revolution in 1950–51. The third and last section will describe the deepening of Barman's commitment under the three decades of the Partyless Panchayat system that led to the second Nepalese revolution in 1990.

BEFORE 1950: THE THAKURI CONQUEST AND THE RANA PATRIMONIAL STATE

Barman was born in 1930 in the village of Thabang (or Thawang), in the north of Rolpa district. At that time the area was the western canton (*thum*)[10] of Pyuthan district and was locally called Kalashes, 'the black heights', the eastern canton being called Gorashes, 'the white heights'. Nepali *shes* designates more precisely a high remote place, with connotations of being somehow residual. This could not better express the feeling of the inhabitants, among whom the Kham Magar constitute the majority.

The Thabang area was covered with forest and the villagers had to provide forced labour (*jara*) to the Pyuthan authorities. In their case, this meant making charcoal. The famous *pyuthane nal*, a type of gun, needed fuel to melt metal for the barrel and good walnut wood for the stock. Once the area was cleared and the wood burnt, it was converted into farming land. In 1848, the Ranas[11] married one of their daughters, Chandra Devi, to Indra Bahadur Shahi ('Captain' to the villagers), the grandson of the last Thakuri king of Rukum.[12] The bride's dowry was Thabang, along with Bahunthana near Rukumkot, as freehold land (*birta*).[13] What this meant for the villagers was that now they owed tax to the *birta*-holder rather than directly to the king.

Indra Bahadur joined the Nepalese army (hence his title of Captain) and entrusted his younger brother, Upendra, to collect the taxes in the area. Like many officials in such a position, Upendra had a reputation for extorting money from villagers with the help of local headmen, or *mukhiya*s, whom he appointed to collect taxes in their respective villages. It seems that the headmen changed often and that this was a source of conflict among Thabangis. Other villages under the more common *raikar* land tenure system also suffered from their headmen, who were entitled to collect taxes for the government. However, even if conflicts were frequent, this office usually fell to the oldest member of the local founding clan and was not the object of intense competition, as seems to have been the case in Thabang. The intrusion of an influential Thakuri to back up his chosen headman could not but make things worse. *Birta* status, unique to Thabang among the Kham-Magar-speaking villages, may well have played its part in the village's exceptional destiny as the Maoist 'capital'.

Barman was a long-awaited son. His parents, who had only daughters, begged the local god Braha to send them a son and sacrificed a ram at the top of Jaljala, one of the highest hills in Rolpa district. Until the Maoists banned this practice, hundreds, if not thousands, of ram sacrifices were made every year to this local god by people of all castes, some of whom came from afar, to ask for offspring and prosperity. Barman associates the first syllable of his name, *bar*, with the 'blessing' or 'gift' granted by Braha to his parents.

The Maoist rebels were not mistaken in symbolically conquering Jaljala. A pillar to the memory of their martyrs was erected on the pass below the mountain top soon after the beginning of the People's War and the name appears in numerous propaganda songs.[14] It is also used in association with the name of another high hill, Sisne, in Rukum district, and designates the first political campaign by the Maoists in 1995, Si-ja Abhiyan.

The pass and its small lake had already been the object of conflict among the gods. A legend tells how Satsalya, a deity coming from the west, wanted to fight with Braha on Jaljala. With the help of two Magar hunters, Braha defeated his competitor. He made the Magars his priests, or *pujari*s, confirming the pre-eminence of this group in the place.[15] Although the identity of the deity Satsalya is unclear, its western origin suggests a parallel between the conflict between the gods and the conquest of the local Magars by the Thakuri from Jumla. This would not be the first Nepalese case where the conquerors entrusted indigenous people with the worship of local gods.[16]

Barman's grandfather was the headman of a nearby village, Jurbang, while his father married in Thabang. Since his wife, Barman's mother, was the only daughter, the couple stayed in her parents' house. Being a 'house son-in-law' (*ghar jamai*) is poorly regarded among the Magars, as among other Nepalis. Moreover, among the Magars wife-takers have a lower status vis-à-vis wife-givers, who remain their eternal creditors for having given their daughters away. This asymmetric relationship is less easily reversed when the son-in-law does not have his own space to be a father-in-law in his turn. Barman, the grandson of a headman, may have felt his ambitions thwarted by being the son of a 'house son-in-law'.

He was still a child when he was sent to look after his father's sheep, a flock of 300 to 400, along with a hired shepherd. The transhumance routes cross the area from the high pastures in the north (well into Dolpo) to the south (as far as Dang, keeping to the ridges). The shepherds rarely stay in the village. They come down from the pastures to celebrate the two festivals of Dasai: Thulo Dasai in the autumn, when returning from the north, and Caite Dasai in the spring, when coming back from the south. Compared to the more sedentary villagers, they are known to be independent, free-spirited, and prone to fighting and gambling (although Barman was never attracted by gambling). They also have a great deal of free time. Barman taught himself how to read and write while he was looking after his animals. He learned the alphabet, drawing letters with a stone in the dust of the trail.

To conclude: Barman spent his formative years under the Rana dictatorship, a time when a Magar villager would have had very little prospect of political participation other than through being chosen as a tax collector by the local Thakuri. As the son of a 'house son-in-law', he was unlikely to have been in a position to obtain even this position and Barman was more inclined to travel with his sheep.

FROM VILLAGE CONFLICTS TO POLITICAL AWARENESS: 1950–59

Transhumance and the Circulation of Ideas

The 'revolution of the year 7' (*satsalko kranti*), that is, the revolution of 1950–51 that overthrew the Ranas, is a landmark in Barman's account. He remembers when he heard about the Congress for the first time, on his way down to Dang with his sheep:

> I used to graze the sheep in Chalikot. Many people from different places would gather there, some with their sheep, some with their cows and buffaloes through the jungle. One day I heard people from Dang shouting: "Congress have come! Congress have come!" (*Kangress ayo*). I wondered what sort of people these were! I thought they might look different from us. Later I understood that leaders from Kathmandu had come to ask the people in Dang to join their group and protest against the Ranas. They were going around shouting: "Death to the Ranas, long live the Nepali Congress!"
>
> There are big landlords (*jamindar*) in Dang. The rumour was that some of them had fifty to sixty armed guards to protect them. Jaikku Prasad Bahun was one of them. He was very rich. Congress sympathizers raided his house. The Gaine musicians used to sing:
>
> The Great King riding [in the]
> Dang jungle
> Grandfather Bahun Jaikku Prasad
> How long [is his] beard![17]
>
> In the past only Tharus could live in the Tarai. Being autochthonous, they were immune to malaria. But gradually clever people from the hills, Bahuns and Chhetris, came down to buy land. The Tharus agreed to work on their fields and to divide the crops with their landlords. The landlords paid the taxes, something the Tharus were too poor to do. During the hot season they would carry all the food to their landlords who stayed in higher cooler places above Dang. They went back and forth like a mother bird feeding her fledglings; the landlords just stayed at home doing nothing.
>
> The Tharus are simple and docile people without any sense of revolt. Their landlords could beat or kill them, and they would say nothing. Their share of crops was not enough to feed them, so they had to borrow grain from their landlords and in this way would find themselves bound to them. For Maghe Sankranti, a big Tharu festival, the landlords would pretend to be generous and give them alcohol so that they would renew their promise to stay on the following year and work for them. In Rukum and Rolpa it is different: there are no landlords, and we work our own fields.

This account shows that the first revolutionary ideas circulated from the southern bazaars in the plains up to the northern hills through the transhumance routes. Barman takes up the analysis provided by the anti-Rana propaganda of the time: the appropriation by high-caste immigrants of the land of the indigenous Tharus, their gradual enslavement to their landlords and the trickery behind the yearly ritual through which the Tharus had their contract renewed. Barman also takes up the contrasted stereotypes respectively associated with the populations in the Tarai and in the hills. While the Tharus are said to be credulous and docile, and the Bahuns and Chhetris devious and experienced in dealing with the state, Barman by contrast remembers wanting to join the army of liberation, or *mukti sena*, in accordance with the warrior ideals conventionally associated with hill people.[18] The army was the natural option for those hillmen who, apart from bringing some cash home, wanted to see the world beyond their village. In fact, Barman was not drawn to this project by political motivations, but rather by curiosity about the outside world:

> Once I ran away from the pastures to join the army of liberation, but the husband of my elder sister caught me on the way and forbade me to go. I wanted to see Kathmandu city and to study. I thought it was useless to remain a shepherd and look after animals all my life. But I did not have any political awareness (*cetan*) at that time, I just thought that it would be fun to travel.

The Shepherds' Association

A new headman, Krishna Bahadur Jhankri, himself the son of a previous headman of Thabang, was appointed in 1952.[19] He was a sympathizer of the Nepali Congress and began to modernize the village. He tried to reform local customs, such as pig rearing, which he banned on sanitary grounds. This measure turned out to be unpopular among the Magars, who have a particular fondness for pork. The main problem, however, was that Krishna took advantage of his position as a tax collector. The freehold land privilege had not yet been abolished and the Thabangis were still required to satisfy the *birta*-holder in Rukumkot. In order to calculate the amount each had to pay, the village had been divided into two approximately equal halves, each half being sub-divided into five groups or divisions (*khandas*). These groups corresponded to 10 exogamous lineages. It seems that the two halves were drawn up simply to provide some kind of demographic balance and to simplify the calculation of the taxes, with each lineage paying a fixed amount.

Until then the Thabangis had not taken into account the land survey (*napi*) documents of 1912, which were compiled under Prime Minister Chandra Shamshere Rana. On the basis of these documents, which specified the measurements of the fields and the names of their owners, Krishna Mukhiya questioned the amounts people used to pay. He then suggested to some villagers that they were entitled to contribute less, given the size or the category of their fields as specified in the documents. He encouraged others to claim their ownership of this or that field cultivated by somebody else. He introduced a different logic, based on individual interest and conformity to written documents, in place of the lineage solidarity that had prevailed up till then.

What Krishna Mukhiya personally gained by sweeping the dust off these documents and creating havoc was the opportunity to appear as the saviour of the oppressed and, Barman suggested, to gain moral credit from those who ended up paying less. Barman openly expressed his discontent at what he saw as an attempt to gain the political high ground and led the opposition to Krishna Mukhiya: "I knew people were afraid of him because he was powerful—appointed by the Thakuri of Rukumkot—but I don't like people who lie and cheat. I don't like people looking down on others."

On the 1st of Jeth, 2011 (June 1954) Barman formed an association of shepherds (*gwala sanghatan*) numbering about 50 to 60 men with a hard core of seven members. When they were not too far away from the village, the shepherds came down from the pastures at night and visited the villagers, inquiring about Krishna Mukhiya and encouraging people to oppose him. Numerous fights took place between Krishna's and Barman's groups. These fights remain vivid in Barman's memory and he enjoys recounting them:

> Once we wanted to trap Krishna Mukhiya at home and force him to come out with his gun, so that we could then accuse him of having threatened us. We threw stones at his house and shot clay bullets with our slings. We did not let the public crier (*katawal*) approach the house and take his instructions from Krishna. Finally, Krishna came out with his gun. We were standing on the hill above the house, shouting in his direction and throwing out our chests, provoking him: "Here, here, shoot here!" Krishna's friends joined him and they ran after us. We escaped through the Blacksmiths' quarter then to the jungle. We ended up in Jurbang village, at the house of a friend called Manjit, where we

> stopped and had beer. Suddenly somebody rushed into the house and warned us: "Hey guys! Your old man is coming!" I remember Manjit, his nose in the bowl of beer. He did not know what to do, finish his beer or run with us! "Wait! Wait! I'm coming!" (laughs).

This was the beginning of a long walk to Pyuthan headquarters, where Barman and his friends had planned to bring a legal case against Krishna. The journey was slowed down by a search for money and a lack of food. When they finally arrived, they saw "people wearing *suruwal*" approaching. The sight of these Nepali trousers (loose in the seat and close-fitting from the knees down), characteristic of government officials and high-caste people, made them run away, but they were finally caught: Krishna had preceded them and already registered a case against Barman for being a Communist.[20] "I knew nothing about the Communist Party at the time", says Barman, "but I have learned."

The Accusation of Communism

The first thing Barman remembers after he and his two friends were arrested is that they were given a snack of soya beans. The provincial governor (*bada hakim*) was standing next to him and also popped a few roasted beans in his mouth. Barman looked at him and asked, "Do you also eat soya beans?" and the governor answered, "If we did not eat this, what would we eat then? We too can die of hunger." Barman did not expect this "important man" (*thulo manche*) to be such an ordinary human being, with the same needs and eating habits as himself, an ordinary villager. It must have been the first time (he was in his early twenties) that he had ever conversed with a government official: "For several days after this meeting my body was shaking with fear" (laughter). Not only was the governor a powerful individual, someone of higher social status, but he also belonged to a higher caste by birth. He incarnated a kind of human being that Barman felt was essentially different from a Magar shepherd. This anecdote reminds us that caste hierarchy is not only an abstract system of social classification. It was embedded in Barman's body and, for him, overcoming his initial fear was the first step towards 'political awakening'.

It soon became clear that Krishna Mukhiya had bribed the governor so that he would win the case and to ensure that Barman would stay in prison, away from the village. Barman's friends begged him to compromise:

> It's useless to fight, we won't get anything that way. Krishna Mukhiya gave a bribe of Rs 3,000 [a substantial amount at the time] to the governor. Let's pay the Rs 3,000 to Krishna. He will withdraw his accusation, the case will be settled, and we will go back home.

Barman stubbornly refused: "If they want to kill us, let them kill us! I shall not go anywhere until I am recognized as innocent [not a Communist]".

Although Barman and his friends were not allowed to leave the district headquarters, they were not imprisoned, unlike the well-known political leaders, Mohan Bikram Singh and his friend Khagulal Gurung, who were there at the same time.[21] Barman remembers hearing them shouting communist slogans two or three times a day and giving the governor a lot of trouble. He did not then know the important role that "Mohan Bikram and his people" (*mohanbikramharu*) were to play in his life and in the future of Thabang.

The governor eventually summoned Barman and Krishna Mukhiya to appear before him together. Lacking evidence—faced with Barman's questions, his opponent remained silent, "scratching his head"—the governor issued a written statement (*tamsuk*) lifting the accusation of communist involvement and treating the case as an ordinary dispute. Barman and his friends were to pay a small fine (Rs 300 for Barman, as the leader of the group, Rs 200 for his associates) as compensation for the trouble they had caused Krishna Mukhiya. Although Barman's group went back to Thabang, Barman himself refused to pay the fine and was more determined than ever to oppose Krishna. The situation was so tense that Barman's family insisted that he spend time in the pastures, away from the village. Barman turned to the other tutelary authority he knew: Upendra Bahadur Shahi, in Rukumkot, the younger brother of Indra 'Captain', Thabang's *birta*-holder. However, the Thakuri turned a deaf ear to Barman's complaints. For Barman, the fine of Rs 300 was not the issue. He wanted fair treatment and recognition of his innocence. It was a question of principle.

Mohan Bikram Singh's Visit to Thabang[22]

In 1956, Mohan Bikram Singh and two friends were released from prison in Salyan. On their walk back to Pyuthan, they stopped in Thabang for a few days and introduced the villagers to the communist ideology:

> They spoke about the evolution of man and about other countries in the world, about Marx and Lenin. We heard about Mao later. Communist books translated into Nepali were circulated and we were encouraged to organize a sort of commune, where everything was done collectively, cooking, eating, and working. I thought: "If educated people are in the Communist Party, why not us as well?"

Informed of the ongoing conflicts between Barman and Krishna Mukhiya, which were dividing the village into two factions, Mohan Bikram Singh persuaded them to reconcile and form a peasant association as a front organization of the banned Communist Party. The resolution of this conflict is reminiscent of the recurrent pattern found in the partly legendary and partly historical accounts of the conquest of Nepal by the Thakuris. Tribal chiefs, especially among the Magar, would call a Thakuri king to rule over their community to end their chronic instability. In the contemporary situation, clandestine affiliation to the Communist Party acted as a temporary social binding for a divided community.

Krishna died of tuberculosis in 1958 and Barman was elected headman by the villagers in his place, a year before the first parliamentary elections. As the election approached, he was contacted by activists from the Gorkha Parishad and the Nepali Congress, who were campaigning for their parties and trying to secure votes from the villagers: "How could they work for the people when they called themselves [respectively] the Ranas' party and King's party? I did not join them". All the Thabangis voted for the Communist candidate, Khagulal Gurung, who had been visiting the village regularly since his first visit with Mohan Bikram Singh in 1956. "Our food is maize, our weapon is the sickle"[23] went the song that celebrated the symbol of the Communist Party at the time. Following the stereotype associated with ethnic communities, the unanimous voting pattern of Thabang must have been attributed to the political ignorance of backward peasants, blindly following their chief. However, the obviously strong communist presence in Thabang also attracted the attention of the authorities.

Barman's First Measure as a Communist Headman (1959)

One communist teaching that Barman made his own—he says that once you are "aware", then ideas come naturally "from inside" yourself, without being imposed from outside—is that impurity is not intrinsic to people; it is only a prejudice:

> Whether it is tasty or not, the tongue tells it.
> Whether it is pure or not, the eye sees it.

In a few words Barman strips the notion of impurity of its symbolic dimension in Hindu thought (all the more powerful for being invisible), and brings it down to its more prosaic version, that is, dirt. The episode of the soya beans conveys how caste hierarchy could be embodied by a young peasant like Barman, who could not at first believe what he saw (a high-caste official eating the same food as himself) and whose body shook with fear after the encounter. What the above adage now evokes, by contrast, is an enlightened person who does not blindly endorse received wisdom but rather trusts his own senses and thinks for himself.

The reforms that Barman implemented did not only concern the way Blacksmiths and Tailor-Musicians were treated in the village. He also allocated them uncultivated land and encouraged them to become independent of their former masters: "In Thabang the Dalits are now farmers, soldiers, or workers abroad like any other caste. People will gradually get rid of the habit of considering them impure. It is only a habit".

The other task of prime importance to Barman was the creation of a school:

> I wrote a fake paper showing that we had the facilities to build and open a school. This was the government procedure to get the permission. B.P. Koirala was the Prime Minister at the time [1959] and the Nepali Congress neglected us because we were known to be Communists. But the permission was finally granted.

As was common in those days, a retired soldier from the Indian Gurkha regiments was the only literate person in the village and was therefore the only available schoolmaster. Later on, Communist activists from Mohan Bikram's group in Pyuthan came to teach in

Thabang, thus securing at the same time a more systematic ideological education, notably through night classes. The school remained an important centre of communist teaching throughout the Panchayat years.[24]

Barman had first been accused of being a Communist by a personal enemy, a Nepali Congress sympathizer. In the climate of village factionalism his embrace of the communist cause looked at first more like a counterattack than a well-thought-out ideological commitment. Barman himself acknowledged the logic of affiliation to political parties among uneducated villagers:

> There always were opposed groups (*dapha*) in the village. Nowadays people know more about [national] politics and join political parties. But the reasons for conflicts are the same as before. If my enemy joined one party, I would join the other one. People are motivated by anger. They are not politically aware.

Right from the beginning of the politicization of the country, old local conflicts found new names. However, in the process, the villagers became connected to a new network of relationships throughout the nation. The political parties opened avenues from the periphery of the country to its centre. Although the Panchayat years drove this process underground, it did not bring it to an end: along with new factors such as rising education and the general opening of the country to the outside world, the traditional ferment of conflict within the village kept feeding it.

FROM UNDERGROUND TO PARLIAMENT: 1960–91

The Panchayat Years: Increasing State Repression Leads to Stronger Political Convictions

This is not the place to trace all the developments of these 30 years of political life. For Barman, they were marked by several elections, both at local and national levels, by clandestine activities, and by a great deal of travelling. King Mahendra dissolved Parliament in 1960 and the first elections for the Panchayat replacement happened one year later. In the course of his many trials, Barman came to know some of the government officials quite well. One of them, Ratna Bahadur Gurung, was the Commissioner of Bheri Zone. Seeing in Barman a local leader with a career ahead of him, he tried to convince him to join the Panchayat system and to stand in the elections. Barman refused. "What would my friends from the Party say if I won? I preferred to remain a shepherd (*gwala*), a Communist *gwala*!" he said with a laugh.

Although he wanted to keep his distance from political activity in the village as long as this was a partyless democracy, the villagers, or at least a majority among them, insisted that he stand in the local elections. He duly did so in 1966 and was elected village chairman, by then called Pradhan Panch, for the second time. However, conflicts arose at the time of the following elections, when his opponent, Ram Kumar Budha, a supporter of the Panchayat system, managed to win, apparently with the help of the election commissioner. Ram Kumar failed to unite the Thabangis and the village was again split into two groups as in the time of Krishna Mukhiya in the 1950s. When he was not in conflict with Barman, Ram Kumar fought with Kaman Jhankri, another Communist supporter.

The 1970s were marked by several legal cases against the Communists. In 1979–80, when a referendum on the Panachayat system was called, Barman, now Pradhan Panch for the third time, was called to Libang, the headquarters of Rolpa district,[25] to campaign for the Partyless side:

> Pashupati Shamshere and Khadga Bahadur K.C. held a meeting in the district hall, asking us to vote for *nirdal* (the Partyless system). I said that I did not know what my people would vote, *nirdal* or *bahudal* (the multi-party system): this was their choice, not mine. I was their representative and could not decide in advance. They insisted that I join them and offered me money and protection. They would act as a shield whatever I did if I went onto their side. But I refused. Other leaders looked at me and asked me to think twice, but I stuck to my position.
>
> Then the CDO and the police inspector came to me and said that Thabang was a dangerous area with all this forest around. They asked me for a good place to build a police station. I sent them to the top of the hill, where the forest is the thickest! (laughs)

This was a declaration of war. Sure enough, Barman continued, Thabang unanimously voted for the multi-party system in May 1980, then boycotted the general elections one year later. The police station was established in the course of a major operation in October 1981. Barman was arrested on a false charge of gambling, which followed a set-up in a teashop. Jailed for 20 days, he was finally declared innocent, but was arrested again, this time under the Public Security Act (which allowed detention without trial for up to 12 months) and spent another seven months in a prison in Libang. He was transferred to Gorahi, the headquarters of neighbouring Dang district, where his detention was extended to 20 months for an anti-state crime that he supposedly committed in Thabang ... while he was in jail: "I'm not a bird that can fly!" This was because of an episode that soon became a legend: the burning of the portrait of King Birendra and Queen Aishwarya in the Panchayat office of Thabang. Barman was presented as the culprit, although the damage to the portrait in fact occurred in the course of a fight between the vice-chairman of the village, a Panchayat supporter, and a Communist villager.[26] What is certain is that a picture of the late king and his family occupied a place of honour in Barman's Kathmandu house until the 2006 uprising, when the prospect of a republic buried the memory of the vanished royals in an irrelevant past.

Knowledge Acquired in Prison: *From Volga to Ganga*

Barman's arrests are like a serial, one episode followed by another in an endless game of hide-and-seek that never leaves him defeated. On the contrary, acts of state repression could not but strengthen his convictions. Barman also acquired knowledge in prison. This is how he came across a book in Hindi about the evolution of man "from the time people lived in caves up to Nehru". Although Barman could not identify this book—the title and the author's name had been lost with the cover—what he remembered was enough to suggest that this was *From Volga to Ganga*, by Rahul Sankrityayan.[27] This is the only book that Barman mentioned in greater detail than the vague and dutiful references to Marx and Lenin, and it may be useful to say a few words about it. It was published in November 1943 and was so successful that a second edition was published a year later, followed by an English translation in 1946. The author, who was Professor of Indology at Leningrad University in the 1930s, popularized a history of humanity through narratives heavily impregnated with communist ideology.

The book develops 19 stories based on different characters, each representative of his or her time. The first chapter describes a small band of blood-related kin around the mother, Nisha, living by hunting on the upper banks of the Volga. The story revolves around the matriarchal state of society at the dawn of humanity, when the necessity of survival in a hostile environment did not allow human sentiments. The descendants of this primordial mother developed into an Aryan clan and migrated towards the east and India through the Himalayas. The last chapter takes place in 1922 and is based on a conversation between two intellectuals: Sofdar, a young and successful lawyer, and Shankar, his friend from school days, a more modest schoolteacher. They discuss the issue of Indian independence within the context of European revolutionary history and Shankar puts forward the shortcomings of Gandhi's peaceful resistance. Sofdar is deeply moved by this conversation and decides to abandon his property along with the British lifestyle that he and his wife have enjoyed so far. The couple join the movement for independence in a communist cell.

Barman may not have been familiar with European history and the urban intellectual milieu, on which the last chapters of the book are based. However, the narrations skilfully provided a number of received wisdoms that Barman still enjoys checking against his own experience. He agreed, for instance, that, unlike plains people, 'Mongolian' hill tribes are brave warriors and like cold places. The evolutionist perspective developed throughout the 19 chapters of the book appeared as a natural truth to him. In the process of reading these overviews on the history of humanity, he acquired the ability to reorganize his own experience of time and to view the current political situation in a long-term perspective. He presumably also saw himself as playing a progressive role in this historical human saga.

'Addiction' to Politics and the Question of the Common Good

During his stay in prison Barman also reflected on his fellow prisoners. They were people from various castes and origins, whom he describes as being all 'addicted' (*nasa*) to something, whether it was to alcohol and women, to money like thieves and businessmen, to religion like the Christians, or to politics like himself. They could not help doing something that in the end was dangerous and possibly destructive, something stronger than practical reason, but that would drive them irresistibly and that, in the end, they enjoyed. If personal suffering or frustration trigger one's commitment to political action— "until people are caught (by the police), they know nothing; until they go to jail and suffer, they are afraid of everything, they are not aware"—it seems that the experience of overcoming this suffering through resistance and struggle fuels the feeling of one's own power. This feeling grows all the more as the reason for resistance is the pursuit of the common good and no longer solely one's own benefit.[28]

Barman likes to repeat that he was not involved in political activities through personal interest, but because he was representing the people. However, it is worth noting that in expressing his political programme and general vision of society, he never used the patronizing or moralizing style of the standard activist discourse (whether of social or political activism, Panchayat, or Communist). This style, forged over the last 50 years of schooling and the dominant development ideology, conveys a conception of villagers as backward people waiting to be civilized.[29] As mentioned earlier, Barman was sent to high pastures with the sheep from an early age and did not receive any formal education. Although he can read and write—reading newspapers is his "daily prayer"—he is not an intellectual alienated from his own society.[30] In this sense, he has remained closer to being a local leader, preoccupied more by his people's welfare than conforming to universal ideals. His independent spirit can be discerned from the way he relates the adventure of the first parliamentary elections in 1991.

The 1991 Elections

Once the ban on political parties was lifted in 1990, an active campaign for the first general elections started on all sides. It must have been clear for the leaders of the United People's Front that Barman was a key candidate likely to achieve success in Rolpa. He was therefore asked to run for the party. It was agreed that he should compete against Bala Ram Gharti Magar, the Rastriya Prajatantra Party's (RPP) strong candidate, in the eastern constituency of Rolpa, even though this was not Barman's own home base. At the same time he could mobilize the western constituency—his own—where another candidate, Krishna Bahadur Mahara, would benefit from his support. Barman hesitated at first:

> I was already old (61 years) and I thought that a younger person would do better. But the UPF leaders insisted. I wanted to walk alone [i.e. not with the entourage that candidates usually recruit during their campaigns]. I went everywhere in the eastern part of Rolpa. I stayed in all the houses, whatever their party was, and whatever their caste was. I would eat there and tell them that although I was fighting for the UPF, they should think about this by themselves and vote for whichever side they thought was better. I would go and see them at work, share their tasks, carry their children, beat the grain, or plough a length of field. I am also a farmer, aren't I? I would joke and say, "You are from another party, but I know that you will end up voting for me!" It was on the radio that I heard that I'd won—I did not go to the headquarters for the counting of the votes. Bala Ram went with his supporters and they tried to cheat. They thought it was still the way it had been under the Panchayat. I went later though and shook hands with him. This is only politics [not personal].

Looking at his campaign from the point of view of marketing and the public image industry, Barman appears to have played the card of authenticity and simplicity. He initiated a style of public relations totally different from the more solemn and hierarchical behaviour usually adopted by politicians and government officials. With nobody to carry his bag or umbrella, Barman walked from village to village armed only with his convictions. He sustained this attitude all the way to Singha Darbar, where the new Parliament met, in Kathmandu. This is the setting of another legend about Barman and, unlike the episode of the burning of the royal portrait, one with a solid foundation.

The First Meeting of Parliament and the Question of Ethnicity

> When I arrived in Kathmandu, my friends [Party supporters] insisted that I change my village dress—the short kilt and the velvet shirt—for the Nepali dress of *daura suruwal*. I refused, accepting only to wear a jacket on top. Then we were called to Singha Darbar in order to prepare the visit of the king the following day. He was coming with the queen to give a speech before the first meeting of the Parliament. The general secretary took me to one side and told me: "You have to wear the national dress for the king's visit tomorrow". I told him: "What I am wearing now, I have always worn and so did my ancestors. If I can't wear this in front of the king, then why should I stay here?

I don't mind going back to the village". The general secretary did not reply. The following day there were a lot of people, everybody with the same dress and the same grey jacket. We were standing in line as the king and the queen walked by us. The king noticed me, a little surprised maybe, but he did not say anything. He gave his speech and all went fine.

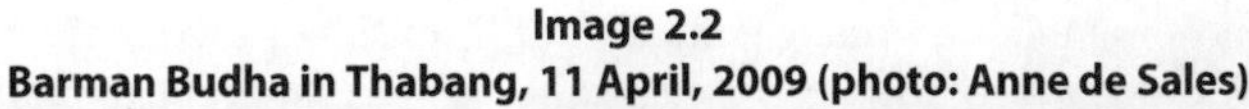

Image 2.2
Barman Budha in Thabang, 11 April, 2009 (photo: Anne de Sales)

Barman's brevity about this episode stands in stark contrast to the extensive public comment the incident generated. How are we to understand his eccentricity on this point? In the general context of the 1991 elections, the ethnic issue provides an obvious first interpretation of what looked like a provocative stand against the dominant Nepali culture, which minorities began to question openly.[31] However, not once in the course of our discussions did Barman claim to represent Magar culture or identity, nor did he claim to be fighting for it. As a matter of fact, mention of ethnic protest was remarkably absent from his discourse. At this point we are left with speculations, and a glance at the Communist position towards minorities may be useful.

Image 2.3
Barman with Santos Budha, and his wife (centre) in Thabang on the day Santos was elected a member of the Constituent Assembly, 11 April, 2009 (photo: Anne de Sales)

Mukta Tamang reminds us that in 1951, just two years after it was founded, the Communist Party of Nepal (CPN) issued clear statements in favour of "the preservation of cultures, the development and fundamental rights of all castes and ethnic groups ... their inclusion in governance and use of mother tongues in education and local bodies".[32] In the following decades, however, the Party focused on 'class struggle' to solve social problems at the same time as it promoted a strong nationalism to fight imperialism. The Communists counted only a few people from ethnic communities and even fewer were influential within the Party. According to Tamang, these leaders ended up leaving the Party out of frustration and embarked on new political career, some of them along ethnic lines, such as the Magar, Gore Bahadur Khapangi. Even when, in the post-1990 period, the Communists reconsidered their position towards culture, caste, and ethnicity, they saw the ethnic movements and their extremist trends as reactionary, bringing Nepal back to the pre-unification stage.

Tamang argues that the Maoists departed from these ideological premises shared by most in the left and were able to assess the post-1990 political situation and aspirations of the people in a more pragmatic way: "Instead of condemning caste/ethnic based movements ... the CPNM has come to recognize (them) as necessary allies" (Tamang, 2006: 284).[33] One of the main reasons for the increasing Maoist support for the ethnic agenda was the important role played by indigenous nationalities in advancing the armed struggle. In 2001, as the guerrilla warfare intensified, the Maoist 14-point programme publicly stressed equality and freedom of the oppressed nationalities and their right to self-determination. Three years later, within the space of a month, they declared nine 'Autonomous Regions', six of which had an ethnic basis, starting with Magarant on 9 January 2004.

The Athara Magarant provided the Maoists with a case in point for their ethnic politics. As mentioned earlier, Kham speakers are a linguistic minority within the Magar group and the Magar elite involved in ethnic issues looked down on them. The Nepal Magar Sangh, founded in 1991, did not count a single Kham speaker in its offices until 1998. For Gore Bahadur Khapangi, secretary of the association at the time, the general lack of education on the part of the Athara Magars (another way of referring to Kham speakers) explained why it was difficult to mobilize them on ethnic issues. The Maoists, by contrast, knew how to make good use of an area neglected by Magar activists. In 2002, they singled out the 14 Kham-speaking Village Development Committees as a 'special district' that would be added to the 75 others created under the Panchayat administration. The Athara Magarant and the obsolescent 'residual heights' of the Kalashes and Gorashes had become the core of the future Autonomous Magarant Region. The chief of the Magarant People's Government, Santos Budha Magar from the village of Thabang, was elected by the Magarant Parliament on the eve of the official declaration of the Magarant Autonomous Region.[34] In this way, with Maoist support, the Athara Magarant stole the show on the ethnic scene that had previously been dominated by the Bahra Magarant.

This being said, though the Maoists have courted the indigenous populations and acknowledged that they had been 'historically oppressed' by the Indo-Aryans, their ultimate goal was always the building of a nation of equal citizens. Santos Budha Magar was very clear on this point:

> We communists are not *jatibadi* (supporters of nationalism); our final purpose is to delete the concept of *jati* (nationalities) and classes and to make all people *samyabad* (supporters of equality)[sic]. However, as our society is half way between feudalism and capitalism, we formed the Autonomous Region as a stage to change the people's consciousness. (Ogura, 2008: 201)

The recognition of ethnic nationalities as distinct cultural-political entities, and the right of these nationalities to self-determination, are seen as a transitional phase in the evolutionary process of economic development and cultural assimilation. According to this view, the contradictions inherent in the historical situation will be resolved in the course of time, when education gradually changes people's consciousness.

The recently elected Constituent Assembly is still working on the new constitution and it is too early to make any predictions about the outcome of the ethnic policy of the Maoists who are now the largest political party. For the time being, the autonomous regions and all the other levels of Maoist 'people's government' that were established during the last years of the People's War are officially abolished. This incursion into the subject was an attempt to clarify Barman's aloofness towards ethnic issues in 1991. We might conclude that his attitude reflected his party's line, one that was already fraught with contradictions, but he had his own way of overcoming them. He did not politicize his identity as a Magar, but his wearing Magar dress in Parliament and taking the oath in Kham made it clear that he had not abandoned it either.

CONCLUSION

At the risk of succumbing to the 'biographical illusion' (Bourdieu, 1994), the dress incident in Parliament may be seen as the outcome of a long process that started 37 years earlier in Pyuthan, during Barman's encounter with the governor. When the quarrelsome young shepherd reached Pyuthan headquarters for the first time with his friends from Thabang, he was out to win. Falsely accused by his village enemy of being a Communist, he wanted to right a wrong. However, the sight of the men in *suruwal* made him and his friends run away out of fear and the presence of the governor got the better of Barman's body, which shook for days afterwards. Nevertheless, this traumatic encounter was also the source of a revelation—the governor was not a demigod but an ordinary human being who ate soya beans like everyone else—that marked the beginning of Barman's career as a political actor. Once he had overcome his fear, Barman felt empowered to fight injustice. The meeting with Mohan Bikram Singh was a turning point in his career and the teachings of the Communist activists provided him with the conceptual tools and the political infrastructure to frame village disputes in terms of a national political struggle. Within a few years the young man whose family had kept him away from home to avoid trouble became the Communist leader of his village, determined to go beyond running village affairs.

It seems that the empowerment Barman associates with the accusation of communism was of a different kind from his earlier wish to fight his long-term village opponent. What Barman calls *chetan*, 'consciousness' or 'awakening', is the key to a total transformation of the self, something potentially dangerous because it leads to transgressions, but enjoyable nevertheless and even intoxicating. Barman speaks of "addiction to politics" (*rajnitik nasa*). Although this inner transformation brought about a certain level of reflexivity in Barman's vision of himself, it did not alienate him from his own society: on the contrary, as suggested earlier, in this respect he remained closer to a traditional local leader than an activist.

In his biography of Tanka Prasad Acharya, the founder of the first Nepalese political party, James Fisher suggests that "the special role of Brahmins is central to the construction of power and agency in Nepal". The Brahmins could not be executed "not just because it was illegal but because it would have been too great a sin to have done so" (Fisher, 1997: 253–4). Although the Brahmins may have had to face physical duress—and they did—the charisma of their caste supported them in the process of their political empowerment. Barman could not rely on such a privilege. Indeed, he had to draw his power from some other source of legitimacy, and for this he turned towards his ancestors. There was no ostentation in Barman's behaviour in Parliament. He was simply being who he was, a representative of the rural population that had so far been too remote, poor, and uneducated to be present among the men in *suruwal*.

NOTES

1. After 1990, several radical communist groups professing Maoist thought, such as CPN Masal (Mohan Bikram Singh group) and CPN Mashal (Mohan Vaidya group) among others, were brought together under the Unity Centre appellation. In 1995 the leader of the Unity Centre, Pushpa Kamal Dahal (alias Prachanda) seceded and formed yet another group, the CPN (Maoist). For a lucid recent discussion of the political parties in Nepal, see Hachhethu (2006).
2. The ostensible purpose of the revolutionaries in contesting the parliamentary elections of 1991 and the local elections of 1992 (where they were seen to be even more successful and therefore a serious threat to the Nepali Congress, traditionally dominant in the west of the country) was to "expose the sham of parliamentary democracy" (Hachhethu, 2006: 10).
3. This chapter is based on about 10 interviews with Barman, who agreed to my proposal to write his biography in 2005. The trip to Nepal was financed by the MIDEA Programme (www.uni-bielefeld.de/midea) and I thank David Gellner and Joanna Pfaff-Czarnecka for making this possible.
4. Ogura's (2007) investigation of the roots of the Maoist movement in Rolpa and Rukum districts confirms Barman's instrumental role. I take this opportunity to thank this author for making her work available to me before publication. Robert Gersony's report (2003) is another comprehensive and generally reliable study, and can be used independently of his consultancy analysis.
5. These publications, all in Nepali, have been analysed by Marie Lecomte-Tilouine (2004, 2009) and Makito Minami (2007). On activism more generally, see Gellner and Karki (2007).
6. The Gurkhas started to recruit in the Kham Magar area only after 1985.
7. March (2002) found the same importance of songs in her work on Tamang women's lives.
8. Among the few biographies available in English, see Fisher (1997) on Tanka Prasad Acharya, the founder of the first political party in Nepal and his wife; Aziz (2001) on the life of Yogamaya and Durga Devi, two social activists under the Ranas; two autobiographies, one by B.P. Koirala, the leader of the Nepali Congress translated into English in 2001 and one by Durga Pokhrel, a human right activist under the Panchayat system (Pokhrel and Willett, 1996). On the subject of the biography as a literary genre in South Asia, see the introduction to Fisher (1997).
9. This point is developed by Levy (1998).
10. The *thum* was an administrative unit encompassing several hamlets, themselves reorganized into named villages and under the jurisdiction of an official from the central government. It usually had natural frontiers and formed a ritual unit (Gaborieau, 1978).
11. The Ranas were a powerful family who ruled the country as dynastic Prime Ministers from 1846 to 1951. Under their dictatorship the king's role was strictly ceremonial.
12. The traditional ruling families in the hills of Nepal are known as Thakuris. They claim descent from the Rajputs who fled to Nepal from Rajasthan to escape the Muslim invaders (fourteenth to sixteenth century). According to Lokendra Bahadur Shah, a descendant of the Thakuri ruler, whom I interviewed in 2005, his ancestors came from Jumla to settle in Rukumkot in the fourteenth century and by trickery

defeated the local king, Bokse Jar. Four centuries later, at the time of Bahadur Shah, the Thakuri kingdom joined the Gorkhali state. Although the Thakuri family had to give up its royal prerogatives, it kept a close alliance with the rulers of Nepal: if Indra Bahadur Shahi married a Rana, their grandson, Kumar Mohan Bahadur Shahi, married Princess Shobha, the younger sister of King Gyanendra. See Ogura (2007) for a more detailed account of the history of the ruling families of Rukum, although the scarcity of documents necessarily makes this a partial attempt.

13. *Birta* refers to a privileged endowment of land on which the king no longer claims rent. One of the first measures taken by the first elected government of Nepal in 1959 was to abolish this form of tenure. By contrast, *raikar* land tenure denotes leasehold land.
14. Some examples are given in de Sales (2003).
15. The Braha priests are Thabangis, members of the Rokha clan. There are four main clans in Thabang—Rokha, Budha, Gharti, and Pun—but the first two outnumber by far the others. The clans (*thar*) are sub-divided into exogamous sub-clans.
16. The most famous example is the worship of Mankamana, the goddess of the Gorkha dynasty, that was entrusted to Magar priests. On the subject of the participation of indigenous populations in the state rituals of Nepal, see Lecomte-Tilouine (2000).
17. *Shri Panc Maharaj Dhiraj sawari bhayo*
    Dangko ghari ghari
    Jaikku prasad bahun bajeko
    Kati lamo dari
18. What Barman calls the *mukti sena* was converted into the Raksha Dal in February 1951 and some elements of it supported K.I. Singh's attempted coup in January 1952 (Joshi and Rose, 1966: 88, 100; Whelpton, 2007: 89).
19. Jhankri here does not designate the Nepali ritual specialist, but an exogamous lineage belonging to the Rokha clan, one of the four Kham Magar clans along with the Budha, the Gharti, and the Pun. Krishna Jhankri (Krishna Mukhiya) is mentioned briefly by Ogura (2007: 456–7).
20. The Communist Party of Nepal, founded in Calcutta in 1949, was banned in Nepal until 1955, then again during the Panchayat period (1960–90) along with the other parties.
21. Mohan Bikram Singh, currently the leader of the CPN (Unity Centre-Masal), joined the underground Communist Party in 1952, organized a communist training camp in Pyuthan in 1953–54, and was jailed in 1954 for 18 months, first in Pyuthan then in Salyan.
22. For complementary information, see Ogura (2007) and Gersony (2003: 25–8).
23. *Makai hamro akar, hasiya hamro hatiyar.*
24. See Ogura (2007: 464–6) on the role of teachers in the expansion of communism in Rolpa and Rukum.
25. Rolpa was separated from Pyuthan and became one of Nepal's 75 districts in 1961.
26. In an earlier publication (de Sales, 2000), I myself took for granted the account that I heard in the neighbouring village of Lukum, a little more than a year after the event. This false rumour reveals how striking imagining any sacrilegious act against the king was at the time.

27. I thank Dilip Menon for this suggestion at the Oxford conference where I presented a first version of this chapter. After I read the book myself, I was able to confirm that some of the stories matched Barman's memories.
28. On the basis of interviews with Maoist activists, Fujikura (2003: 24) developed the idea that joining the movement was not simply a reaction to personal grievances, but to the aspiration to "bring about a particular form of collective future".
29. See Shneiderman, this volume. For a general analysis of the development ideology and its reception by villagers, see Pigg (1992).
30. On this subject, see Krauskopff (2009).
31. Barman was one of a number of new MPs who took the oath of allegiance in their mother tongues, not in Nepali, which was likewise much commented on. It is interesting however that Barman never mentioned this himself.
32. Report from the first CPN conference in 1951 in Calcutta, quoted in Tamang (2006: 274).
33. See also Lecomte-Tilouine's (2004) analysis of ethnic demands in the Maoists' discourse between 1990 and 2001. She brings out the contradictions inherent to the questions of territorial autonomy, nationality, and class with a special focus on Magar activists at the revolutionary end of the spectrum.
34. For a detailed account of the formation of the Magarant Autonomous Region, see Ogura (2008).

REFERENCES

Aziz, B. 2001. *Heir to a Silent Song: Two Rebel Women of Nepal.* Kirtipur: Centre for Nepal and Asian Studies.

Bourdieu, P. 1994. 'L'illusion biographique', chapter 3, in P. Bourdieu (ed.), *Raisons pratiques: Sur la théorie de l'action.* Paris: Seuil.

de Sales, A. 2000. 'The Kham-Magar Country, Nepal: Between Ethnic Claims and Maoism', *European Bulletin of Himalayan Research*, 19: 41–72. Also published in D.N. Gellner (ed.). 2003. *Resistance and the State: Nepalese Experiences.* New Delhi: Social Science Press, and in D. Thapa (ed.). 2003. *Understanding the Maoist Movement of Nepal.* Kathmandu: Martin Chautari.

———. 2003. 'Remarks on Revolutionary Songs and Iconography', *European Bulletin of Himalayan Research*, 24: 5–24.

Fisher, J.F. 1997. *Living Martyrs: Individuals and Revolution in Nepal.* New Delhi: Oxford University Press.

Fujikura, T. 2003. 'The Role of the Collective Imagination in the Maoist Conflict in Nepal', *Himalaya*, 23(1): 21–30.

Gaborieau, M. 1978. 'Le partage du pouvoir entre les lignages dans une localité du Népal Central', *L'Homme*, 18(1–2): 37–67.

Gellner, D.N. and M.B. Karki. 2007. 'The Sociology of Activism in Nepal: Some Preliminary Considerations', in H. Ishii, D.N. Gellner, and K. Nawa (eds), *Political and Social Transformations in North India and Nepal*, pp. 361–97. New Delhi: Manohar Books.

Gersony, R. 2003. 'Sowing the Wind ... History and Dynamics of the Maoist Revolt in Nepal's Rapti Hills' (report submitted to Mercy Corps International, October 2003), available at www.un.org.np (accessed on 8 March 2008).

Hachhethu, K. 2006. *Political Parties of Nepal*. Kathmandu: Social Science Baha Occasional Papers.

Joshi, B.L. and L. Rose. 1966. *Democratic Innovations in Nepal: A Case Study of Political Acculturation*. Berkeley: University of California Press.

Koirala, B.P. 2001. *Atmabrittanta: Late Life Recollections*. Kathmandu: Himal Books.

Krauskopff, G. 2009. 'Intellectuals and Ethnic Activism: Writings on the Tharu Past', in D. Gellner (ed.), *Ethnic Activism and Civil Society in South Asia*, pp. 241–68. New Delhi: SAGE Publications.

Lecomte-Tilouine, M. 2000. 'The Enigmatic Pig: On Magar Participation in the State Rituals of Nepal', *Studies in Nepali History and Society*, 5(1): 3–41.

———. 2004. 'Ethnic Demands within Maoism: Questions of Magar Territorial Autonomy, Nationality and Class', in M. Hutt (ed.), *Himalayan 'People's War': Nepal's Maoist Rebellion*, pp. 112–35. London: Hurst & Company.

———. 2009. 'Ruling Social Groups—From Species to Nations: Reflections on Changing Conceptualizations of Caste and Ethnicity in Nepal', in D.N. Gellner (ed.), *Ethnic Activism and Civil Society in South Asia*, pp. 291–336. New Delhi: SAGE Publications.

Levy, R. 1998. 'Selves in Motion', in D. Skinner, A. Pach III, and D. Holland (eds), *Selves in Time and Space: Identities, Experience, and History in Nepal*, pp. 321–29. Lanham: Rowman & Littlefield Publishers.

March, K. 2002. *'If Each Comes Half Way': Meeting Tamang Women in Nepal*. Ithaca: Cornell University Press.

Minami, M. 2007. 'From Tika to Kata? Ethnic Movements among the Magars in an Age of Globalization', H. Ishii, D. Gellner, and K. Nawa (eds), *Nepalis Inside and Outside Nepal*, pp. 443–66. New Delhi: Manohar.

Ogura, K. 2007. 'Maoists, People, and the State as Seen from Rolpa and Rukum', in H. Ishii, D.N. Gellner, and K. Nawa (eds), *Political and Social Transformations in North India and Nepal*, pp. 435–75. New Delhi: Manohar Books.

———. 2008. 'Maoist People's Governments, 2001–05: The Power in Wartime', in D.N. Gellner and K. Hachhethu (eds), *Local Democracy in South Asia: Microprocesses of Democratization in Nepal and its Neighbours*, pp. 175–231. New Delhi: SAGE Publications.

Pigg, S.L. 1992. 'Inventing Social Categories through Place: Social Representations and Development in Nepal', *Comparative Studies in Society and History*, 34(3): 491–513.

Pokhrel, D. and D. Willett. 1996. *Shadow over Shangrila: A Woman's Quest for Freedom*. Dulles: Brassey's.

Sankrityayana, R. 1947. *From Volga to Ganga: A Picture in Nineteen Stories of the Historical, Economic and Political Evolution of the Human Society from 6,000 BC to 1922 AD*. Bombay: People's Publishing House Ltd.

Tamang, M. 2006. 'Culture, Caste and Ethnicity in the Maoist Movement', *Studies in Nepalí History and Society*, 11(2): 271–301.

Whelpton, J. 2007. *A History of Nepal*. Cambridge: Cambridge University Press.

Chapter 3

Creating 'Civilized' Communists

A Quarter of a Century of Politicization in Rural Nepal

SARA SHNEIDERMAN

INTRODUCTION

By the time Nepal's Maoist insurgency reached its tenth anniversary in February 2006, it had only recently begun to garner consistent international attention.[1] Many early discussions of the 'People's War' in Nepal treated radical communism as if it were a newly introduced ideology which common citizens were unlikely to understand, much less believe. Yet communism had been one of the country's central political forces since the advent of party politics in the early 1950s. This paradox is in part due to the fact that, as Nepali political scientist Krishna Hachhethu has stated, "research on political parties at the local level is completely lacking in the literature on Nepali politics and parties so far" (2003: 136). In agreement with Hachhethu, I suggest here that we cannot understand contemporary politics in Nepal without taking a closer look at how political discourse, ideology, and practice have been deployed by leftist parties in local Nepali contexts over time. This chapter therefore seeks to provide a piece of historical background to the country's recent upheaval by considering the role of communist parties in the process of politicization that many citizens of rural Nepal have experienced over the last quarter century.

Both of Nepal's mainstream parties—the Nepali Congress (hereafter NC) and the Communist Party of Nepal (hereafter CPN)—have been involved in the ongoing project of raising political consciousness among Nepal's citizens since the early 1950s.[2] In this chapter, I focus specifically on the activities of the Communist Party of Nepal (Marxist-Leninist) (hereafter CPN-ML) in the eastern districts of Sindhupalchok and Dolakha, where cadres first began actively 'educating' villagers in the late 1970s. On the run from persecution under the pre-1990 partyless Panchayat system, CPN-ML activists chose several villages in the region as their 'underground' hideouts and used the opportunity to spread communist ideology among local people.[3] One such village was Piskar, in Sindhupalchok district, predominantly inhabited by the poor and disenfranchized Thangmi ethnic group.[4] As subsistence farmers who had long been exploited by the wealthy landowners whose land they sharecropped, many Thangmi were sympathetic to the communist project. The area soon developed a reputation as a hotbed for revolutionary ideas, and the village of Piskar gained national notoriety when government forces ambushed a local festival there in January 1984, killing two Thangmi villagers and injuring many more. In the next several months scores of villagers were arrested for their alleged participation in this event, and held in custody for up to three years without trial. After the fact, the so-called Piskar Massacre (*piskar hatyakand*) became a rallying point for a range of communist factions operating in the area, including today's Communist Party of Nepal (Maoist) (hereafter CPN-M).

I have described elsewhere the aftermath of the Piskar Massacre, and how the ensuing events shaped local attitudes towards the Maoists when they appeared on the scene in the mid-1990s (Shneiderman, 2009a). Here, I look back in time to examine the activities of CPN-ML activists in the years leading up to the Piskar Massacre. In particular, I consider the relationships between party cadres and residents of the Piskar area in the late 1970s and early 1980s, so as to understand how communist ideas were introduced and received at the local level. An analysis of these relationships suggests that Piskar's history as an early CPN-ML base area had produced a heightened political consciousness, which meant that Maoist ideology, when introduced in the late 1990s, was attractive to many villagers who had long been communist supporters but were disillusioned by the mainstream Communist Party's shift to the centre after the 1990 democracy movement. CPN-ML activists had done the difficult work of politicizing the populace, but then disappeared to pursue their own paths to power at the centre, leaving the villagers of Piskar open to Maoist recruitment.

My discussion of the early years of communist political activity in Piskar brings out the way in which socialism is a civilizing project linked to the production of dominant 'modern' identities. The attitudes of the cadres who interacted with Thangmi villagers in Piskar during the early phase of the communist politicization project there reveal a great deal about the internalized class and caste prejudices that motivated many communist activists, despite their ideological disavowals of such differences. They saw themselves as the architects of a radical social transformation that required all participants to give up 'primitive', localized ethnic identities in favour of a 'modern', homogeneous national identity.[5] From the beginning of their attempts to create a modern peasantry through the discourse of class struggle, the CPN has consistently viewed the competing discourse of ethnic empowerment as secondary.[6] This is hardly surprising, given the fact that the CPN has always espoused an orthodox communist line when it comes to the evolutionary model of historical materialism, which suggests that ethnic, national, and other group identities are simply artifacts of class hierarchy, which will disappear naturally as a side effect of class struggle.[7] Mukta Tamang has raised these issues in an analysis of CPN's policy documents on caste and ethnic issues over time, arguing that, "despite the policy formulation during the formative periods, the issue of caste and ethnicity remained marginal in the party discourse and practice in the whole history of the communist political movement until 1990" (2004a: 2). Yet there remains little documentation of how these tendencies played out on the ground as party cadres from dominant groups came in contact with ethnic minority peasants through the process of politicization. Here I show how such cadres saw themselves as part of a civilizing mission to create modern, national Nepalis, who would rise up in class struggle leaving their outmoded ethnic identities behind.

METHODOLOGY AND SOURCES

One of my primary sources for the present discussion is an extensive interview with Amrit Kumar Bohara and Asta Laxmi Shakya, conducted in Kathmandu in November 2004. Bohara and Shakya, a husband and wife team, were some of the first CPN-ML cadres to reside in Piskar during the early 1980s and were both major players in the events leading up to the massacre. After the 1990 *jan andolan*, or People's Movement for the Restoration of Democracy, they became important figures in the newly unified CPN (Unified Marxist-Leninist) (CPN-UML) party and remain Central Committee members of this mainstream opposition party. Both served as cabinet ministers during Nepal's multi-party democracy phase from 1991 to 2005.[8] In the 2008 Constituent Assembly election, Shakya ran for a first-past-the-post seat from Kathmandu's 8th district, but lost to Nabindra Raj Joshi of the NC. She was later appointed as Minister for Industry. Bohara served as acting general secretary of the UML for several months after Madhav Kumar Nepal stepped down in the wake of their party's poor electoral showing.

Other textual sources include two articles on the Piskar Massacre published in Nepali by Thangmi ethno-political organizations (NPTS, 1997; TBTSUK, 1999), a book about the event published the following year in Nepali by the CPN-ML (HPP, 1984), and English-language human rights reports on the massacre published by Amnesty International (1987) and Informal Sector Service Centre (INSEC), a Nepali human rights NGO (1995). These materials are complemented by a series of interviews with Thangmi residents of the Piskar area conducted between 1998 and 2000, and additional interviews conducted in Kathmandu between 2000 and 2005.

BACKGROUND: CPN PARTY HISTORY

The CPN has split and reunified several times. A basic understanding of these dynamics provides essential context for interpreting villagers' experiences. I rely heavily on the seminal work on Nepal's political parties done by Hoftun, Raeper, and Whelpton (1999) and Hachhethu (2002, 2003) to provide an overview of the history of the party here.

The CPN was officially founded in 1949 by Pushpa Lal Shrestha in Calcutta. Previously a member of NC, Pushpa Lal was influenced by Mao Zedong, and called for mass mobilization of the peasantry and violent struggle against Nepal's partyless Panchayat system. Pushpa Lal and his supporters returned to Nepal in 1951 after the fall of the Rana ruling family, but were quickly banned in 1952 for their violent activities. They operated underground for four years between 1952 and 1956, during which time they focused primarily on peasant issues, such as redistribution of land, tenancy rights, and the abolition of compulsory unpaid labour (cf. Hachhethu, 2002: 34–5). The CPN was legalized again in the late 1950s, and stood in the 1959 elections, but won only 4 seats out of 48 contested (compared to 78 out of 108 for the NC).

In 1960 King Mahendra terminated Nepal's first experiment with democracy. All political parties were once again banned, and the CPN and NC alike went underground. During the 1960s and 1970s, the CPN underwent multiple splits, based on ideological, pragmatic, and personal differences. One of the most important factions to emerge during this period was the 'Jhapeli' group, which operated in the eastern border district of Jhapa and followed the Indian Naxalite doctrine developed by Charu Mazumdar, which drew heavily on Maoist ideology.[9] Active in the early 1970s, this group took the hard line that 'annihilation of the class enemy' was the only way to effect political transformation. They were for all practical purposes Maoists, since they, "advocated the application of the Chinese way of armed revolution in Nepal to establish New Democracy [*naulo janbad* in Nepali] according to the Chinese model" (Hachhethu, 2002: 36). After killing at least eight landlords, and experiencing several casualties among their own activists, the Jhapeli group eventually shifted away from the Naxalite line and began forging alliances with other less radical communist factions. Despite this ideological shift, the Jhapelis remained well respected within Nepali leftist circles, and they formed the nucleus of the CPN-ML at its establishment in 1978 (Hoftun et al., 1999: 84).

It was during this period of change between the late 1970s and the mid-1980s that CPN-ML cadres first travelled to the Piskar area, as part of the party's programme to identify suitable 'base areas' and develop support there (Hachhethu, 2002: 59). As we shall see, the party's ambivalence at the central level during this period about whether to pursue violence or not had important implications for Piskar villagers' early experience of communism.

As part of their transformation in the late 1980s, the CPN-ML turned away from the demand for a one-party communist state. Along with other communist factions, they accepted the proposition that "conventional multi-party democracy could be a stage on the road to achieving *naulo janbad*" (Hoftun et al., 1999: 238), as an alternative to armed struggle. Under this aegis, the CPN-ML became one of seven communist factions allied as the United Left Front (ULF), which fought alongside the NC during the 1990 movement for the restoration of democracy. After the success of that movement, in 1991 the CPN-ML merged with the CPN (Marxist) to become the CPN (Unified Marxist-Leninist) (CPN-UML, usually known simply as the UML). This combined party then fully adopted the concept of 'multi-party democracy' (*bahudaliya janbad*) as an end in itself, in place of *naulo janbad*, and became the mainstream opposition party in competition with the NC. The UML came to power at the national level for the first time in the November 1994 elections, forming a minority government for nine months, but were ousted in a vote of no confidence in September 1995. For those nine months, Nepal had the world's only democratically elected communist Hindu monarchy. The party split again in March 1998, largely due to personal differences within the top leadership. The larger faction retained the UML name. The CPN-ML—now a very different entity than the pre-1990 CPN-ML, the popularity of which was inherited and maintained by the UML—was unable to gain the name recognition or popular support necessary to consolidate power. In 2002, these two factions reunited once again as CPN-UML.

In the meantime, the Communist Party of Nepal (Maoist) (CPN-M), which was established as such by 'Prachanda' (Pushpa Kamal Dahal) in 1995, had emerged as a major force to be reckoned with. The CPN-M officially launched their People's War in February 1996, after presenting a 40-point list of demands to the central government and receiving no response. By the end of the civil war in 2006, over 13,000 people had died in the conflict between the insurgents and state security forces, with the Royal Nepal Army (RNA) deployed to fight the Maoists in 2001 after the police suffered severe losses. Thousands more were injured, displaced, disappeared, and otherwise adversely affected. The CPN-M won de facto control of base areas in the far western parts of the country and rural areas of much of the rest of the country, but was never able to hold any district capitals or major cities through military operations. The Maoist agenda and the lack of a coordinated political response to it were important features of Nepal's crisis right up to the Second People's Movement of 2006.

After the UML accepted the notion of multi-party democracy as an end in itself (rather than as a means to an end) in the early 1990s, they had trouble maintaining their radical communist ideological edge. It became harder to differentiate the UML from the NC by their policies, particularly because the NC had always portrayed itself as a socialist party at the economic level. As Hachhethu puts it, "the NC is a liberal democratic party but with a socialist trademark and the UML is a communist party but with allegiance to multi-party democracy" (2003: 137). The UML had difficulty maintaining its emphasis on activism and positive change for peasants at the grassroots level after 1990. This situation became particularly acute in the face of the Maoists' erstwhile 'successes': if the UML was indeed a genuine peasants' party, why then were they unable to maintain their mass support? Why did many of those who supported the UML in an earlier era later turn towards the CPN-M instead? Looking at the Piskar story from an ethno-historical perspective helps answer these questions.

JOINING THE PARTY: BOHARA AND SHAKYA AS YOUNG IDEALISTS

It was during the formative years of communist thought in Nepal in the 1960s–70s—as the party leadership was struggling to intertwine Naxalite, Maoist, and democratic ideologies and reconcile this mixture with practical mobilization strategies suited to Nepal's context—that young activists like Amrit Kumar Bohara and Asta Laxmi Shakya emerged. Bohara was born in Piskar, Sindhupalchok in 1948 into a landholding Chhetri family that was part of the Hindu rural elite against which he later fought, and Shakya was born in 1954 in Kathmandu to a middle-class urban Newar Buddhist goldsmithing family. Their respective backgrounds determined the different manners in which they were initiated into the CPN, and these divergent experiences demonstrate clearly that the gap between rural and urban Nepal—which is often cited as one of the underlying causes of the Maoist insurgency—was already substantial in the 1970s.

Bohara was a rural youth angry with the exploitation he saw around him while growing up in the village. He was particularly struck by the plight of Thangmi sharecroppers, who were intentionally kept illiterate by the landlords they worked for so that they could not understand land use and loan documents they signed. As Bohara put it, "We abhorred from deep inside the feudal exploitation and injustice. But how were we to liberate the people?"[10] His maternal uncle had been an early social worker in the area. Although not affiliated with a political party, this uncle was devoted to educating villagers and raising social awareness, against the wishes of his own family and other village elites. Bohara had long been influenced by his uncle's activities, and when he came into contact with CPN party workers in the town of Dolakha while completing his secondary studies there, he felt that he had finally found the answer to his burning questions about injustice and exploitation. In 1966, at the age of 16, he became a member of the underground Pushpa Lal faction of the CPN. He imagined that he would continue with his college studies and work with the party at the same time. But when he went to meet Pushpa Lal in Banaras some time later and explained this plan, the party leader told him that further studies would only bring him personal security and comfort, not liberation from injustice and exploitation in the manner that full-time Communist Party work could. Pushpa Lal instructed the young man to leave college, and Bohara was convinced: "After he said this I decided then and there that I would quit my studies and give up everything including my home and my family. I took a vow that I would get involved in politics". He was soon assigned to a village-level cell and sent to "organize the people" from his home area. By 1980, he was the top CPN-ML party leader for the entire Bagmati zone.[11]

One of seven daughters and three sons in a well-to-do urban family, Shakya lived a very sheltered life. After taking her School Leaving Certificate (SLC) exam in 1972 at the age of 18, she had several months of free time while waiting for the results.[12] By chance, she stumbled upon a library maintained by the Chinese diplomatic mission to Nepal. She enrolled in Chinese language lessons, began to read Chinese literature, and in her words, "learned that China was a good country and that the communist party was good". She had been acutely aware of her own privileged position from a young age, and had desired to help the poor people who worked as servants for her family. But, "it was difficult to form those kinds of ideas having been born in a family like that", so when she came in contact with communist literature, she finally felt that she had found her place. Shakya continued her Chinese lessons after enrolling in college, and soon developed a network of like-minded friends. They became associated with the CPN through the Shyam Prasad faction, but after some months Shakya and her friends became disillusioned because "it could not work according to our aspirations, so we rebelled and left the group". Instead, they formed their own study group of fifty or so young people, and continued reading Chinese texts, especially Mao Zedong's *Little Red Book*. They learned from reading Mao that villages held the key to transforming the country, and that they would have to go to the villages and raise consciousness there if they wished to be true communists.

There was only one problem. As Shakya explained, perhaps with some exaggeration, "We had not seen a village, so we did not know what a village was like. We did not know what kind of people lived in the village and how one should deal with them." Urban youths like Shakya had never been to the villages where over 90 per cent of their fellow citizens lived, mostly in abject poverty.[13] The interest that she and her comrades had in visiting villages like Bohara's was more of an exception than the norm, and following this desire to visit villages and raise consciousness there required Shakya to make a break from her family. In 1980, at the age of 26, she ran away from home in order to evade an arranged marriage. At that point, she finally took the plunge and became a full-fledged CPN-ML member. Since she joined the party in the Bagmati zone, she came under Bohara's jurisdiction, and soon after she took the party oath he came to meet her to evaluate her skills and determine how to deploy her. He was sceptical of this well-off city girl's commitment to communist ideology, and as a test of her loyalty, he immediately assigned her to 'serve the people' in Piskar. This meant going underground, and for the next three years, Shakya, Bohara, and a third cadre, Madhav Paudel, lived in close quarters in the village environment.

During this period, Shakya and Bohara spent a great deal of time together. They married in 1981; apparently she had passed the test that he had set for her, on both political and personal levels. Shakya described the circumstances of their party-sanctioned marriage in Piskar:

> As I worked there I would meet him often. I liked his habits. I liked his perseverance. I saw him getting involved in the party with sincerity and working for the people. I saw that he endured a lot of suffering. When I saw this I felt that the two of us should get together and I should help him. Then we became attracted to each other. In 1981 we took an oath under the party flag. We could do this only after getting permission from the party. The two of us liking each other was not enough. So we got permission from the party and took an oath under the party flag that the two of us would move ahead together and get [more deeply] involved in the party.

Bohara and Shakya's marriage was a quintessential CPN alliance, which was held up as an example for other cadres. As their divergent narratives of communist initiation show, they represented several defining oppositions that the CPN was working to overcome in order to create a broad-based movement that emphasized Nepali national identity as a whole: rural versus urban, agricultural versus artisanal modes of production, poor versus rich, uneducated versus educated, caste Hindu versus non-Hindu, and even male versus female. Their union and ensuing work in Piskar was a powerful symbol of such party goals at the time.[14]

PISKAR: A 'BASE AREA' IN THE MAKING

What did the CPN-ML see in Piskar that convinced them to choose it as one of their first base areas for political activity in the immediate wake of the party's formal establishment in 1978? According to Hachhethu, "While exploring potential base areas, the ML had considered two factors, one was proletariat people like the landless, agricultural labourers and poor peasants, and the other was area—the remoteness of the villages from the headquarters of the districts" (2002: 59). Piskar met both of these criteria. Its population was overwhelmingly comprised of poor farmers who owned little or no land, who served as indentured labourers to a tiny group of landlords who owned the majority of productive land. The village was located in the eastern corner of Sindhupalchok district close to the border with Dolakha, far away from the district headquarters of Chautara.[15] Although it felt quite remote due to the hilly terrain, poverty, and lack of infrastructure, Piskar was also relatively close to Kathmandu (3–4 days' walk, or one day's bus journey once the Arniko highway opened in the mid-1960s), so cadres could travel back and forth between the political nerve centre in the city and this model 'village of the masses' fairly easily.

In addition, the importance of Bohara's personal connection to Piskar should not be underestimated. He was already in charge of the party's Bagmati zone operations before the Piskar agitation began, and he had a strong say in the choice of base areas in his zone. As a local boy who had risen through the party ranks, he could portray himself as a 'son of the soil' who was genuinely working for the masses in his home village, rather than as an outsider importing alien ideas. Bohara knew that his capacity to portray himself as an 'organic intellectual', in the Gramscian sense, would be an asset in achieving the party's objectives in the area. Moreover, it would satisfy him personally to see an end to exploitation in his home village more than anywhere else.

Piskar's Thangmi villagers had suffered from various forms of exploitation at the hands of predominantly Bahun, Chhetri, and Newar landholders. Highly inequitable landholding relations were at the root of other forms of exploitation, such as indentured labour and usurious money-lending practices. Table 3.1, published in 1985 by the CPN-ML, shows the distribution of land in Piskar at the time cadres began working there in the late 1970s.

Table 3.1
Ownership of Land in Piskar by Class (1970s)

Class	*Families (%)*	*Ownership of Land (%)*
Landlords	1.32	16
Rich Farmers	5.26	31
Middle-class Farmers	19.74	22
Poor Farmers	63.15	29
Landless Farmers	10.53	2
Total	100	100

Source: HPP (1984: 4), translated by Suren Thami.

To summarize the key points, 1.32 per cent of the families were landlords owning 16 per cent of the land, while another 5.26 per cent were rich farmers who owned a further 31 per cent of the land. Adding these two groups together, we can see that 6.58 per cent of the population owned 47 per cent of the land, while 73.68 per cent of the population was classified as poor or landless, and altogether owned only 31 per cent of the land.

The majority of poor and landless farmers had no alternative but to work as sharecroppers for the small number of wealthy landlords. There were two primary systems of land tenure: *adhiya*, by which the sharecroppers were required to give the landowners half of the harvest every year regardless of yield, and *kut*, by which the sharecroppers were required to give the landowners a fixed amount of grain every year, once again regardless of yield.[16] Both of these systems, especially *kut*, led to a situation where the grain that sharecroppers received in exchange for their labour was usually not enough to feed their families for a full year. This compelled the poor farmers to seek out additional cash income, in order to purchase food supplies. However, cash-earning opportunities were almost non-existent in the agricultural economy of Nepal's hills, and in desperation poor families would ask for loans from the same wealthy families for whom they already worked. Loans would be granted, but at extremely high interest rates of up to 5–6 per cent per month (60–72 per cent p.a.). When the farmers could not repay their loans within the stipulated time, the moneylenders would foreclose on their remaining land, if any. If the borrower had no land, he would be required to work on the lender's land with no compensation as punishment. In addition, lenders would often take advantage of illiterate borrowers by falsifying loan papers to show an inflated amount which the borrower could not read. All of these conditions led to a situation where the poor were continually getting poorer and losing land, while the rich were getting richer and consolidating property holdings.

As might be expected, the figures published by CPN-ML do not show the ethnic or caste identity of Piskar's residents, but rather focus on their class position. At the time, the Nepal census also did not collect information on ethnic and caste identity: this was done for the first time only in the 1991 census. For these reasons, there is no concrete statistical data available to demonstrate that most of the poor farmers targeted for politicization by the CPN-ML in the 1970s–80s belonged to the Thangmi ethnic group. However, this is a reasonable assumption based on anecdotal evidence and recent population figures that demonstrate the high Thangmi population of the area, as well as the Thangmi position at the bottom of the economic heap. In the interview, Amrit Bohara claimed that during his childhood in the 1950s–60s the population of Piskar was at least 60 per cent Thangmi. The 2001 Nepal census showed 834 Thangmi residents in Piskar Village Development Committee (VDC) or 38 per cent of the population (HMG, 2002: 73).[17] In the adjacent VDC of Chokati, Thangmi accounted for 46 per cent of the population (HMG, 2002: 69).[18] Based on my own survey work in these areas, I believe these numbers to be substantially lower than the actual Thangmi population.[19] In any case, Thangmi currently constitute an important population block in the region, and most likely their numbers were approximately the same or higher during the earlier period under discussion.

A 1999 survey of property ownership in Alampu, another VDC in the region with a majority Thangmi population, sheds some light on how land was probably distributed along ethnic/caste lines in Piskar.[20] The information collected by a Dolakha-based NGO shows that while Thangmi in Alampu constituted 90 per cent of the population, 75 per cent of Thangmi villagers owned only 0–5 *ropani* of land, and no Thangmi landholder owned over 20 *ropani* (ICDM, 1999).[21] In contrast, 67 per cent of Bahun and Chhetri villagers owned over 20 *ropani* of land and none owned less than 5 *ropani* (ICDM, 1999).

These numbers show that Piskar was a suitable microcosm in which to put communist ideas and actions to the test: it was what the CPN-ML liked to call a 'semi-feudal, semi-colonial' village environment. When Bohara returned to his home village in 1978, he found that there was already a "smouldering class hatred" (HPP, 1984: 7) among the Thangmi farmers, which could be harnessed to serve the broader purposes of the nascent communist movement. Thangmi villagers had long been aware of their exploitation at the hands of landowners, a feeling expressed in a substantial corpus of songs, poetry, and stories in the Thangmi language that articulates these issues and calls for justice. Many older Thangmi told me that they were involved in small-scale acts of resistance against their landlords long before they had ever heard of communism.[22] However, their frustrations had neither been linked to a clear ideological agenda that extended beyond the village, nor expressed in a manner that incurred the wrath of the state and implicated the villagers in a much broader web of political intrigue at the national level.

ENTER THE COMMUNISTS

The two publications on Piskar's history put out by Thangmi ethno-political organizations link the emergence of political consciousness in the area to the arrival of CPN-ML cadres in 1978 (NPTS, 1997: 67).[23] Amrit Kumar Bohara is given credit for being the first activist in the area, introducing other influential cadres to the villagers, and beginning the process of consciousness raising that enabled the Thangmi population to rise up in revolt, ultimately resulting in the Piskar Massacre. Both Thangmi publications suggest that Bohara was and remains a respected figure who was instrumental in organizing the villagers:

> The name of Amrit Kumar Bohara is well-known to the Piskar people, a very responsible underground contemporary Communist leader (recently Minister of Local Development), who was also from Piskar VDC in Sindhupalchok district. Amrit Kumar Bohara had brought to this same village of Piskar a very prominent, honest, and active member of the Communist Party, Madhav Paudel (recently district chairman of Lalitpur)... Awareness of [the importance of] education was increasing and the gap between the rich and poor, and the exploiter and exploited, was widening among the farmers. As a result, an anti-aristocratic and anti-exploitation movement arose among the local peasants in 1987 (VS 2054). (NPTS, 1997: 67)

> The communist minister Amrit Kumar Bohara, who was born in Piskar, returned to Bhumi at his birthplace and became active. The local people gave him support from their hearts. The people were becoming aware of natural rights, human rights, justice, equality, sovereignty, and so forth. They were becoming organized. (TBTSUK, 1999: 67)

The former publication also mentions Shakya:

> Asta Laxmi Shakya arrived in Piskar and spent almost one and a half years underground hiding in the above-mentioned Piskar area. Her work and motivation left a big impression on the locals and motivated them also. (NPTS, 1997: 69)

Several features of these quotations deserve further comment. First of all, it is intriguing that both of them mention with apparent pride Bohara's stint as a Minister within the UML government of 1994–95. This suggests that the people of Piskar saw him as a local boy made good—he is said to have returned to Bhumi, the territorial deity, or literally 'earth'—and that his presence in the national government increased their sense of actual representation in a democratic system. At the same time, these publications elsewhere display an ambivalence about the abilities of the central government to actually follow through on its promises to local people, and increasing disillusionment about the participation of local heroes like Bohara in such questionable ruling structures. Second, although Madhav Paudel, who was not a Piskar local (he was from the city of Lalitpur, to the south of Kathmandu), in fact did much of the early political work in Bohara's absence; Bohara as the local is ultimately given credit for bringing such an 'honest' and 'active' cadre to the village to work there in his stead. Finally, although these publications recognize local people's agency in agitating against the exploiters, the causal relationship between the appearance of CPN-ML cadres on the scene and the beginnings of these activities is made clear. The project was not just about agitating for their own rights, but about 'supporting' Bohara as well—which I interpret to mean supporting his larger political agenda and aspirations for personal advancement within the party. Villagers' frustrations were genuine and were already being expressed through other means, but a broader political consciousness that deployed communist ideology to counter hegemonic powers at the local and national level was Bohara's creation. The extraordinary efforts he put into politicizing the village appear to have emerged partly out of his genuine concern for the well-being of the villagers and his belief in the power of class struggle to transform their situation, and partly as an attempt to increase his own political stature.[24]

DISCOURSES OF DOMESTICATION AND DEVELOPMENT

What did Bohara and Shakya actually do when they arrived in the village? Their descriptions of the process of gaining people's basic trust and laying the groundwork for direct political action expose a great deal about their own class and caste/ethnic positionalities, and the way that these perspectives affected their interactions with villagers. Such details are conspicuously absent from the official accounts published by both the CPN-ML and Thangmi organizations. In addition to the objectives of raising consciousness and garnering personal support as described earlier, a central aim of these activists' early work in Piskar appears to have been the domestication of what Bohara and Shakya saw as the 'wild' Thangmi population, through simple development initiatives that would improve their basic livelihoods.

Bohara had clear impressions of 'the Thangmi' that dated to his childhood in Piskar. Despite having a strong social conscience, he was still a high-caste Hindu and saw the Thangmi, a non-Hindu, Tibeto-Burman language-speaking population, as distinctly other. Speaking of his late childhood years spent studying in the village primary school, he reminisced:

> Since by now there was a primary school in the village, we would call the Thangmi children to come to school. We had to plead with them to come to school. Otherwise they would not come, saying that they were Thangmi children and they had no use of education as it was meant for the rich; the Thangmi children should be looking after the animals.... They would say that they had to go work in the fields and there was no use learning to read and write. We were finally able to convince them and they began to read a little. That way social awareness was introduced to the villagers. Slowly they started becoming politically conscious too.

Although Bohara's claim that he was already introducing social awareness to villagers as a child is clearly exaggerated, the description of the Thangmi as largely illiterate and uneducated is accurate. There is no question that elite landholders conspired to keep their Thangmi sharecroppers from learning to read so that the latter could not challenge exploitative practices. Given this history, Thangmi families were likely to think that the new opportunity for primary education was yet another strategy for exploitation and stayed away from it, saying "it was meant for the rich".

Yet basic literacy was one of the fundamental prerequisites for building political consciousness, so when Bohara returned to the village as an adult with a political agenda, developing literacy within the Thangmi community was one of his first tasks, along with teaching the fundamentals of hygiene and sanitation:

> We began our work with such activities: We conducted adult literacy classes in the mornings and evenings. We taught them that they must keep the paths to their homes clean and keep the area around water taps clean. They used to keep their environment dirty. They would live and eat in such an environment. They did not take baths or wash their clothes. They lived and died like that. We taught them to make their living area clean. That is how we began our work.

However, this was not an easy task:

> But they said that they could not understand such things, and could not understand the lectures of big people (*thulo manche*).[25] They said that they could not fight against the big people and that was the way they were. They said that it was their fate to be poor and lead difficult lives. They were not supposed to have comfortable lives and all that we were suggesting was not possible. They said what we were talking

> about was for bigger people and they should not follow what we were telling them. They wouldn't listen to us. When we said something they would say, "yes, yes", but later they would say that they would not get to eat without working, and therefore they would not come for the literacy classes. They felt that we were trying to disrupt their lives and that we scolded them. It was much later that they began to trust us. Only later did they realize that we were trying to do good.

These details complicate the story of immediate understanding and easy trust between Bohara and the Thangmi villagers recounted elsewhere. Many Thangmi individuals first saw the activists as 'big people' from outside, who could not understand their situation and might in fact be trying to take advantage of them like all the other 'big people' they had come in contact with. Bohara may have been a Piskar native and a communist, but he was not a Thangmi. Until he proved otherwise through his actions, villagers had no grounds on which to believe that he was not out to exploit them just as his forefathers had.

Interviews with Thangmi villagers confirm this view of events. As one man put it:

> We had no reason to trust them. When people like him [Bohara] left the village we said farewell happily, when they came back we worried what they would do next. People were suspicious of new ideas and did not understand why they even bothered to talk with us. They didn't understand our way of life and even though later I understood that he was trying to help us, at first I thought he was like all of the others. Eventually I became interested in communist ideas and I learned to read through the classes Bohara started.

The emphasis on literacy had both symbolic and practical elements: teaching Thangmi individuals to read was symbolically powerful since it flew in the face of the landlords' attempts to keep them illiterate, and it was practically important since it enabled villagers to begin reading political publications on their own and to communicate with like-minded villagers elsewhere through letters. Literacy was linked to a discourse of development and modernity: reading itself was not enough, but along with implementing basic hygiene and developing a sense of pride in one's environment, it was one of the keys to becoming a 'politically conscious' and 'modern' Nepali citizen.

Unlike Bohara, Shakya had no preconceived notions of what village life in general or Thangmi life in particular was like. Her first night in a Thangmi house was a shocking experience, but one which further convinced her that she had taken the right path in becoming a party member:

> We got there exactly at midnight. It was a Thangmi village. We knocked on a door. We went inside a Thangmi house. I felt very strange as soon as I saw the room. I was born in a city. I lived in a city. I realized that this was also Nepal, this was also our country.... It was a dark and small room. There were no mattresses or blankets. When we got there we were hungry, we had not eaten anything. Then a woman comrade wearing dirty clothes got up, shook my hand, and told me to sit down. She said that I must be hungry and asked me what I wanted to eat. There was nothing to eat, only some flour. She poured some water on it and put some salt in it and gave it to us. I came to realize what the love of the people means.

For Shakya, the Thangmi were a wild 'other' in need of domestication before even basic political activities could be carried out. The prospect of imparting communist education seemed impossible until the potential students in question—the Thangmi—began to think of themselves as full-fledged humans entitled to basic dignity and rights:

> They never took a bath. They did not know that the pot they cooked food in should be cleaned. After they cooked the food they would keep it just like that and there would be flies all over the pot the whole day. In the evening they would pour water in it, cook and eat. I would stay inside and clean the pots. They would go to the fields to work, and to collect fodder for the animals. When they came home in the evenings they would see everything clean. It's nice to see everything clean. That's how they learned. I combed their hair and they learned that hair should be combed.... There was no soap to wash clothes. I taught them how to wash clothes. I did not teach only about politics because there was a need to change the economic situation, the social situation, their ideas, and their lifestyle.... They ate beef and we taught them that they should not eat it.

Shakya's social work appears to have been well intentioned, arising out of a genuine concern for the welfare of the people she encountered. But there was also an element of ethnic prejudice in it that saw most Thangmi traditions and habits as unclean and unacceptable, rather than as fundamental aspects of Thangmi life. This is most evident in Shakya's pride in teaching Thangmi villagers not to eat beef.

Killing cows was strictly illegal in pre-2006 Hindu Nepal, and consuming the flesh of cows that have died of natural causes was and remains a marker of low social status. Nonetheless, the practice is still an important marker of Thangmi identity. An act of resistance against the Hindu world that dominates them, Thangmi men and women take pride in eating beef and go to great lengths to maintain this tradition despite strong pressure to end it. What Shakya attempted to teach them, then, was not just how to be communists, but how to subjugate their ethnic identity to an emerging national identity as 'modern' Nepalis who complied with dominant expectations.

PICTURE BOOKS, SONGS, AND SPEECHES

Once the basic hurdles were overcome and trust was gained, Bohara and Shakya both began holding literacy and general education sessions. Since none of the villagers were literate at the beginning, the main teaching tools they used to explain communist concepts were picture books. Shakya explained:

> I took a lot of picture books with stories in which people come together and rise against scoundrels, where people get together to solve their problems. We would explain on the basis of these picture books. There were a lot of picture books in Chinese available then. We ourselves would write picture books which had characters who were the people's enemies.

The next step was getting the people to express their anger about their own oppression, which was best done through songs and other non-literary forms. But, according to Bohara, even these modes of expression had to be introduced to them:

> We taught the women to read, sing songs, recite poems, write, to give speeches, to speak up. We taught them in caves, jungles, and other shelters in the night. We did all that. Otherwise how would they have been able to stand up and speak?

Since songs and poems are widespread traditional Thangmi cultural practices, one wonders whether Bohara and company can actually claim credit for teaching Thangmi women about these forms of expression. Perhaps the activists were indeed the first to suggest to

Thangmi individuals that their songs might be good for more than intra-ethnic communication and entertainment, and could in fact be used as a mode of protest against others. The Thangmi publications on Piskar concur that songs were a central aspect of the emerging political movement:

> The main source of public awareness was the 'people's song', so they went to caves to listen to songs secretly in the evening. For this purpose they purchased a cassette recorder with money from selling wild honey. Through listening to the songs, the farmers realized that there had been serious class suppression. (NPTS, 1997: 67)[26]

Most likely, the communists can claim credit for suggesting to Thangmi villagers that they begin singing and reciting poems in Nepali, rather than in their ethnic language, so that their complaints could be understood by the landlords against whom they were directed. Once again, the cadres' presence worked to inculcate a sense of agency as national political actors, at the same time discrediting the value of indigenous Thangmi-language activities, which did not qualify as 'standing up and speaking'.

SUFFERING AND REDEMPTION

Both Bohara and Shakya felt that they experienced great personal suffering in the process of bringing political awareness to the Thangmi of Piskar and empowering them to 'speak out'. For Bohara, this took the shape of state persecution against his own family in the village:

> Our family has struggled a lot for them [the Thangmi] so that they would not have to be dependent on anyone, so that they would not be exploited by anyone and they could lead their own lives. Our house was locked up for having done that. The government at the time confiscated all our property. They jailed my brother and his wife. They chased us away from our home, they demolished our house and destroyed our garden. That's what they did during the Panchayat era. I could not even see my father when he died. I could not go there.

Shakya described her suffering more as a test of internal strength in adverse conditions, epitomized by the experience of having to eat rotten meat served to her by Thangmi villagers in order to gain their trust:

> I could not eat the meat. I thought that I could not stay there. I thought that I could not work with him [Bohara]. Tears rolled down my face but I somehow ate it. Later I told them that we must live, we do not have money for medicines and if they died early who would bring about a revolution, who would build up an organisation. So we should not eat it, let's continue to live.... I told them this after I ate it. If I had told them earlier, they would have chased me away. They would not have trusted me. Now they could consider me one of them.

All of this suffering was not without its results, and ultimately being 'one of them' paid off. Both Shakya and Bohara acknowledged that their political careers would never have taken off without the support of Piskar's people, and the repute they gained as genuine communist revolutionaries in the aftermath of the Piskar Massacre. As Shakya put it, "Piskar brought me up to here"—'here' being a seat on the UML central committee and a ministerial portfolio in the UML government of 1994–95.

THE MASSACRE: ONE SQUAD ACTION AND BEYOND

How did all of this communist education affect Piskar's Thangmi villagers? As early as 1978, villagers began taking action against landowners and experienced retaliation from state security forces. The massacre of 1984 was not the beginning of the movement, but rather the culmination of a long series of encounters between villagers and the police. The actions in which villagers were engaged, such as 'stealing' property and grain from wealthy landlords, refusing to work for them, and tearing up loan documents, conformed to the broader CPN-ML policy of "escalat[ing] its one squad action .... in some of its base areas in Ilam, Sankhuwasabha, Sindhupalchok, Mahotari and Dang districts in 1978–79" (Hachhethu, 2002: 59).

One of the Thangmi activist publications from the 1990s recounts three different events in the late 1970s in which Thangmi activists pillaged landlords' houses and property, and consequently faced police retaliation (NPTS, 1997). Often it seemed that the police had been called in by the landlords, and that it was these local big men who were using their influence to command the state authorities rather than the other way around. In response to the last incident, 105 Thangmi villagers were listed as 'terrorists' by the government, and warrants were put out for their arrest (NPTS, 1997: 68). In late

1979 a company of 80 policemen came to arrest these individuals, but the villagers resisted them violently. Three Thangmi protesters were badly injured in the incident, and the stakes were further raised.

The villagers of Piskar were not alone in incurring the state's wrath in reaction to their nascent protest movement. The CPN-ML had been instigating similar kinds of actions in other rural base areas throughout the country, and often the results were violent. Ultimately, this compelled the party leadership to rethink their tactics, and a policy change was made at the central level. As Hachhethu explains:

> ... the ML was unable to resist when the government used suppressive measures in areas where the party's one-squad action had disrupted the law and order situation. The Khalsa belt of Dhankuta was an extreme case in which the government used the army with a major operation for 11 days in November 1979 in which 15 persons were shot dead, 200 women raped, 55 arrested and the rest of the villagers left their homes. Consequently, the ML's central leaders were compelled to review their dogmatic strategy. (Hachhethu, 2002: 60)[27]

But despite this change at the central level, the local unit in Piskar led by Bohara, Shakya, and Paudel did not follow suit. They continued with their 'one squad action' throughout the early 1980s, although they knew they were under increased government surveillance, and although they were receiving warnings from within the party to desist.

So when the annual Thangmi festival of Maghe Sankranti came around in January 1984 it was no surprise to anyone that it contained a political element, or that it was brutally suppressed by the police. As Bohara explained:

> Seven days before the 15 January incident, Madhav Paudel and I had gone to Piskar. We had organized a meeting on behalf of the party.... We made arrangements for a cultural programme on 15 January and talked about a progressive type of programme that would make the people conscious, in which they would sing songs against feudalism and stage plays.

Bohara and Paudel were making strategic use of the traditional festival day of Maghe Sankranti—on which the Thangmi community of the region always gathered at the Piskar Mahadevsthan—to communicate communist concepts to a large group of villagers beyond the already politicized core individuals with whom they had been working for several years. About 2,000 people turned up at the festival and, according to one of the Thangmi publications, it was a joyous cultural event—albeit with a not-so-subtle political element—that went sour:

> On the above-mentioned day at the *jatra* [festival], around 2,000 villagers and devotees from all around the vicinity as well as other places were present. The enthusiastic villagers had also prepared a stage for presenting an entertainment programme.... The audience was deeply engaged in the appealing programme of dances, skits, plays, songs, and so forth. The freezing cold of Magh [January–February] didn't bother them at all. Those who were hungry were busy enjoying soybeans and yams distributed by the organizers. Piskar's environment was entranced by the rhythm of the *madal* [drum] and the melodious sound of the bamboo flute. By around three in the morning the programme had finished peacefully, but the festival continued.
>
> Forgetting their daily lives, the villagers had been enjoying the festival, each in their own way. The time was about four in the morning. No one had any clue that the conspirators in their well-planned style had been encircling the site of the programme from all directions with lethal arms, and they were moving forward. According to the premeditated plan, the bloodsuckers were marching alertly on the paths from Chitrepati and Changtha [nearby villages]. The group of police who had come along with the DSP [Deputy Superintendent of Police] had arrested Madhav Paudel and Tara Pant [another cadre], but Madhav was successful in escaping from the police grip. Immediately after he skipped out like that, the police called the attack on the *jatra*. Overturning all of the lamps, destroying the stage, and randomly lathi [baton] charging, the situation became more and more frightening.
>
> Bir Bahadur Thami and Ile Thami stepped forward to take control of the frightened and terrorized trembling masses. The bloody attack went on and on for about half an hour non-stop. (TBTSUK, 1999: 63–4)

Both Bir Bahadur Thami and Ile Thami were killed as the police opened fire on the villagers, and these two men were subsequently declared martyrs by the CPN-ML. Fifteen others were injured, five of whom succumbed to their wounds and died in the following weeks. Several hundred villagers were also arrested and held for up to three years without charges.

These events constituted a massive rupture in daily life for Piskar's villagers. Families were torn apart, as all those who had been present at the festival (and many who weren't) were branded as 'extremists' or 'terrorists' and went into hiding to avoid arrest. Strangely, Amrit Bohara was not there on the day of the massacre.[28] He had returned to Kathmandu just a few days before, and heard about the events there. Bohara rushed back to the village to hold 'condolence meetings' for the new Thangmi martyrs. Even so, many of the villagers became suspicious that the party leaders had been tipped off about the impending police action, and had saved their own skins by leaving, while putting Thangmi lives on the line in the name of communist revolution. In our interview, Bohara admitted that he was aware of the possibility of retaliatory action from the police, but suggested that his actions had minimized the potential damage:

> Once the government starts getting suspicious it begins acting. Political activities increased and people started getting organized. The government mobilized soldiers. They were planning to have a big battle. Their base was Piskar. They said that the communists were coming ... since the forces in the district were not adequate they brought more from the capital and suppressed us. We knew a little of what was going to happen. Friends had warned us to be careful. That's why only two people died. Otherwise hundreds would have died. They had encircled us.

Although he identifies himself with those present at the festival—"they had encircled *us*"—his absence on the day of the event planted the first seeds of doubt in many villagers' minds that Bohara's political activism was intended solely to benefit them and improve their livelihoods. For some local Thangmi who had become CPN-ML activists, the massacre only hardened their resolve to fight against exploitation and the violent state through communism. Others, however, began to worry that the revolution was not so much about them as about politicians fighting for power at the centre. As one young man from Piskar whose father was arrested put it, "It was Bohara's fault that innocent people suffered, and we cannot forgive him for that".

Human rights reports about the event tried to give the villagers the benefit of the doubt by portraying them as victims of outside agitators who used local people for their own political ends. As the Amnesty International report on the incident explains, "The authorities of the Piskar area are understood to have been concerned for some time about the influence and activities of radical groups who ... were 'defaming' local landowners" (1987: 15). As I have argued elsewhere (Shneiderman, 2009a), I do not believe that this is an entirely accurate portrayal of the situation: the specific political terms through which the villagers' frustrations were expressed had indeed been introduced over the preceding five years by activists like Bohara, but the villagers' grievances against the landlords were genuine and homegrown, and might well have come to be articulated through other means had communism not appeared on the scene. Yet given the circumstances surrounding the event, Bohara and his comrades do seem to bear substantial responsibility for the loss of life and ensuing social fragmentation that occurred in the village, while they were lauded as 'heroes' by the party for their work in mobilizing Piskar's masses.

AFTER THE FACT: STATE POWER FOR THE PARTY, DISILLUSIONMENT IN THE VILLAGE

The massacre and its after-effects put a temporary end to explicit political activism and one squad action in the Piskar area. Most of the village leaders were in jail, and the rest were afraid for their lives. Bohara and Paudel stopped spending much time in the village and began to focus increasingly on building the party at the central level, especially as the movement for the restoration of democracy began to heat up in Kathmandu in the late 1980s. Although many Piskar villagers remained CPN-ML members, they became increasingly sceptical of the limited role the leadership envisioned for them within the party as village-level cadres rather than key party members at the national level. Furthermore, it seemed that the very party leaders who had taught the villagers about the value of violent class struggle were beginning to lose their ideological edge, as the CPN-ML joined the United People's Front and adopted 'multi-party democracy' (*bahudaliya janbad*) as their goal, in place of the Maoist concept of 'new democracy' (*naulo janbad*). As one Thangmi villager who had been an active CPN-ML cadre until the early 1980s put it:

> That was the moment when we knew they were not thinking of us any more. We had come to believe in the value of new democracy through

> violent class struggle, and suddenly those who had got us involved in the first place deserted us. It looked like they were only interested in gaining power in Kathmandu and had forgotten our suffering. That's when I left the party.

Bohara and Shakya were highly aware of such accusations, and made a point of defending themselves by asserting their continued concern for the villagers of Piskar. Bohara in particular defended his actions as a cabinet minister in the 1990s, but acknowledged the limits of his capacity to effect change in Piskar from his position of central power:

> The condition of the people is still the same. We have not been able to bring about change in their suffering. There is a lot of discontent. We have tried to work for them so that their economic condition improves a little, and they get their political rights. The party respects them and has given them status.... I have become a member of parliament and have become a Minister two times. When I am leading such a comfortable life, I remember the people of Piskar and understand their suffering. Sometimes people accuse me of being a retrograde and say that I have earned a lot of money. They ask me what I have earned. They say that I have forgotten the people. I still feel for them and I have not forgotten them.... It is because of the people there that we are here today. They brought us here. I would not be alive if they had not hidden me and saved me when the Panchayat system tried to shoot me. I would not have been alive if they had not hidden food in their clothes and given it to us. So how can I forget them when I am living a comfortable life now?... It is not easy to go there now but I have not forgotten. I tried to help them when I could and when I was in the government. I tried to have some construction work done in the village there so that the people would benefit economically. I tried to do this through different government agencies. But the class difference there will not end just like that. That could take a very long time. There is a need for a very big social transformation.

One wonders who could effect the kind of 'social transformation' Bohara speaks of, and how.

By joining the fight for multi-party democracy and then participating in governance within the new system after 1990, the UML demonstrated that they were no longer a revolutionary party, but rather a mainstream democratic party that was struggling to maintain its populist image. As Hachhethu explains, throughout the 1990s both major parties began to lose credibility due to internal power struggles, corruption scandals, and an over-emphasis on power at the centre to the detriment of grassroots concerns:

> Parties are increasingly becoming an instrument for self-aggrandizement of the power elites and vested interest groups. This has a negative impact on the parties' advocacy of the collective interests of society. Nepali political parties have failed miserably in their basic duty of linking citizens' preferences with public policy.... Beset by these problems, the NC and the UML seem headed towards a reverse course as protectors of the status quo rather than as instruments of change. Their existence among the people and in the society at the grassroots level is mainly confined to physical presence not functional activity. So the mainstream parties themselves are creating a vacuum, ideologically and politically, in society. (Hachhethu, 2003: 173)

Many of Piskar's villagers shared the sense that the UML was becoming part of the status quo rather than continuing to work for social transformation, and the party therefore began to lose its appeal to many of the villagers it had worked so hard to politicize.

The concept of 'democracy' in particular seemed to have delivered little to those who had worked so hard for it. In the version of the Piskar story published by a politically centrist Thangmi cultural committee, the two Thangmi 'martyrs' from the village are initially represented as sacrificing their lives in the interest of national democracy. By the end of the polemic, however, a clear sense of frustration emerges with the central government's refusal to acknowledge their contribution to the democratic struggle. At the outset, the martyr Bir Bahadur is described as follows: "A poor village boy, fiercely defending himself against the enemy, he proudly sacrificed his life for his country as a true nationalist" (TBTSUK, 1999: 65). The closing sentence of the article, however, poses the question, "Isn't it an insult that the country has hesitated to put the names of these heroes who sacrificed their lives for democracy on the list of national martyrs?" (TBTSUK, 1999: 68). UML leaders like Bohara had taken on ministerial positions and become part of the state apparatus, yet they had failed to secure adequate compensation for Piskar's villagers. While democracy was the ideology of choice as long as it appeared to promise positive change in villagers' lives, when the democratic system was perceived to fail the very villagers who had fought for it, the space was open for other alternatives.

A quotation from the other, more radical, Thangmi publication from 1997 drives this point home:

> Was the intention of these patriots [the Piskar martyrs] to establish a multi-party system instead of the Panchayat? Why then are the same old leeches sucking the poor dry? This is absolutely wrong, so to fulfil the lack of representation in the common interest, in the coming days we will definitely see the blood of the people of Piskar flow again. (NPTS, 1997: 68)

Indeed, the UML's shift to the centre had created a serious ideological and political vacuum, which the CPN-M—the Maoists—stepped in to fill in 1996.

THE EMERGENCE OF NEW REVOLUTIONARIES

By early 2001, Piskar was a regional Maoist base, or *adhar ilaka*, and it had even become a show village where Maoist propagandists took foreign reporters (Liu and Roberts, 2001). The village's history had produced a heightened political consciousness which meant that when the Maoists finally arrived on the scene, their ideology was seen to be essentially congruent with the existing agendas of many villagers. In short, CPN-ML activists had done the difficult work of politicizing the populace, and then disappeared to pursue their own paths to power at the centre, leaving the villagers of Piskar a perfect target for Maoist recruitment. When the Maoists held their first meetings in Piskar in 1998, their agenda sounded very much like the CPN-ML platform 20 years earlier. Despite everything the village had been through in the 1970s and 1980s, very little had changed in terms of economic or social structure, and it is hardly surprising that the same type of people who had reacted positively to the CPN-ML rhetoric in an earlier era, and then felt let down by the party's shift to the centre, would once again be attracted by this new version of hard-line communist ideology. Some prominent villagers who had supported the CPN-ML in the early days remained party members, especially those who had been involved at higher levels in the district-level party committee. But others were disillusioned, particularly the younger generation who had witnessed their parents' arrests after the massacre in 1984, and who had no personal allegiance to the earlier generation of CPN-ML activists. Some of these individuals began to support the

Maoists, either by directly joining their People's Liberation Army, or by acting as village-level militia and informers.

The suggestion that the Maoists were responsible for politicizing the people of Piskar and mobilizing them for revolutionary action was anathema to Bohara and Shakya. It was difficult for them to acknowledge that in fact a substantial number of villagers who had originally comprised their base might have now defected to the new revolutionaries:

> Bohara: The Maoists are calling the Piskar area and the Thangmi settlement in Dolakha their base area. There is no truth in this. They may be staying there by force but it was not they who made the people there socially and politically conscious.
>
> Shakya: Today the Maoists say that the Thangmi in the settlements of Dolakha and Sindhupalchok have become socially and politically conscious because of them. That is a lie. It was our party that started organizing the Thangmi politically in very difficult circumstances in Sindhupalchok and Dolakha districts. Our party started working from the beginning, from ground zero, from nothing. Our party is working there even now. Some might have become involved with Maoists, I don't know. They might have got involved for various reasons. I do not want to comment on their independence. But until today, it remains we who worked from the beginning to build the organization there.

There is no question that it was the CPN-ML activists who first built a communist consciousness in the area, which the CPN-M took advantage of later. The Maoists are nonetheless unashamed of using the Piskar Massacre as a propaganda tool. 'Piskar' is a rallying cry in their mass meetings throughout the region. They claim that the massacre was 'their' event and that they will avenge the Thangmi martyrs' death through their revolutionary actions.[29] Although the first part of this statement is historically unfounded, the second part of the statement has proven to be a winning gambit with the disillusioned Thangmi community of the area. It is telling that the sons of both Bir Bahadur Thangmi and Ile Thangmi, the two martyrs of the Piskar Massacre, became involved with the Maoists, one as a high-level area commander. Apparently the Maoists were able to rekindle interest by promising a revolutionary social transformation that villagers no longer trusted the mainstream wing of the CPN to deliver.

At the time of writing in 2005, the UML leadership was disturbed by this situation, and was doing everything they could to win back their past supporters. At a May 2005 convention held by the Nepal Thami Samaj in Kathmandu, a national Thangmi ethno-political organization, one of the invited speakers was none other than Madhav Paudel, now Lalitpur district chairman. He pulled out a dog-eared copy of the 1984 Himali Prakashan Parivar book about the Piskar Massacre published by the UML (HPP, 1984, as cited earlier) and presented it to the convention's organizers, all of whom were relatively young Thangmi who would have been children at the time of the massacre. "This is your history," he said, "[A]ll of Nepal knows that the Thangmi are brave martyrs fighting for their country." Although Paudel did not explicitly mention the UML, his speech was clearly intended to attract young Thangmi to the party. It had mixed effects: the 26-year-old general secretary of the Thangmi organization later told me that he was very uncomfortable with the way both the Thangmi ethnic name and the village of Piskar were deployed for political purposes. "All of the parties have promised us things", he said, "especially the UML. We still want to think that they have something to offer us, but how can we trust them any more? Many young Thangmi lie about their ethnic affiliation because they do not want to be seen as communists or Maoists, especially in the current situation [i.e. post 1 February 2005]".

However, other young people who did not take part in activities of the Nepal Thami Samaj were instead proud of their membership in the Thami Mukti Morcha, a Maoist-affiliated alternative ethnic organization. Although the CPN-M does not differ from earlier CPN groups at an ideological level (all of them claim to give precedence to class over ethnic struggle), Maoist cadres have been significantly more successful at engaging in and expediently manipulating ethnic discourse. The Maoists hardly had a choice: by the time they emerged as a full-fledged political force in the mid-1990s, Nepal's ethnic rights movement, or *janjati andolan*, had developed as a significant alternative social movement that could no longer be ignored.[30] By establishing nominally independent organizations that represent each ethnic group within the party, encouraging cultural performances of 'indigenous' song and dance at political meetings, and carefully appointing individuals from locally prevalent ethnic minority groups to the leadership of their 'people's government' councils (*jan sarkar*) in each area, the Maoists have made a show of being sensitive to grievances voiced in an ethnic, rather than class, idiom.[31] These gestures still only go so far; many Thangmi and members of other minority groups who were first attracted to the Maoist movement by precisely such measures soon found that they were often cosmetic. The glass ceiling remains when it comes to the higher levels of CPN-M party leadership, which is dominated by Bahuns.[32] Furthermore, the Maoist platform for political change is ultimately a radical nationalist one predicated on the erasure of both class and ethnicity.

For UML leaders like Paudel, Bohara, and Shakya, who have joined the mainstream, Piskar remains a symbol of what they once were. According to Bohara, "Piskar is a village that gives birth to martyrs. It gives inspiration for political work". Indeed, the early work of politicization and consciousness raising that these activists carried out in Piskar appears to have inspired a whole new generation of revolutionaries. But they will have to work even harder than their predecessors to avoid falling out of favour with a highly politicized populace more aware than ever of their ethnic and economic rights.

NOTES

1. The research presented here was conducted in 1999–2000 with funding from a Fulbright Fellowship (Shneiderman, 2009b), and in 2001–05 under a National Science Foundation Graduate Research Fellowship. Additional funds were provided by the Department of Anthropology and the Einaudi Center for International Studies at Cornell University. I thank Bir Bahadur Thami, Man Bahadur Thami, and Mark Turin, as well as the members of the Nepal Thami Samaj, for their invaluable support and contributions to my research. Finally I thank Dambar Chemjong, David Gellner, Krishna Hachhethu, David Holmberg, Kathryn March, Frank Pieke, and Mukta Tamang for influential conversations and comments on earlier drafts of this chapter.

   This chapter was originally written in 2005. I have not been able to update it fully to incorporate an analysis of more recent events, such as the CPN-M's April 2008 electoral victory. Since the focus of my discussion here is largely historical, for the most part I have left the text in its original form. At key moments, I have added footnotes to indicate areas where recent events warrant future research.
2. The CPN has undergone several splits and reunifications over time. These will be detailed in the following; here I refer to the 'parent' party as a whole.
3. All political parties were illegal until 1990.
4. Thangmi is the indigenous ethnonym used by members of the group to refer to themselves. Thami is the Nepali derivative which is used in official documents and most literature on the group. I use 'Thangmi' when referring to the group in my own work, but Thami when citing ethnic organizations who use the term in their title, or other writings on the group which use this term.
5. See Tamang (2002) and Pigg (1992, 1996) for detailed analyses of how such national ideals were constructed during the Panchayat period. Although both

of these authors emphasize the role of development discourse and practice in creating the generic 'modern Nepali', there is no question that political parties such as the CPN conceptualized the ideal national Nepali in a similar fashion during this period, and the relationship between development and political discourses in Nepal is worthy of further examination. See also Liechty (2003) for a general discussion of the consumption of 'modernity' in urban Nepal.

6. Several authors have addressed the relationship between class and ethnicity in shaping the history of party politics in Nepal. See especially Lawoti (2003) and Tamang (2004 a, b). After the 2006 Comprehensive Peace Agreement, the CPN-M began emphasizing the concept of ethnic federalism with a proposal for nine states, but in the wake of their 2008 election win, this agenda has again taken second place to that of economic reform. It remains to be seen whether or not the CPN-M-led government can adequately satisfy ethnic demands.
7. See Connor (1984) for an overview of these issues in Marxist-Leninist ideology.
8. Both Bohara and Shakya were placed under house arrest on 1 February 2005, when King Gyanendra assumed full power in a military coup. Shakya was released after one month, but Bohara was held for almost three months. Shakya was re-arrested in January 2006.
9. See Richard Bownas (2003) for details of Naxalism and its relationship with Nepali Maoism.
10. All direct quotations of Bohara and Shakya come from an interview conducted in Nepali on 10 November 2004 in Kathmandu. It was transcribed by Bir Bahadur Thami and translated into English by Manesh Shrestha.
11. Nepal is divided into 14 administrative zones and 75 districts. Bagmati is a particularly influential zone as it includes the urban area of Kathmandu.
12. The very fact that she was sent to school through SLC level as a girl from such a large family demonstrates the wealth and relative open-mindedness of her family; during that era very few girls studied at the secondary level, and large families with limited resources would be likely to send only their sons to school.
13. These attitudes match well with Pigg's (1992) description of the ways in which development discourse, laid atop ingrained forms of caste and class stratification in Nepal, has constructed 'the village' as a metaphorical place identified with all things 'backward' in opposition to the 'developed' urban centre.
14. There are several other well-known examples of Bahun and Chhetri men marrying Newar women within Nepal's communist circles. These include the late Man Mohan Adhikari and Sadhana Pradhan, as well as Baburam Bhattarai and Hisila Yami.
15. Areas near district border lines have always been popular choices for political activity in Nepal and continued to be so for the Maoists. Until recently, Nepal's security forces were commanded from district headquarters by officers who only had jurisdiction over only one district. Therefore if the situation got tense and party cadres expected punitive action from the state, they could simply cross the district border to buy time while information and orders got communicated from one district-level command to another. This loophole was closed in 2003, when the security forces introduced the new Unified Command concept, under which certain companies of police, military police, and army were commanded from the centre and could cross district lines.

16. See Regmi (1976) for additional details on these and other land tenure systems in Nepal.
17. Village Development Committees (VDCs) are currently the smallest administrative unit in modern Nepal. They were established only after 1990, replacing the earlier panchayats.
18. Although the massacre itself occurred in Piskar, CPN-ML cadres were active in other Thangmi villages throughout the area, particularly in Chokati, Dhuskun, and Tauthali.
19. See also Turin (2000) for an explanation of Thangmi census figures.
20. Unfortunately comparable statistics from Piskar itself are not available.
21. A *ropani* is a standard Nepali measurement equivalent to 5,476 square feet or 508 square metres.
22. The other common reaction to the high level of oppression that Thangmi villagers experienced was to leave the area entirely and emigrate to Bhutan or India, primarily to the north-eastern areas of Darjeeling, Assam, and Sikkim. My research with the Thangmi community in India confirmed that many of the earliest Thangmi settlers who left Nepal did so because they could no longer stand the exploitation they experienced in their home villages. My doctoral dissertation addresses these dynamics in further detail (2009).
23. Nepal Pragitisil Thami Samaj (NPTS) was linked with far left elements of the CPN, while Thami Bhasa Tatha Sanskriti Utthan Kendra (TBTSUK) was a centrist organization with ties to the NC. Both have now been integrated into the national Nepal Thami Samaj, which represents the interests of the group within the Nepal Federation of Indigenous Nationalities (NEFIN).
24. Whether or not Bohara himself made this distinction is unclear, but we will see that the villagers of Piskar came to make it on his behalf.
25. The connotation of *thulo manche*, which literally means 'big people', is of high-caste, high-status outsiders.
26 De Sales (2003) has described the importance of leftist 'revolutionary songs' in generating political consciousness in western Nepal. Indeed, music has been a favoured medium for political mobilization across the country.
27. Martin Gaenszle is conducting an ongoing research on this event, known as the 'Chintang incident'.
28. Asta Laxmi Shakya, by then Bohara's wife, had left Piskar permanently a few months earlier in late 1983 after she gave birth to their daughter.
29. Personal communications from Gabriele Tautscher and Deepak Thapa, both of whom observed such meetings.
30. See Fisher (1993, 2001), Guneratne (2002), and Gellner et al. (1997) for overviews of the ethnic rights movement and its relationship with broader political developments in Nepal during the 1990s.
31. See Ogura (2008) on the topic of ethnic representation within Maoist 'people's [local] governments' at the local level.
32. Members of the Magar ethnic group are an exception to this rule, having played a prominent role in the 'people's war' which began in parts of western Nepal with a majority Magar population.

REFERENCES

Amnesty International. 1987. *Nepal: A Pattern of Human Rights Violations*. New York: Amnesty International National Office.

Bownas, Richard. 2003. 'The Nepalese Maoist Movement in Comparative Perspective: Learning from the History of Naxalism in India', *Himalaya: The Journal of the Association for Nepal and Himalayan Studies*, 23(1): 31–7.

Connor, Walker. 1984. *The National Question in Marxist-Leninist Theory and Strategy*. Princeton, NJ: Princeton University Press.

de Sales, Anne. 2003. 'Remarks on Revolutionary Songs and Iconography', *European Bulletin of Himalayan Research*, 24: 5–25.

Fisher, William. 1993. 'Nationalism and the Janajati', *Himal*, 6(2): 11–14.

———. 2001. *Fluid Boundaries: Forming and Transforming Identity in Nepal*. New York: Columbia University Press.

Gellner, David N., Joanna Pfaff-Czarnecka, and John Whelpton (eds). 1997. *Nationalism and Ethnicity in a Hindu Kingdom: The Politics of Culture in Contemporary Nepal*. Amsterdam: Harwood.

Guneratne, Arjun. 2002. *Many Tongues, One People: The Making of Tharu Identity in Nepal*. Ithaca: Cornell University Press.

Hachhethu, Krishna. 2002. *Party Building in Nepal: Organization, Leadership and People*. Kathmandu: Mandala Book Point.

———. 2003. 'Nepali Politics: People-Parties Interface', in D.N. Gellner (ed.), *Resistance and the State: Nepalese Experiences*, pp. 133–76. New Delhi: Social Science Press.

His Majesty's Government (HMG). 2002. *Nepal Population Report 2002*. Kathmandu: Central Bureau of Statistics.

Himali Prakasan Parivar (HPP). 1984 (VS 2041). *Piskar: Daman ra Pratirodhko Katha* [Piskar: The Story of Oppression and Resistance]. Varanasi: Janata Press.

Hoftun, Martin, William Raeper, and John Whelpton. 1999. *People, Politics & Ideology: Democracy and Social Change in Nepal*. Kathmandu: Mandala Book Point.

Integrated Community Development Movement (ICDM). 1999. *Profile of the Village Development Committee of Alampu*. Dolakha: Nepal Integrated Community Development Movement.

Informal Sector Service Centre (INSEC). 1995. 'Appendix 3: Peasant Movement in Nepal', in *Human Rights Yearbook 1995*. Kathmandu: Informal Sector Service Centre.

Lawoti, Mahendra. 2003. 'The Maoists and Minorities: Overlap of Interests or a Case of Exploitation?' *Studies in Nepali History and Society*, 8(1): 67–97.

Liechty, Mark. 2003. *Suitably Modern: Making Middle-Class Culture in a New Consumer Society*. Princeton: Princeton University Press.

Liu, Melinda and Patricia Roberts. 2001. 'Nepal's Maoist Threat', *Newsweek*, June 18: 26–7.

Niko Pragatisil Thami Samaj (NPTS). 1997 (VS 2054). 'Piskar Hatyakand' [The Piskar massacre], *Nan Ni Patuko*, pp. 65–85. Kathmandu: Niko Pragatisil Thami Samaj.

Ogura, Kiyoko. 2008. 'Maoist People's Governments, 2001–2005: The Power in Wartime', in D.N. Gellner and K. Hachhethu (eds), *Local Democracy in South Asia: Microprocesses of Democratization in Nepal and its Neighbours*, pp. 175–231. New Delhi: SAGE Publications.

Pigg, Stacy Leigh. 1992. 'Inventing Social Categories through Place: Social Representations and Development in Nepal', *Comparative Studies in Society and History*, 34(3): 491–513.

———. 1996. 'The Credible and the Credulous: The Question of "Villagers' Beliefs" in Nepal', *Cultural Anthropology*, 11(2): 160–201.

Regmi, M.C. 1976. *Landownership in Nepal*. Berkeley: University of California Press.

Shneiderman, Sara. 2009a. 'The Formation of Political Consciousness in Rural Nepal', *Dialectical Anthropology*, 33(3–4): 287–308.

———. 2009b. 'Rituals of Ethnicity: Mixing, Making and Migrating Thangmi Identities across Himalayan Borders', unpublished PhD thesis, Cornell University, Ithaca, NY, USA.

Tamang, Mukta S. 2004a. 'Communist Party of Nepal (UML) Jatiya Mamila Bibhag (Division of Caste and Ethnic Affairs)'. Case study draft. GSEA Research.

———. 2004b. 'Nepali Congress (NC) Nepal Adibasi Janajati Sangh (Nepal Indigenous Nationalities Association)'. Case study draft. GSEA Research.

Tamang, Seira. 2002. 'The Politics of "Developing" Nepali Women', in Kanak Mani Dixit and Shashi Ramachandaran (eds), *State of Nepal*, pp. 161–75. Kathmandu: Himal Books.

Thami Bhasa Tatha Sanskriti Utthan Kendra (TBTSUK). 1999 (VS 2056). 'Thami jatiko ragatle lekhieko Piskar parba' [The Piskar Massacre was Written in Thami Blood], *Dolakhareng*, pp. 63–8. Jhapa, Nepal: TBTSUK.

Turin, Mark. 2000. 'Time for a True Population Census: The Case of the Miscounted Thangmi', *Nagarik* (Kathmandu), August–September, 2(4): 14–19.

Chapter 4

Youth and Political Engagement in Sri Lanka

SIRIPALA HETTIGE

INTRODUCTION

It may not be an exaggeration to say that youth have dominated the political landscape of Sri Lanka over the last four decades. Though young people participated in political movements in the country even prior to political independence in 1948, the emergence of political movements dominated by youth is a post-independence phenomenon. The demographic, socio-economic, and political factors that prepared the ground for the emergence of such political movements have already been discussed by many social scientists. What should be pointed out at the outset is that social and political conflicts in the country in recent decades have centred around youth political movements. Moreover, the persistence of violent political conflict in Sri Lanka to this day is also integrally connected with the co-existence of several youth constituencies that have conflicting ideologies and interests. This chapter examines the question as to why these conflicting youth constituencies remain largely intact in spite of rapid socio-economic change over the last three decades. The hypothesis that is advanced and examined here is that the recent socio-economic changes have not undermined the post-independence youth constituencies due to a lack of a radical transformation of the structural basis of the relevant social formations. The focus of attention of the chapter is on the post-1977 period as it is during this period that state domination of the economy ended giving rise to a strong private corporate sector that has made inroads even into social sectors like education, health, transportation, and housing.

The chapter is divided into several sections. In the first, word only an attempt is made to outline the socio-economic transformation after 1977 and to discuss the largely superficial nature of the shift that has taken place. Then I discuss the fact that the socio-economic transformation further marginalized the core youth constituencies embedded in youth political movements. In the final section the con tinuing pre-occupation of marginalized youth with territory and state power is discussed in terms of the uncertainties created by the de-territorializing tendencies of the market and the increasing dominance of the new urban middle class that came into prominence after 1977.[1]

THE POST-1977 SOCIO-ECONOMIC TRANSFORMATION

The transformation of the Sri Lankan economy following the adoption of liberal, open, economic policies in 1977 has already been the subject of many publications.[2] What I wish to do here is to examine the nature of this transformation sociologically, in order to emphasize the fact that the changes were in fact partial and superficial, leaving significant areas largely untouched, thereby creating significant structural inequities within the social system. These inequities have undermined the social and moral order that came into being after independence. What is this social and moral order?

As is well documented, the system of social stratification that evolved during the latter part of the British colonial rule was characterized by structural inequities, largely based on the distribution of land rights and access to education and employment. The domination of the colonial economy and society by a privileged, westernized propertied class became the most contentious issue in the immediate aftermath of political independence. Post-colonial economic and social policies increasingly sought to address the foregoing inequities. The Paddy Lands Act (1958), the Official Language legislation (1956), the nationalization of foreign-owned plantations (1962), the Land Development Ordinance (1935), the take-over of private schools (1960s), and so on, were all aimed at creating the conditions conducive for the emergence of a new, post-colonial social and moral order that emphasized equality of opportunity, a fair distribution of life chances across social strata, and a sense of social justice in the minds of the hitherto marginalized groups. However, the fact that colonial society was not just vertically differentiated but was also characterized by horizontal divisions based on ethnicity, caste, and religion made the transition from the colonial to a post-colonial social order more complex and contentious. As a multi-ethnic society, post-colonial political struggles in the country did not simply follow social class lines but involved competition and conflict among ethno-linguistic groups as well. The triumph in 1956 of the left-of-centre coalition led by S.W.R.D. Bandaranaike was a victory for the marginalized Sinhala-Buddhist groups. The same victory was considered by the Tamil minority as a major setback for its members.

The left-leaning policies adopted by the 1956 government laid the foundation for a state-dominated economy that flourished in the next two decades. With more and more economic resources coming under its purview, the state became the main source of redress for a whole host of problems faced by underprivileged groups. When state institutions, including the nationalized enterprises, gradually adopted Sinhala as the language of business, educated Sinhala youth could find state sector employment with relative ease. With the expansion of the education system after independence, even underprivileged youth could secure educational qualifications free of charge and move into various positions within the state sector. While youth with higher educational qualifications, despite being monolingual, moved into highly prestigious positions in the civil service (later the Sri Lanka Administrative Service), planning service, universities, medical and legal professions, state banks, etc., those with lesser qualifications found their way into a whole host of lower rung positions such as teaching, clerical, and book keeping. The expansion of the state sector due to import substitution industrialization[3] and nationalization of private enterprises from the late 1950s to the early 1970s resulted in a proliferation of employment opportunities for *swabhasha*-educated (literally 'own-language-educated') Sinhala youth. On the other hand, rapid population growth in the 1960s and the 1970s coupled with an equally rapid expansion of education following the introduction of free education in the early 1940s led to an increasing gap between the demand for and supply of the type of employment desired by educated youth, a malaise referred to by an International Labour Organization (ILO) mission in 1972 led by Dudley Seers as a mismatch between education and employment. Yet, for educated rural youth originating from lowly social backgrounds, much-desired white-collar employment in the state sector was the only way to move away from poverty and social marginality and achieve upward social mobility. When prospects for such mobility were bleak, they were ready to join hands with anti-systemic movements that promised revolutionary change. As is well documented (Obeyesekere, 1974) a majority of youth who took part in the 1971 Janatha Vimukthi Peramuna (JVP)-led youth uprising were, in fact, educated Sinhalese youth from lowly social backgrounds.

In the face of high rates of youth unemployment, scarcity of basic consumer goods, and widespread poverty, the incumbent left-of-centre United Front government was challenged in the mid-1970s by the emerging free-market-oriented United National Party (UNP) leadership. Frustrated voters gave a landslide victory to the UNP at the 1977 general elections. Economic reforms that followed created a liberal economic environment conducive for private investment, import–export trade, mobility of labour, both internal and external, and overseas travel for business, educational, and employment purposes. Yet no clear and explicit policies were formulated to reform the social sectors like education and health. On the other hand, reforms in the other sectors began to impact on the social sectors, thereby bringing about significant change.

New inequalities emerged in the education sector with significant implications for access and equity (Hettige, 2004a). Privately funded institutions sprang up in various guises, offering new educational opportunities to children from affluent families. The newly established international schools, private colleges, and other more specialized educational establishments began to impart instruction in English. Most state sector schools had few English teachers capable of teaching English as a second language. The few privileged public schools in the urban centres that had more facilities became so popular and attractive that parents from all parts of the country joined the competition to admit their children to these schools. Bribery, political influence, and other unlawful methods to admit children became endemic, leading to frustration, anger, and even litigation.

The expansion of the private sector with an increasingly transnational orientation resulted in a proliferation of employment opportunities, particularly for youth with English-language skills. The private corporate sector based in Colombo continued to use English as the language of business in spite of the adoption of Sinhala as the official language in 1956 and the medium of instruction in schools in the late 1950s. The sector that contracted due to the inhospitable policy environment in the country in the two decades following political independence continued to recruit its managerial staff largely through social and old-boy networks. When the sector began to expand after 1977, the increasing demand could now be met by youth passing out from international schools, private colleges, and those returning home from abroad after their education in foreign universities.

After several decades of *swabhasha* education in the country, most schoolteachers had also become monolingual. With the establishment of many private schools, the demand for English-educated teachers also increased. The result was that even the few public school teachers who were fluent in English left the public system to join more lucrative private sector establishments, or migrated abroad, further depleting the supply of English-educated teachers in the state sector. In spite of a growing desire to learn English among schoolchildren in all parts of the country, they have had no opportunity to do so. The proliferation of private English tuition classes in rural as well as urban areas has not made much of a difference as instruction in most of these classes is of a very low quality. In any case, youth with a little knowledge of the English language can hardly compete with English-speaking youth graduating from private institutions. This situation has compelled youths securing their educational qualifications from state-funded institutions to look for state-sector employment that does not usually require an English education. Hence, the continuing political pressure on the government to recruit *swabhasha*-educated youth to public institutions.[4]

The annual budgetary allocations for education that have remained stagnant over the last several decades have been adequate just to maintain the system. The structural changes required to address the new challenges would have necessitated a significant increase in public expenditure on education. On the other hand, affluent and more influential sections of society no longer rely on poorly equipped state schools and do not feel the need to revamp the public education system. They either rely on private schools or send their children to privileged urban public schools. With a bilingual education, their children experience no difficulties in finding lucrative employment in any sector. The vast majority of youth in the country who receive a monolingual, *swabhasha* education find conventional paths to upward social mobility virtually closed in the emergent liberal economic environment, hence their continued commitment to conventional anti-systemic politics.

The liberal economic policies were advocated by their proponents as a way of promoting private investment to generate employment for youth (Hettige, 2004b). The unemployment rate did indeed decline in the 1980s, following the implementation of liberal economic policies. On the other hand, much of the employment created was in unskilled and semi-skilled categories in the Free Trade Zones, in the Middle East, and the urban informal sector. More and more rural youth, even with secondary educational qualifications, accepted such employment as this was preferable to remaining unemployed. Yet, such employment did not offer opportunities for professional or career development. In fact, low-level employment in the private sector, particularly for women, has remained a transitory source of income, till they return to their villages in a few years and often settle down as housewives or go abroad for overseas employment. For men, unskilled and semi-skilled employment has not necessarily amounted to upward social mobility. Youth with aspirations for upward mobility remain unemployed for several years, till they find desirable types of employment. This is particularly true for university graduates.

The shift from state domination to market domination over the economy following the adoption of liberal economic policies has brought about significant changes in opportunity structures. Yet, the publicly funded education system that mediated between the economy and society in significant ways in the past was not revamped to enable it to play a similar role in the new economic environment. In other words, the dominant role it played in facilitating upward social mobility in the decades following political independence is no longer feasible. This is due to two main reasons. First, most of those who secure educational qualifications from within the state-funded education system cannot find employment in keeping with their qualifications and aspirations. Second, the public education system plays a relatively insignificant role in preparing youth for private sector employment. On the other hand, those who have no resources to access private education remain almost totally dependent on the publicly funded education system, in spite of its serious gaps and weaknesses. The educational qualifications they obtain do not often help them achieve their life goals.

THE MARGINALIZATION OF CORE YOUTH CONSTITUENCIES

The left-leaning economic and social policies adopted after independence were aimed at creating an egalitarian environment in economic and social terms. Land reforms, food and other subsidies, free education, provision of employment, etc., were part and parcel of the foregoing policies. On the other hand, these policies did not produce social and political contentment as the rising aspirations and expectations of a large upwardly mobile youth constituency could not be fulfilled due to various circumstances.

The policy shift in the late 1970s in the form of a package of liberal, market-friendly measures created an economic environment where the market began to guide the allocation of resources including labour. The expanding private sector began to operate side by side with the state sector, creating a more competitive environment. The virtual state monopoly in the education sector came to an end with the proliferation of private educational institutions catering to more affluent strata of society. The non-affluent social strata continued to rely on a stagnant, conventional education system funded by the state.[5] A contracting or stagnant state sector could no longer create employment opportunities to meet the rising demand from educated youth leaving publicly funded educational institutions. These mostly non-English-speaking youth are usually excluded from white collar employment in the private, corporate sector that, as mentioned before, usually recruits English-educated youth from elite educational institutions.

What is noteworthy here is that the youth who are marginalized in the new economy constitute a large majority of youth in the country. As the statistical data clearly show, affluent urban youth attending private schools constitute a small minority in relative terms, though their absolute numbers have increased over the last two decades. In fact, they constitute just over 2 per cent of the total school student population in the country (Hettige, 2004b).

The marginalized youth constituencies are highly significant not only in numerical terms but also in terms of their socio-cultural orientation. Their primary and secondary socialization that takes place in an ethno-linguistically segregated institutional environment is a critical factor influencing their identity formation and ideological orientation. The strong ethno-nationalist orientation displayed by youth constituencies belonging to both majority and minority ethnic groups in the country reflects the foregoing state of affairs. As is well known, an ethno-linguistically segregated education system and ethnically homogeneous settlement pattern in most parts of the country (both in the south as well as in the north and east), reinforced by public policies as well as post-independence political conflicts, have facilitated the formation of monolingual youth constituencies. These constituencies rarely interpenetrate even at the national level largely due to linguistic barriers. While most universities in the country are ethno-linguistically segregated, even where students from different ethnic groups do congregate, there is little or no interaction across ethnic boundaries. They continue to reproduce or reinforce their separate identities through formal as well as informal activities such as segregated classrooms, ethnic and religious fraternities, social and cultural practices, and informal group formation. Being mostly monolingual, they have no opportunities to interact across ethnic boundaries. Being confined to classes conducted by staff members belonging to one's own ethnic community, most students often have no contact with teachers from another ethnic group. In other words, students coming from ethno-linguistically segregated rural settlements often do not cross community boundaries even when they go for higher education at a national university. The situation is much worse if one goes to a university where the only medium of instruction is one's own native language.

Politically active university students have played a catalytic role in national and regional politics in Sri Lanka. Almost all political parties in the country have mobilized university students through their youth and student wings. It is a well-known fact that many university student groups have their affiliations to political parties and usually actively participate in national electoral campaigns in support of their respective parties. The leftist parties that played a vibrant and highly visible role in the national political arena in the aftermath of political independence attracted many university students. The leaders and key activists of the parties like the Communist Party and the Lanka Sama Samaja Party (LSSP) were bilingual, often having had their education in the English medium. Students who were attracted to these parties, therefore, did not belong to one ethnic community. The fact that many students themselves were mostly bilingual would have facilitated interaction across ethnic groups.

The traditional leftist parties mentioned earlier gradually lost popular support in the country in the 1970s when the new left-leaning JVP emerged as an alternative. More and more *swabhasha*-educated Sinhalese youth, in particular university students, began to show their allegiance to the new party. Student groups affiliated to the JVP have been able to dominate student politics in most universities in the south. The fact that the leaders of the JVP also hailed from similar social backgrounds is no doubt a critical factor here. A similar pattern is evident in the north-east of the country as well. Youth in general and university students in particular have been attracted to more militant political parties or groups there.

As I have discussed elsewhere (Hettige, 2004b), the two main radical youth political movements in the country, namely the JVP and the Liberation Tigers of Tamil Eelam (LTTE), have pursued two mutually antithetical political projects. While the JVP advocated a Sinhala Buddhist-dominated unitary state for Sri Lanka, the LTTE campaigned for a separate state in the north and east for the minority Tamil community. Their commitment to such contradictory positions can be explained in terms of their identities, political socialization, and their perceived and real interests as two important constituencies. On the other hand, a closer examination of their values, ideological orientations, and lived experiences shows that these two seemingly divergent youth constituencies also have a lot in common. In fact, their social and cultural orientations have some clear parallels. It is significant that both are committed to egalitarian ideologies and have similar grievances against the dominant strata or elite segments of society. In short, they are alienated from mainstream society, defined, of course, in different ways, depending on the community to which they belong.

In the context of post-1977 developments that followed the liberalization of the economy and the re-integration of Sri Lanka into the global economic system, the youth constituency that the JVP represents, no matter how large it is in numerical terms, is clearly marginalized from the mainstream urban economy dominated by local and global capital. This is clearly evident from the fact that most of the *swabhasha*-educated graduates passing out from the local universities did not find employment in the expanding private corporate sector. Their numbers continued to increase over the years until the backlog reached an unprecedented 52,000 by 2004.

One of the key demands of the JVP to join the coalition government formed in 2004 was to absorb these unemployed graduates into the state sector. In other words, state power is critical to address the grievances of these marginalized youth constituencies. This brings me to the last issue that I wish to discuss in this chapter, namely the continuing pre-occupation of marginalized youth constituencies with territoriality and state power.

YOUTH, TERRITORIALITY, AND STATE POWER

As mentioned earlier, political engagement of Sri Lankan youth took a militant turn in the early 1970s. This is a clear departure from the path followed by revolutionary Marxist leaders in the country in the immediate aftermath of political independence. Their political practice, oriented towards parliamentary democracy, was radically different from their political rhetoric that emphasized revolutionary change. On the other hand, as partners in left-of-centre coalition governments since 1956, they committed themselves to a reformist agenda and campaigned for social and economic change through progressive state policies. In fact, most of the social and economic reforms in post-independence Sri Lanka can be attributed to the efforts of left-oriented leaders.

The decline in the 1970s of the traditional left represented by the two main Marxist parties at the time coincided with the entrenchment of two dominant parties in national politics, namely the Sri Lanka Freedom Party (SLFP) and the United National Party (UNP). There was no third force in sight, making prospects of an alternative parliamentary party challenging the hegemony of the two parties a remote possibility. None of the candidates fielded by the traditional left parties at the 1977 general elections could win a seat in parliament (cf. Spencer, 1990).

The JVP that led the 1971 armed uprising emerged as a visible political force only when its leaders who were jailed following the insurrection were released by the newly elected UNP government in 1977. Its leader contested the 1982 presidential elections but did not attract significant popular support. Those who voted for him appeared to be mostly Sinhalese youth loyal to the party. The party's violent campaign against the Indo-Lanka Accord that laid the foundation for the establishment of Provincial Councils to devolve power to the regions reaffirmed its commitment to a centralized unitary state.

The anti-government armed struggle that the JVP launched in the late 1980s, resulting in thousands of deaths of political activists, leaders, and civilians, was eventually suppressed by the government forces with brutal force, eliminating most of its front-line leaders.[6] The younger and second-tier leaders who survived managed to reinvigorate the party and its cadres in the mid-1990s and enter the democratic process, contesting elections held in 1999. They also won scores of seats at provincial and local council elections in subsequent years. It reached its highest level of democratic representation at the general election held in 2004 when it contested as a key partner of the coalition led by the SLFP.[7] It joined hands with the other coalition parties to form a government led by the SLFP in 2004.[8] However, the JVP left the coalition in 2006 when the newly elected president brought in a similar but more Sinhala nationalist party, namely Jathika Hela Urumaya, and a breakaway of group of parliamentarians from the main opposition party, the UNP, to form a wider coalition. Thereafter, the JVP remained part of the parliamentary opposition, as an independent group.

The tensions within the ruling coalition became obvious when the JVP continued to criticize its dominant partner for failing to live up to people's expectations. The points of contention were mainly related to issues connected with good governance, economic policy, and later the approach that the government should take to resolve the long-standing ethnic conflict. The JVP policy against the privatization of state enterprises was revealed in no uncertain terms when it mobilized its trade unions in many state organizations against privatization and the government could not go ahead with the reforms advocated by multilateral lending agencies.

The JVP's opposition to privatization in almost all sectors cannot be interpreted entirely in terms of their political ideology. Its opposition to it is as much motivated by pragmatic political considerations as by its ideological commitments. Disadvantaged rural youth, the JVP's support base, perceive the corporate private sector as discriminatory towards them[9] on account of their lack of cultural capital,[10] so the preservation of the state sector is the ultimate refuge for them. It is also significant that, when the new coalition government was formed in 2004 with JVP participation, the party leaders opted for ministerial positions that fell within sectors that had strong connections to key JVP constituencies such as rural peasants, fishermen, small rural enterprises, and indigenous artists and artisans. The JVP also successfully negotiated for state-sector employment for about 50,000 university graduates who had been unemployed for several years. If not for the privatization of many large state enterprises such as commercial plantations, and government-owned service and productive industries, many of these graduates would have found employment in such state enterprises. Once privatized, the new owners of these enterprises have the freedom to recruit personnel on criteria that they determined with no consideration given to political or social imperatives. This is already evident in the privatized plantations.

When the privately owned plantations were nationalized in the early 1970s, leading to the establishment of state-owned plantation corporations, many university graduates were recruited as trainee managers who eventually reached higher managerial positions. This was in contrast to the earlier practice under private ownership of recruiting close acquaintances on the basis of social and personal connections. The recruits then were usually school leavers belonging to the families closely connected to those of owners and managers. Recent developments in the plantation sector following privatization indicate that the new owners have already adopted the old recruitment practices. The new recruits to managerial positions in the plantation companies have been drawn from urban middle-class backgrounds. Even if the university graduates respond to advertisements appearing in English-language newspapers, most of them could hardly face the interviews that are invariably conducted in English. This pattern prevails in the corporate private sector in general.

Given the developments outlined earlier, it is understandable that the large, *swabhasha*-educated youth constituencies, in spite of their numerical superiority, feel that they are marginalized in the new liberal economic environment. Thus, it is reasonable to assume that they would rally round political parties that advocate state intervention on their behalf. It is in this sense that the state is critical for them to safeguard their interests. Hence, they are suspicious of and even antagonistic towards the non-state actors like non-governmental organizations (NGOs) and private entrepreneurs.

However, what is also noteworthy is that more and more youths, instead of resisting liberal economic reforms, have increasingly adapted to the changing socio-economic circumstances. As one would expect, youth from affluent urban backgrounds have by and large embraced the new economy that offers them not only lucrative income sources but also, many opportunities for adopting new lifestyles and consumption patterns. On the other hand, lower-class youth, both rural and urban, in particular those who leave the education system early, have taken up income opportunities in both the formal industrial sector as well as in the urban informal sector. Yet, given the strong affinities they have with educated youth from disadvantaged backgrounds, often coming from the same families, their political role does not seem to be determined entirely by economic pragmatism. There is evidence to suggest that radical youth activists have considerable support among young industrial workers as well as among informal sector activists. Most of the militant young Buddhist monks also hail from lower-class families.

Sinhala nationalist youth activists who have rallied round the nationalist parties like the JVP and Hela Urumaya perceive their future as integrally connected to a strong nationalist state that defends their interests against those who operate outside the framework of the Sri Lankan state, in particular the Tamil separatists who challenge the hegemony of the Sri Lankan state as it is conceived by Sinhala nationalists. Hence, their resistance to any attempt to weaken the centre. On the other hand, those who fight for greater autonomy from the centre or for a separate state perceive Sinhala nationalist resistance as the biggest obstacle to achieving their goal (cf. Wimmer, 2002). Extremists on both sides of the ethnic divide appear to be willing to sacrifice their lives for their course. As is well known, the Tamil separatist group, the LTTE recruits disadvantaged Tamil youths as combatants, some of whom are known as suicide bombers. The latter have carried out hundreds of suicide missions in all parts of the country. Sri Lankan security forces recruit their rank-and-file members mostly from among disadvantaged Sinhala youths from rural area. Though their main motivation in joining the forces is to secure livelihoods, Sinhala nationalist parties and groups hail them as heroes who are prepared to sacrifice their lives to safeguard the nation. While large banners and posters hailing and thanking security forces for their sacrifices can be found in many parts of the country, including Colombo, many events and functions are organized by nationalist groups to bestow divine protection on soldiers and support the latter in other ways such as blood donations and collection of food rations and medicines to be sent to the battle front.

IDEAS, INTERESTS, AND YOUTH POLITICAL ENGAGEMENT

As mentioned earlier, post-1977 economic reforms have brought about significant socio-economic change over the last three decades. While some long-established livelihood opportunities declined, certain new employment and income opportunities were created by the new policies. Increasing integration of the local economy with the rest of the world created many business opportunities for the expanding private, corporate sector. Expansion of the transnationally oriented corporate sector largely prepared the ground for the rise of the new urban middle-class. The growth of private and overseas educational opportunities also contributed to the expansion of this class.

The establishment of export-oriented, labour-intensive industries, liberalization of the transport sector, expansion of service industries like telecommunications, and the liberalization of imports created many income opportunities for youth. The increasing demand for Sri Lankan labour in overseas labour markets, particularly in the Middle East, also persuaded low-income groups to travel abroad for employment. The steady devaluation of the Sri Lankan rupee after liberalization, the rising cost of living, and increasing consumer aspirations motivated people to take up new income-earning opportunities even though some of these continued to be stigmatized by more affluent segments of society. Such stigmatized areas of employment included garment-factory work, domestic work in the Middle East, and pavement hawking. In the 1980s the JVP criticized liberal economic policies arguing that the types of employment created by such policies were dehumanizing and lowly. Their widely used slogan "pavement for boys, garments for girls" graphically illustrated their point. Yet, thousands of rural Sinhalese youths, both male and female, had no choice but take up such income opportunities. In the process, they also adopted new consumption patterns and lifestyles. These, however, did not help most of them to move away from their lower-class identity.

As mentioned earlier, the JVP mobilized underprivileged yet educated youths with aspirations for upward social mobility. The youthful JVP leaders travelled around the country, conducting political classes for prospective cadres. Some youths joined the party as full-time activists, many others as part-time cadres.

They engaged in organizational work such as organizing rallies, selling the party newspapers, conducting classes for new recruits, putting up posters, and collecting funds. University students and graduates who were party members played a highly significant role in the villages as they were respected by the less educated, ordinary villagers.

How have the significant socio-economic changes mentioned earlier impacted on the JVP's support base in the country? In order to find an answer to the question, the author conducted in-depth interviews with a number of JVP activists drawn from several areas in the country.[11] It is significant that they are all from underprivileged rural families.

It is noteworthy that all activists interviewed had participated in political classes conducted by party leaders and senior cadres. They have participated in these classes in their own villages, indicating that the JVP, which started conducting political education classes in the late 1960s, has continued to maintain this tradition to this day. They also continue to recruit full-time and part-time party activists who help the party in its organizational and propaganda work.

The increasing cost of living faced by lower-class youths and their families has persuaded the latter to engage in whatever income-earning activities they could find including self-employment. Some engage in petty trade, giving private tuition to schoolchildren, etc. These economic activities have reduced the time available for party work let alone engaging in party work on a full-time basis. On the other hand, full-time activists are assisted by the party to meet their personal expenses such as food and transportation.

What attracts youths to the JVP? The fact that it presents itself as an alternative to the two mainstream political parties is a key point here. The two parties have ruled the country over the last 60 years, taking turns to form governments, often in coalition with smaller parties. This has been particularly so after 1977 when the 1978 constitution introduced an electoral system based on proportional representation, making it very difficult for a single party win enough seats in parliament to form a strong government with a sizable majority. The JVP has consistently articulated the view that these parties represent the elite interests and marginalize the underprivileged strata. While the UNP is branded as the party representing urban upper classes, the SLFP is portrayed as a party dominated by traditional aristocratic families such as the Bandaranaikes. In more recent years, the decline in governance standards, exemplified by rampant corruption, abuse of power, electoral malpractices, nepotism, political patronage, and politicization of public institutions, has become a key slogan of the JVP and has attracted considerable support. In 2001, the JVP used its sizable parliamentary presence to introduce an amendment to the constitution (17th Amendment) to establish a Constitutional Council with powers to appoint independent commissions to manage elections. The incumbent government, which depended on the JVP for its political survival at the time, had no choice but agree to vote for the amendment jointly mooted by the JVP and the main opposition party, the UNP. The JVP also put pressure on the government to reduce the size of the cabinet of ministers, which stood around 76 at the time.

The JVP's widely popular slogan *Unuth Ekai, Munuth Ekai* ('both parties are the same') resonated well with the ordinary voting public. The foregoing moves have also given them considerable credibility. Party activists interviewed also emphasized the fact that the JVP represents a better political alternative to the two leading Sinhala-dominated mainstream political parties on account of its commitment to good governance, equality, and social justice.

Interviews conducted with party activists show clearly that the latter come primarily from disadvantaged rural backgrounds. They are also relatively well educated, at least with a secondary education. Many of the party activists are undergraduates or graduates, largely from a liberal arts background.

It is also significant that the families of many JVP activists have faced injustices, discrimination, and even violence at the hands of public officials, politicians, and law-enforcement officers. In some cases, family members were killed when the Sri Lankan security forces crushed the JVP in 1971 and the late 1980s. Such threats have not prevented younger family members from becoming party activists in recent years.

Most of them have had their general education from rural schools and were only competent in their mother tongue. Their initial political education came from their exposure to material distributed by the party itself but later from local newspapers and the media. It is also significant that peer groups have played a crucial role in initial political socialization of party activists.

> The JVP prepared the ground for making our society better. It is unimaginable how pathetic this country would have been if not for the actions of our party. (Sanath, 33, religious schoolteacher)

As the foregoing quotation indicates, party activists are convinced that the JVP is a positive and progressive political force in Sri Lanka today. They do not agree with the view that JVP is a Sinhala nationalist party. They do not feel that it is any more nationalist than the two mainstream Sinhala-dominated parties. The general view they articulate is that it is a socialist party that strives to offer equal opportunities to everybody, irrespective of their class, ethnic, and caste backgrounds.

> Today everybody thinks that the JVP is a Sinhala nationalist party. This is due to the fact the JVP talks a lot about nationalism. The allegation is also put forward on the basis that the party base is a lower-class, Sinhala Buddhist constituency. Moreover, when the JVP emerged in the South, LTTE also emerged in the North as a Tamil nationalist group. While the JVP had legitimate grievances to stage an anti-government insurgency, the LTTE also had a justification to go to war. JVP's biggest challenge today is to get rid of its Sinhala nationalist label. (Rev. Sarana, 25, undergraduate)

> I do not expect any personal benefits from the party. In fact, I work hard for the party, without expecting any personal gains. Our families have also made sacrifices because of the party. (Nimal, 28, undergraduate)

Many JVP activists interviewed feel that people who work for many other parties do so expecting some personal favours for themselves and their family members. They tend to highlight the selfless nature of their political engagement and lament that they cannot do more, due to economic difficulties and pressing social/family obligations.

> I do not expect anything from the party. If the people in general benefit from our party, that is enough, at least to our children. So far I have not sought any favour from the party. ... A main function of the party is to reveal the misdeeds of other parties. As a result, there is some check on corruption now. You know more about it than I do. (Janaka, 33, petty trader)

Overall, the data gathered from in-depth interviews indicate that the JVP activists continue to be drawn from lower-class, rural Sinhala backgrounds in spite of the fact that rapid socio-economic changes after economic liberalization have had a significant impact on them. While liberal economic policies have created new income opportunities for rural lower-class families, increasing economic pressures have not changed their sense of relative deprivation as urban privileged groups have gained a great deal in terms of not only material wealth but also ideological power that determines the new social hierarchy in a neo-liberal economic environment. Given the increasingly transnational nature of economic, social, political, and cultural relations today, rural underprivileged groups tend to feel more marginalized, not less. Hence, their increasing antipathy towards transnational groups such as urban-based NGOs, westernized liberal intellectuals, transnational corporations, and international agencies. It is perhaps no coincidence that the recently appointed parliamentary select committee on NGOs is headed by a leading member of the JVP.

CONCLUSIONS

In this chapter, I have attempted to draw the broad contours of political engagement of youth in post-independence Sri Lanka with particular reference to recent developments. My intention here has been to offer a structural explanation of the emergence of specific youth constituencies and their participation in the political process. This is not an attempt to ignore the significance of many other, endogenous and exogenous factors, that have influenced recent political developments but to emphasize the critical importance of the changing opportunity structures in post-independence Sri Lanka that have had a differential impact on the life chances of different youth constituencies. The rapid socio-economic changes that followed economic liberalization in the late 1970s have altered the life chances of different segments of society but have not altered the sense of relative deprivation felt by underprivileged rural social strata. In fact, increasing rural–urban disparities have reinforced the sense of relative deprivation and marginalization. The declining governance standards over the last several decades have also frustrated disadvantaged youth, persuading them to align themselves with radical political parties like the JVP which continues to attract new members in spite of large-scale death and disappearance of its members in the past at the hands of Sri Lankan security forces.

Increasing economic pressure has also contributed to the sense of marginalization among disadvantaged groups but it has also forced the latter to take up less desirable income opportunities. Livelihood activities have taken away the time available for political work, but not necessarily their commitment to a political movement they consider to be critically important to address social, economic, and political issues that they feel are not addressed by other political parties. Hence, their continued commitment to the political party of their choice, namely, the JVP.

POSTSCRIPT (FEBRUARY 2010)

This chapter was originally drafted in 2006 and subsequently revised in 2008. Since then, the political landscape of Sri Lanka has changed substantially. The LTTE, which was locked in a brutal armed conflict with the Sri Lankan security forces and carried out suicide attacks against military and civilian targets in many parts of the country, faced a major crisis when the movement split after several prominent activists broke away and sided with the government. Consequently, the government forces were able to defeat the LTTE in the eastern part of the country, confining them to parts of the Northern Province. When elections were held in 2007 to elect the Eastern Provincial Council, the leaders of the breakaway faction of the LTTE captured political power in the province and one of the former military commanders became the chief minister there. Sri Lankan security forces continued their military campaign against the LTTE in the northern part of the country and, by early 2009, the LTTE was militarily defeated and its leaders were killed. Many civilians in the conflict-affected areas ended up in internal refugee camps established by the government to temporarily accommodate them.

Meanwhile the People's Liberation Front (Janatha Vimukthi Peramuna), which formed a key constituent partner of the ruling coalition led by the Sri Lanka Freedom Party from 2004 onwards, left the coalition government in 2006 and became an independent group in opposition. In the same way as the LTTE split, several frontline members of the JVP broke away from the party and aligned themselves with the ruling party, a few of them even becoming ministers of the central government. This naturally weakened the JVP and tarnished its public image. When the coalition government led by the incumbent President Mahinda Rajapaksha launched the military campaign to defeat the LTTE in 2005 and completed its mission in 2009, the JVP's public image as a Sinhala nationalist party could no longer be maintained. When the party aligned itself with the main opposition that had maintained a close relationship with ethnic minority parties, their nationalist credentials suffered even more. Moreover, the populist measures adopted by the government to appease disadvantaged rural voters—agricultural subsidies, government jobs to unemployed rural graduates, rural infrastructure development, etc.—further eroded the popular base of the JVP.

So, the two main youth political movements in the country that mobilized a large part of the disaffected young population in rural areas for anti-systemic political activism from the early 1970s onwards faced the biggest challenge to their survival from 2005 onwards. The military defeat of the LTTE leading to the elimination of its entire leadership and the weakening of the JVP as a radical, nationalist party representing disadvantaged Sinhalese youth have changed the political landscape of the country to a great extent. How the youth constituencies that these two political movements inspired and gave leadership to will engage in politics in the coming years is a question that cannot easily be answered at the present juncture. Though the recent socio-political history of the country can provide some clues in this regard, empirical research is indispensable in any attempt to provide a reasonable answer to the question.

NOTES

1. For analysis of social class formation following economic liberalization, see Hettige (1998).
2. See Lakshman (1997, 2002) and Shastri (2004).
3. There was hardly any industrialization in the country during the British period. Following independence, successive governments, particularly after 1956, took steps to establish import substitution industries to produce such commodities as sugar, cement, steel, textiles, paper, and chemicals.
4. The establishment of several new universities in the 1980s and 1990s resulted in a significant increase in university enrolments while neo-liberal economic policies led to a contraction of state-sector employment. The result has been increasing unemployment among university graduates. Continuing political agitations by unemployed graduates supported by the JVP compelled governments to devise various strategies to provide employment to university graduates including mass recruitment of graduates as schoolteachers and low-level functionaries in government and semi-government institutions.

5. Public expenditure on education declined substantially after economic liberalization. Allocation for education declined from 15 per cent of the government budget in 1970 to 5.6 per cent in 1983 (Lakshman, 1986).
6. The insurgency and the counter-insurgency measures taken by the government forces resulted in the destruction of an estimated 60,000 lives within a period of about three years. For good analyses of the JVP movement, see Obeyesekere (1974), Janatha (1977), and Gunaratna (1990).
7. The JVP won 39 seats out of 106 gained by the coalition that formed the government.
8. The JVP position in the government was weakened when several other minor parties joined the government leading to a substantial reduction in their influence. This naturally frustrated them, persuading them to leave.
9. The National Youth Survey of 1999 found that a majority of youth in the country held this view (Hettige, 2002).
10. Private sector leaders have often expressed the view that graduates passing out from local universities do not speak English, do not have the right attitudes and other desired psychological predispositions required to fit in to the corporate work environment.
11. Interviews were drawn from Southern, North-central, Western, Uva, and Central provinces.

REFERENCES

Gunaratna, R. 1990. *Sri Lanka, A Lost Revolution? The Inside Story of the JVP*. Kandy: Institute of Fundamental Studies.

Hettige, S.T. 1998. 'Global Integration and the Disadvantaged Youth: From the Centre Stage to the Margins of Society', in S.T. Hettige (ed.), *Globalization, Social Change and Youth*, pp. 71–104. Colombo: German Cultural Institute.

———. 2002. 'Sri Lankan Youth: Profiles and Perspectives', in S.T. Hettige and M. Mayer (eds), *Sri Lankan Youth: Challenge and Response*, pp. 13–50. Colombo: Frederic Ebert Stiftung.

———. 2004a. 'From Social Justice to Market Competition: Impact of Globalization on Education in Sri Lanka', paper presented at the 18th Modern South Asian Studies Conference, 6–8 July 2004, Lund, Sweden.

———. 2004b. 'Economic Policy, Changing Opportunities for Youth and the Ethnic Conflict in Sri Lanka', in D. Winslow and M. Woost (eds), *Economy, Culture, and Civil War in Sri Lanka*, pp. 115–30. Bloomington: Indian University Press.

Janatha. 1977. *Aprel Negiteema* [1971 April Uprising]. Dehiwala: Janatha Sangamaya.

Lakshman, W.D. 1986. 'State Policy and Its Impact', *Upanathi*, 1(1): 5–38.

———. 1997. *Dilemmas of Development: Fifty Years of Economic Change in Sri Lanka*. Colombo: Sri Lanka Association of Economists.

———. 2002. 'A Holistic View of Youth Unemployment in Sri Lanka: An Exploratory Study', in S.T. Hettige and M. Mayer (eds), *Sri Lankan Youth: Challenge and Response*, pp. 57–88. Colombo: Frederic Ebert Stiftung.

Obeyesekere, G. 1974. 'On Social Backgrounds of the April 1971 Insurgency in Sri Lanka', *Journal of Asian Studies*, 33(3): 367–80.
Shastri, A. 2004. 'An Open Economy in a Time of Intense Civil War: Sri Lanka 1994–2000', in D. Winslow and M. Woost (eds), *Economy, Culture, and Civil War in Sri Lanka*, pp. 73–94. Bloomington: Indiana University Press.
Spencer, J. 1990. *A Sinhala Village in a Time of Trouble: Politics and Change in Rural Sri Lanka*. New Delhi: Oxford University Press.
Wimmer, A. 2002. *Nationalist Exclusion and Ethnic Conflict: Shadows of Modernity*. Cambridge: Cambridge University Press.

Chapter 5

Can Women be Mobilized to Participate in Indian Local Politics?

STEFANIE STRULIK

Following the 73rd and 74th Amendments in 1993 that implemented a 33 per cent women's quota for local governance, by 2003 about 2 million women had been elected to the different panchayat institutions at the village, block, and district levels (Mathew, 2000). After the mid-1990s, almost literally overnight, huge numbers of women were invited, pushed, or grudgingly admitted to local political arenas. In many cases previous stakeholders sought to hold on to their power by trying to turn the newly elected women into their 'proxies' or, if that was not possible, tried to marginalize them by sidelining, ridiculing, or even harassing them.[1] At the same time, many women's organizations, non-governmental organizations (NGOs), governmental initiatives, etc., encouraged women to stand for the election, to fight for their entitlements, and to perceive the reservations as a rightful and long-overdue chance to participate in local governance.

This chapter will discuss the different entry points that women have into local politics. Special attention will be given to the question of how 'activists'—above all non-governmental activists—are involved in women's 'political mobilization'. Becoming 'mobilized' by activists, however, is just one way of entering local politics. To substantiate my argument, I will discuss the range of relevant actors by examining the role of six different types of social actors who are influential in the process of women becoming active in local politics. In the course of the argument it will become clear that it is difficult to identify a particular 'political entry point' and that indeed it would be more interesting for further analysis to think in terms of women's political trajectories.[2]

The second part of this chapter elaborates the idea of political trajectories and discusses the limits of being 'mobilized' by activists by contrasting it with the importance of multilayered gendered support networks in the politicization of women. Finally, the question whether such inclusivist reforms are bound to fail because of the nature of the state at the local level will be addressed.

LOCAL GOVERNANCE AND PANCHAYATI RAJ

The 73rd and 74th Amendments to the Indian Constitution were an attempt to revitalize the so-called 'Modern Panchayati Raj Institutions' of local self-governance through village councils. These councils are often claimed to have forebears in the subcontinent that go back earlier even than 1000 BCE (Kuhn, 1998: 241).[3] After independence, local self-governance through panchayat bodies was incorporated into the first constitution, but politics and administration continued to be dominated by centralized state government. Hardly any devolution of power or funds took place and the influence and scope for self-governance for panchayati raj bodies remained limited (Mathew, 1994). Whatever powers the *gram* panchayat held were concentrated in the hands of local elites (i.e., male representatives of the locally dominant, landholding castes) and were often used to maintain exploitative local power relations (Girtler, 1972).

Apart from devolving funds and development responsibilities to the local level, the constitutional amendments of 1993 intended to remedy these asymmetries. They aimed at the empowerment of hitherto marginalized sections by introducing a 33 per cent quota for women and reservations for low castes (SCs), Adivasis (STs), and so-called 'Other Backward Classes' (OBCs) according to their local demographic strength. The 'new panchayats', which meet bi-monthly, discuss village affairs and evaluate ongoing development initiatives. Moreover, elected members, together with the *pradhan* (the head of the village council)[4] and the village secretary (a local bureaucrat), plan, prioritize, and subsequently apply for financial support for development schemes. Among many very varied responsibilities, *gram* panchayats are also active in the mediation of local conflicts.[5] The *pradhan* plays a crucial role in the implementation, management, and supervision of government's development programmes. Whereas the *pradhan* is accountable to the panchayat council, the panchayat council in turn is answerable to the village assembly (*gram sabha*) in its bi-annual meetings.[6]

The panchayat system, moreover, is now hierarchically organized on three levels, of which the *gram* panchayat is at the lowest tier, followed by the block panchayat and, at the district level, by the *zilla parishad*. The prioritized applications for funds and development schemes are handed up to the next tier, and the *zilla parishad*, in cooperation with the District Planning Committee (DPC), finally decides on the prioritized lists and formulates a draft development plan on which basis money will be sanctioned and eventually funds are transferred down, back to the *gram* panchayats. Reservations for women, SCs, STs, and OBCs are valid on all three levels on a rotating basis, including reservations for the head of the respective bodies.

A TYPOLOGY OF ACTORS

In order to delineate the complexity of the local political arena that the constitutional amendments sought to transform I distinguish analytically between six different types of social actors who are of particular importance for women's initial electoral nomination, as well as women's political self-assertion. The different actors are *(a)* local bureaucrats, *(b)* politicians, *(c)* urban feminist activists, *(d)* women from local women's groups, *(e)* patrons, and *(f)* family members. These groups will be illustrated in turn by examples from my own empirical material.[7] These characterizations have to be understood as 'ideal types' (Kluge, 1999) as they are often crosscut by kinship, caste, and patron–client relations. The types should not be seen as mutually exclusive. In fact, actors from at least several types generally play a role in women's gradual assertion within political institutions. Furthermore, since politicization is a process, it often happens that some sorts of actors play a prominent role at certain stages and later fade into the background, or they may be selectively called upon depending on the situation.

Local Bureaucrats

Women who are elected to panchayat bodies generally come into contact with local bureaucrats only after their election. Therefore, local bureaucrats play a less important role in the initial phase of women's political trajectory. However, they are important brokers to the formal political field (Bierschenk and de Sardan, 2003: 46) and become crucial counterparts, especially to *pradhans*, after the election.

One characteristic of local bureaucrats (e.g. the village secretary[8] but also other officials from the block office, including the BDO) is that, although they are perceived as representing the state, they are also socially and discursively embedded within kinship and caste relations in the localities where they work.[9] Consequently, they share in the widespread complacency about enacting the constitutional amendments or may even be in complicity in deliberately undermining them.

During my fieldwork in eastern Uttar Pradesh (2000–03), I found the collaboration of husbands and officials in sidelining elected women to be symptomatic of the problem. Most of the officials are from the higher castes themselves and come from families where *purdah* is observed. One secretary justified his habit of working with the husband and not attempting to involve the woman-*pradhan* as follows:

> These reservations are impossible to combine with our culture, the government does not know anything about our life here. I know that if I were the pradhan, I wouldn't send my wife out to do the work either. Because, she would not be able to do the work, she doesn't understand anything about this work, about schemes and politics, you know, she is not educated nor is she interested in politics. Even if she learned and became knowledgeable [about politics], how will she talk to the villagers? My family and I would become a joke. People would talk very badly about our family, how advanced we are. They would not give the due respect to my wife and our family—how could I tolerate that? [...] Here men have always been pradhans and good at it—why should it be changed? [...] If I had to work with a woman pradhan, I would have to work twice as long, explaining each and every bit to her.

However, during my fieldwork, I also encountered exceptional cases. In fact, in Himachal Pradesh the majority of secretaries insisted on working together with the elected women, rather than going through their husbands or male patrons. But, even in eastern Uttar Pradesh, there were some secretaries who took the time to explain formal procedures to the newly elected women or made an effort to argue with reluctant relatives to permit the woman to attend panchayat meetings. Both in Himachal and in Uttar Pradesh the majority of secretaries were men. But in those rare cases where the secretary happened to be a woman it improved the rapport between *pradhan* and secretary in many ways. Women *pradhans* explained that they felt more at ease with female secretaries: not only while sitting down and working over books and reports together, but also when asking questions, women felt less pressure to legitimize their election by pretending to be already conversant with all the technical details. As a further major advantage, it was mentioned that families tend to object less when the *pradhan* toured the sub-villages of the panchayat with another woman. In those cases where secretaries and *pradhans* have a good personal rapport it is obvious that it will help the newly elected women to understand the political field better, both in terms of technical and legal knowledge, and also with regard to building up the cultural capital needed for day-to-day participation in politics (e.g. how to deal with corruption; cf. Gupta, 1995).

The relation to local bureaucrats other than the secretary is just as complex. If a woman can rely on an ally at the block office, she will have access to the latest information on certain schemes coming up and may count on preferential treatment when negotiating her panchayat's claims at the block level. Moreover, due to the bureaucracy's hierarchical organization her secretary probably will also feel more obliged to cooperate with her. However, very few women have a supporter at the block level. Whereas men usually either enter local politics through a network of kinship, caste, or patron–client-based distributive coalitions (cf. Pfaff-Czarnecka, 1999, 2008), or understand the importance of establishing and nurturing such networks of mutual favours and sharing legitimate and illegitimate spoils, women are often inexperienced in how to broach such issues or even deliberately make it a point to stay clear of these 'dirty' aspects of politics. Often, those villagers who held crucial positions of power before 1993 try to continue siphoning government funds by bypassing the elected women—frequently with the cooperation of local officials. In such cases, it is indispensable that the elected women know who to turn to in the upper echelons of district or state-level bureaucracies to have the local bureaucrats reprimanded.

To sum up, if there is no rapport between women and local bureaucrats, and the latter refuse to implement the reservations, the chances for women's political participation offered by the amendments are considerably diminished. On the other hand, if women succeed in establishing good working relationships with supportive local bureaucrats, this will constitute one important avenue of entry into the formal political sphere. Such alliances give women access to different stocks of knowledge and offer significant opportunities to transform the political arena either by circumventing or by tapping into already existing power relations and distributive coalitions.

Politicians

For a very few women the road to participation in panchayat institutions goes via prior active involvement in party politics. Whether women receive party support depends generally on other (male) family members who are already affiliated with a political party. In such cases political parties may organize and even financially support the election campaign of female candidates.

Being supported by a political party mostly means being the *protégé* of an influential politician, preferably a member of the legislative assembly (MLA), who functions as patron during a woman's election campaign and particularly after she takes up office. At the same time he/she expects the woman to be loyal to him/her personally and to rally supporters during state-level legislative elections. In exchange, the woman gains access to development funds controlled by the MLA. The political patron may even mobilize what Indians call musclemen to manhandle or intimidate her opponents in situations of crisis. Most importantly, the woman enjoys patronage at the district level where ultimately the funds for development programmes are prioritized and sanctioned. Political parties generally have a 'women's wing' and women who are elected on the basis of party support, without being considered symbolic 'stand-ins' for male relatives and their nepotistic party networks, begin their political careers through them.

A typical example is Pramilla Devi, a Rajput woman from Himachal Pradesh, who established her local reputation by starting up a local savings and credit group. Later, through her position as head of several women's groups, she became the contact person for the Himachal government for the implementation of several development schemes (e.g. afforestation, introduction of smokeless cooking stoves). In turn, her function as a broker between the government and local women's groups drew the attention of the Bharatiya Janata Party's (BJP) women's wing.[10] They invited her to attend various party programmes and workshops which gave her the opportunity to extend her network of political friends and 'sisters'. It was also on one such occasion that she became aware of the possibilities for women to stand for the panchayat elections. At one of these programmes, she was introduced to the MLA who assisted her later in running a successful campaign for her election to the Block Development Committee (BDC).[11] The posters for her campaign were printed using BJP funds. In villages that she visited during her election campaign she was received by BJP supporters shouting slogans and assisting her in door-to-door canvassing.[12]

Pramilla was proud to point out that after her election, due to her good personal relations with the MLA and with her 'sisters' in the BJP's women's wing, she was able to bring additional funds (e.g. for the construction of a panchayat building) to her constituency. However, her attempt to be elected president of the BDC failed. Another Rajput woman, wife of a local Congress politician, was elected instead. The following description by Pramilla Devi highlights the ambivalence of political parties and their mobilization as well as support of certain women in panchayat politics. It illustrates the dangers of walking a tightrope between being instrumentalized for party interests, being dependent on 'buy it all' party funds for campaigning, and attempts to voice and practise a gender-sensitive vision of local governance despite party protection:

> See, Girija Devi [the successful Congress candidate] spent Rs 200,000 for her campaign and she got that money through her party. She gave huge gifts to the other members of the BDC—for instance one SC lady was given a motorbike costing Rs 65,000 to vote for Girija Devi. Even though she is the chairman, she hardly had any experience, neither is she efficient nor does she know things. It was because of party politics that she won. Although she does not know anything, she has her party men behind her who will suggest to her whatever she should do next—in fact her husband is in the Congress party as well. Although she chairs the meetings, it is through her husband that she is given directions.

Of course this quote illustrates the ongoing rivalry between the two women, but it also shows the pitfalls of entering panchayat politics dependent on the support of a political party. On the one hand, having access to the formal political field and its information networks, knowledge, and resources through vertical support structures helps women to carve out new spaces for manoeuvre. But, on the other hand, both the examples together have shown that only those women who can rely on an already established varied support network and are not exclusively dependent on one particular type of supporter are in a position to further their own agenda.

Urban (Feminist) Activists

There are many initiatives in India to mobilize women for panchayat politics. Many of these initiatives are funded by international development cooperation and are run by Indian NGOs and rely above all on so-called 'capacity-building programmes'. The capacity-building programmes in turn focus mostly on 'legal literacy', politicization, awareness raising (rights, entitlements, responsibilities), and building 'leadership qualities'.[13] Most of the more professionalized NGOs working in this field are urban based with an executive staff consisting of women with feminist activist backgrounds. But many smaller rural NGOs, hitherto working in different fields, lured by the availability of funds, have incorporated at least some 'capacity-building projects' for newly elected women into their ongoing programmes.

Despite the fact that there are large numbers of NGOs working in the field of capacity-building programmes, these NGOs are not spread evenly throughout the country. In fact, in both the blocks in Uttar Pradesh and Himachal Pradesh where I carried out the major part of my fieldwork, no NGO was running a specific programme to mobilize and train women for panchayat work. In Latur district, Maharashtra, the area where I initially started research work on panchayati raj,[14] however, one Mumbai-based feminist NGO had been active since the earthquake in 1993 with capacity-building programmes intended to organize women in groups and involve them in local governance. The NGO was otherwise engaged in consultancy work for international donor agencies, including the World Bank, in the field of relief and reconstruction work from a gender perspective. The NGO also participated in global feminist networks, and their staff were part of the 'development jet-set', attending conferences all over the world. In Latur district they were working together with 'local field staff' who functioned as brokers to local communities and as implementers of the major part of the programme.

After the 73rd and 74th Amendments, building upon the already established network of local women's groups, a new emphasis was laid on mobilizing women from these groups to stand for panchayat elections. They ran programmes to impart the necessary legal as well as practical knowledge to those women who had succeeded in being elected to the *gram* panchayats. In addition, the need for cooperation between women's groups and elected panchayat members to engender local governance beyond panchayat politics was highlighted, and strategies for effective collaboration between women's groups and elected panchayat members were part of the agenda. In many villages this approach of organizing and mobilizing women for local governance beyond its narrow conceptualization of formal participation in panchayati raj bodies produced interesting synergy effects: women *sarpanch*es had a support group to rely on as a buffer, as well as visible legitimization against male vested interests. On the other hand, by means of close cooperation with the *sarpanch*es, women's groups had the opportunity to bring their concerns with regard to development schemes or to local disputes into the local political arena.[15]

However, despite the training workshops being open to non-group members and the capacity-building programmes targeting all elected women, I realized, after several weeks in the area and many introductions to 'success stories' later, that, surprisingly, many *sarpanch*es and panchayat members were neither members of one of the groups, nor worked explicitly with the support of these groups. It turned out that in many villages the 'mobilization' of village women in fact had been so successful that the women's groups not only did not see it to be necessary to work together with the female members of the panchayat but went directly to the (male) *pradhan*. In those cases where the *pradhan* was a woman whom they did not consider particularly capable, they preferred to deal straight away with her husband or with block officials. Interestingly, precisely in those villages were the women's groups had become really vociferous and strong, they did not have the patience to enrol the *sarpanch* in their projects and were bypassing 'unenlightened', 'slow', or 'incapable' female panchayat members and *pradhan*s.

Women who were elected to the panchayat bodies but did not participate in local women's groups generally explained their reluctance either by pointing out that there were personal animosities with some of the group's members or, more often, by saying that there was no women's group of their own caste in the village and that they did not feel comfortable in, or wanted by, the existing groups.

Mobilization via various programmes by urban activists working for the 'empowerment' of women definitely offers an opportunity for the organization of women and putting women's issues on the agenda in local governance. Moreover, it gives women access to alternative discourses on gender and development and may help to establish a crucial support network. However, not all women are attracted to this option. In cases where mobilization fails to overcome caste barriers, its success is likely to be limited. Groups of women who are vocal and already well organized may prefer to go 'the easy way' to realize their own agenda, which may not be the agenda of all other women within the panchayat—nor the one envisioned by the urban feminists. The sidelining of 'inefficient' or 'non-cooperating' women may create a parallel structure of local governance, albeit one that responds to women's concerns.

Since a common strategy to marginalize elected women is to represent them as ignorant and incapable, trainings provided by NGOs are nonetheless important, insofar as they serve to offset such allegations by imparting knowledge of the legal framework on which women can draw in order to legitimize their actions. However, it is also necessary to realize that people are successful in representing women as 'ignorant' only because they exaggerate the importance of formal (male) political knowledge.[16] Women are knowledgeable as well—their stocks of knowledge are merely 'constructed' as less relevant (Lachenmann, 1996, 2004). Therefore, initiatives for 'mobilizing for political participation programmes' and 'capacity building' by feminist/NGO activists should not focus exclusively on women. Instead, they should aim to disseminate alternative discourses on gender, knowledge, politics, rights, and entitlements to the entire local community.[17]

Members of Local Women's Groups

The political trajectories of those women who are not merely elected to panchayat bodies, but succeed in getting a foothold in local politics and manage to shape local governance show certain similarities. The majority of such women have been members or even founders of local women's groups long before they were elected as representatives for their panchayat. This suggests that the interaction with fellow members of local women's groups is of significance for its role in drawing women into local governance.

It would be useful to differentiate between members of local women's groups (like Mahila Mandals, Saving and Credit Groups (SCGs), self-help groups (SHGs)), on the one hand, and urban (feminist) activists, on the other, as constituting two different types of relevant actors. The prime objective of members of local women's groups is not to mobilize fellow members for local governance, but rather they are preoccupied with income generation and credit and saving activities, games and songs, and establishing solidarity networks. The members' rationales for organizing as a group or participating in the group's activities range from enthusiasm to do some 'social work', to being attracted to possible personal 'benefits' (getting access to certain schemes, etc.), to primarily enjoying the company of other women and the chance to discuss matters of common interest with women outside their own kinship network. Furthermore, these women's group members tend to take a less assertive stand in explicitly (verbally) challenging discourses on politics or gender. Many of these groups are founded as a result of the initiative of village women, and others are encouraged by local NGOs in the context of implementing development projects.

The following example of Bimla Devi, an SC woman from Himachal Pradesh, is meant to illustrate how the interaction and joint activities with fellow women group members are important both as path-breaking experiences on the way to being elected, as well as crucial for shaping consciousness and agendas for later work as a panchayat member, and thus form part of a process of making local governance gender-sensitive.

Bimla's first contact with a local women's group was in her twenties, a couple of years after her marriage. She was encouraged to join by an educated older woman from a neighbouring village who wanted to educate and organize women through the newly established Mahila Mandals scheme. These groups started by organizing leisure activities (for instance playing games, such as musical chairs) and competing in these with other similar groups on block and district levels. Apart from playing games the women discussed livelihood matters and occasionally utilized government funds for development schemes (e.g. planting trees). In the late 1980s Bimla's group also followed the then-emerging trend and turned itself into an SCG. Bimla, being one of the more experienced members with regard to savings and credit schemes, started to interact with other women's groups beyond the district boundaries, attended various governmental and NGO training programmes, and eventually became a 'multiplicator', founding new groups in surrounding villages. In 2000 the women of her group suggested to her that she should stand in the next panchayat election, "because she is so good at organizing". Bimla's initial reaction was that *gram* panchayat politics and women's groups are two different things. But the women insisted and told her, "Look, if you see it as social work, the panchayat work is not so different after all," and assured her that she need not worry. Finally, they persuaded Bimla and, 'taking permission' from her husband, she filed the nomination paper. During the election campaign, she walked around the five sub-villages of her *gram* panchayat, escorted not only by women from her own group, but also by women of those groups she had founded in the area. The way the women described participation in the election made it clear that they had derived much enjoyment from travelling and working together.

After her election, Bimla continued to work closely with her friends from the women's group. Together with her fellow group members, they share views of local governance and then strategize and plan together how these things should be achieved. The villagers' initial reaction to her different, 'typically female' working style was to make fun of her and to tell her repeatedly that "This is not the way politics is done." However, with time, the opposition subsided, since she managed to have development funds sanctioned.[18]

In her interviews with me, Bimla gave many more examples of how, in times of crisis, when attempts were made to de-legitimize her with negative rumours, the women were there to comfort her and to confer on what should be done next. In return, through Bimla, they had the opportunity not only to discuss their individual and common problems and frustrations, but also to draw attention to these in the panchayat meetings and *gram sabha*s.

In short, the women who constitute this fourth type can be seen as crucial companions in the process of becoming a successful *pradhan* or panchayat member. Through the continuous process of mutual discussion, by lending a sympathetic ear, but also through open criticism, an important female political space is created. Through the elected woman, who is moving in different political, above all male-dominated political arenas, this female political space is linked with the formal political field. This, in turn, may offer the opportunity gradually to transform the local political arena in the long run, that is, to open local governance up to women and to change long-established discourses on politics and gender.

Patrons

Yet another type of actor that plays a role in women's decisions to stand for election, as well as in later outlining the scope of possible action, is constituted by what could be summarized as 'patrons'. In the context of panchayati raj, patrons are almost exclusively men who are linked by dyadic ties with the woman who is or was elected to the panchayat. Although the patron may seem to be benevolently performing favours for his client, in fact the flow of goods and services is generally in favour of the patron. Although the relationship is one of interdependence, the power balance generally is advantageous to the patron. Patrons could be members of the landholding elite, influential members of caste panchayats, mafia, or local politicians.[19] Often patrons play an important role in suggesting or even pressuring a woman to stand in panchayat elections. They either promise to 'take care of everything' before and after the election, or to support the woman in her subsequent panchayat work. In most of these cases the intention of the patron is to circumvent the new legal norms which 'block' certain seats with reservations in order to extend his own sphere of influence. The inherent power asymmetries of the patron–client relationship, and the common attempts by patrons to install women as their 'proxies', suggest the need to be wary about the potential of this kind of 'mobilization' for engendering governance. Nevertheless, some women succeed in shifting some of the boundaries of the patron–client relationship and extend their room for manoeuvre. Moreover, there are rare cases of patrons who support women because they believe in the need and desirability of the empowerment of women or members of low castes. They sincerely try to impart knowledge and extend support to enable women to craft their own political career. However, in most of the cases the patron's rationales are selfish rather than altruistic or idealistic, as is illustrated in the following example of Rita Devi, a 48-year-old SC woman in Himachal Pradesh.

Rita Devi lives in a remote *pahari*[20] village together with her two daughters-in-law and five grandchildren, while her sons and husband are working in different lumber camps all over Himachal Pradesh. Rita Devi never went to school and her family struggled hard to make ends meet. Their indebtedness began with the need to build a *pakka* house (solid, baked-brick house) when her first son got married, for which they borrowed Rs 20,000 from a rich Rajput farmer, Ghanshyam Singh, on whose fields Rita and her family worked occasionally as seasonal agricultural labourers. Rita had to take another loan in order to be able to pay for the dowry and wedding for her two daughters. Then, a few years later, her son fell ill and had to be hospitalized in the district capital for which yet another loan had to be taken from the same Rajput farmer, who by now had become the *pradhan* of the panchayat. These days, her family is so heavily indebted that they barely manage to pay back the interest. Rita's family lives under continuous threat that the Rajput farmer will seize the small landholding on which they depend for subsistence production.

In 2000, Ghanshyam Singh, then *pradhan*, came to Rita Devi's house and told her to sign some forms to stand for election as representative for her SC ward to the panchayat. Rita Devi replied that she did not think herself to be suitable for such a responsibility because she was illiterate and already overburdened with organizing the survival of her family in the absence of her husband and sons.[21] She requested Ghanshyam Singh to ask other more educated women, whom she considered much more suited for the work as a panchayat member.

The *pradhan* assured her that she "shouldn't worry at all", that he "would do all the work for her", that he would stand for the *up-pradhan*'s (vice-pradhan's) seat in the upcoming election and that he would brief her before every panchayat meeting when to raise her hand and that, apart from that, she "wouldn't have to do anything".[22] Yet, Rita Devi remained reluctant, well aware that she "might get into something she wouldn't be able to handle". She was especially fearful of being caught between the interests of the people of her ward and those of the 'big people'. But finally she agreed, following subtle hints about her family's indebtedness, that if she would not do this small favour to the *pradhan*, in future he might be also deaf to her pleas. Ultimately Ghanshyam Singh financed her election campaign (gifts, sweets, etc.) and also the post-election celebration. It should be mentioned that Ghanshyam Singh's political engineering was eventually so successful that he managed not only to co-opt one more SC woman candidate but also installed his sister as the panchayat's *pradhan*.

Even Rita, who otherwise is so uninformed about panchayat matters, is well aware why it is attractive to be the *pradhan*—or, as in this case, to be the *up-pradhan* and the brother of the *pradhan*: "If you are the pradhan, you get the respect from the people, because they need your benevolence if they want to get any of their work to be done. And there is money in that, too!"

At the time of my research, Rita had been in office for two years, and she agreed that overall she enjoyed the campaigning. She also asserted that now she likes being elected to the panchayat, that going and sitting there in the meetings is interesting, and that overall her relation to Ghanshyam Singh has improved. However, she is also aware that Ghanshyam's benevolence rests upon her 'cooperation', and that she cannot dare to vote against him during the meetings. She is happy that the Ghanshyam Singh is bringing some development schemes to her ward so that so far she has not yet drawn the anger of her own ward's people upon her.

Since the majority of patrons I came across during my fieldwork tended to work on similar agendas as Ghanshyam Singh, it seems to be justified to claim that despite patrons being instrumental for the electoral victory of some women, there are, based on the relation's inherent power asymmetries, decisive limitations to such mobilization. Being 'mobilized' by a patron for candidature may open the door to local governance for some women. But departing from the default path behind that door—as envisioned by the patron—might be extremely difficult given economic (or other) dependencies. Some women may succeed in carving out a small space for manoeuvre by a gruelling and continuous negotiation—but many remain resigned to fulfilling the patron's expectations.

Family Members

Due to their immediacy, relationships with family members are arguably the most crucial support structures for female participation in politics in rural India. To have the support, encouragement, or at least permission from one's own family is essential for women leaders.[23] Hardly any of the women I interviewed went explicitly against their families' wishes in joining local politics.

For women who are already elected, the support from other female household members in particular is important. Panchayat work is time consuming, and it is almost impossible to work as a *pradhan* if one does not have other family members who take over previous duties (e.g. cooking, looking after children in absence, grass cutting). Most of the time, these chores are taken care of by sisters-in-law, daughters-in-law, or even more often by daughters. The support of daughters is particularly important in other ways as well. In many cases, initially illiterate women learned how to read and write, as well as how to handle panchayat manuals from their daughters. Moreover, adult but unmarried daughters often had the most progressive views on women's entitlement for 'empowerment' and 'a right to have a voice in local governance'. Consequently, the enthusiastic daughters tended to push their mothers 'to give it a try' and to stand in the election.

However, kinship relations can be both enabling and highly constraining. They provide affectionate support and encouragement, knowledge, information, and assistance with household chores. Furthermore, technicalities of the panchayat and extended kinship and caste networks can be helpful in election campaigns, *gram sabha*s, etc. Yet, they also can present an obstacle in the process of women's political assertion, if women are denied the mobility needed for the completion of their office's responsibilities, and if the attempts to challenge gendered expectation (e.g. gender segregation) are heavily sanctified. 'Harmony' and 'happiness' within the family is presented as superseding all personal ambitions by the majority of women.[24] If a woman's political aspirations, or her assumptions about the newly assumed political office, are not acceptable to the family and result in conflicts and tension, many women would rather prefer not to contest family hierarchies too directly by overriding gendered expectations of 'proper' behaviour for a wife or daughter-in-law. Generally, women will prefer a non-offensive subtle approach to negotiate ambitions and may accept certain limits, not necessarily feeling uncomfortable with them.

Therefore, it becomes difficult for the woman to discharge her responsibilities independently, if there is somebody in the family, particularly the husband, who suggests his wife's candidature with the objective to usurp her seat after the election, or to more subtly steer local politics through her. However, even in the 'worst case scenario', in which the husband or some other family member tries to install a woman as a mere 'proxy', even then, some subtle changes may still take place, as the following example of Manju Devi, a Rajput woman in her mid-forties in eastern Uttar Pradesh illustrates.

Manju had never been to any of the panchayat meetings. In fact, since her in-laws observe *purdah* she had hardly left the house after her marriage, and all villagers—including herself—told me that all political activities were managed by her husband. Village men and most of the village women, including Manju herself, were convinced that this was the right way to deal with these 'silly reservations', because her husband, so it was assumed, was so much better equipped to deal with village matters.

Manju was initially against her own nomination, because she was very apprehensive about 'dirty politics', and feared that her name might be blackened by the things done in her name, and which might not be 'right' later. However, she started to take a genuine interest in what was going on at the panchayat level. Her rationale for agreeing to be nominated was her husband's 'happiness' and her family's status, as well as the possibility to influence local politics in her family's interests. During the election campaign, her husband made her speak inside the house, to a group of selected male and female (fictive) 'village' relatives. However, of course she could not take part in the public campaigning, which she left to her husband and other male family members.

Talking about panchayat work, she referred to it as "work done by us" and identified herself with her "outside representation" through her husband. After her election she tried to inform herself by talking and questioning everyone who came to her house, mostly women or younger relatives, but also by gathering information and other people's views through her children. Being herself a school dropout, she went through some panchayat manuals with the help of her daughter, because she felt she should know "what all this panchayat thing is about". She had to leave the house and "*purdah* has become a little bit open", because it was necessary to go to the bank, and she also had to go to the block office a couple of times to sign some papers. However, "*purdah* also had become less open" than she had initially expected.[25] Nevertheless, Manju seemed to be rather resigned about that and enjoyed whatever small exciting opportunities had come up, rather than being interested in challenging and pushing things further.

Village women came to Manju's house to speak to her, because they were afraid or rather 'too shy' to interact directly with her husband. Manju is proud that she could do something for the women at all in her role as mediator. She relished being addressed as *pradhanji* and enjoyed the fact that even the other women in the house called her *pradhanji* teasingly. She pointed out happily that everybody in the village knew her name, and not only as 'wife of so-and-so'.

When her husband held meetings with male family members or outsiders, Manju would eavesdrop from behind the curtain (*saree-purdah*) that divided the inner courtyard of the house. On the other hand, Manju and her husband themselves usually discussed politics, and the village women's concerns at night in bed. Because of gender segregation decreed by *purdah* ideals like 'respect', 'honour', and 'decency', this is the only space, where she can talk to her husband—thus rendering the most 'private' into a locus for village politics, that is, the 'public'.

Manju's example shows that some changes occur even in the every-day lives of women who could otherwise be represented as proxies, and that certain boundaries around the construction of gender are, very subtly, shifted. Through the woman *pradhan*, even if she is observing *purdah*, 'alternative publics' (Frazer, 1992) or female political spaces are linked to the dominant, almost exclusively male, political space, and the latter is thus, even if in a rudimentary way, transformed.[26]

However, Manju's example, also highlights the limits of 'strong support' by a male family member (here the husband). He encouraged her to stand for the election and allowed for certain re-interpretations of gendered expectations where they were necessary for his own political ends. In principle, many variations of this theme are empirically observable. The nature of the conjugal relationship, the husband's own political aspirations, but also, on the other hand, the husband's willingness to accept his wife's political ambitions and consequent re-interpretations of societal expectations, set the parameters for women's political participation. It is then left to women's skilful handling of day-to-day interaction gradually to extend her room for manoeuvre in an ongoing process of negotiation.

CONCLUSION

In this chapter I have discussed six types of actors who play a role in the process of women becoming politically active in panchayati raj institutions. A comparison of the six types suggests the following three observations regarding *mobilization*, *political trajectories*, and the *importance of multilayer support networks*.

Looking at the different actors and the ways in which they are related to women's political participation in panchayati raj institutions showed that 'mobilization' by activists plays a secondary role for women getting involved in local governance. On the contrary, the empirical material shows that precisely those women who had started establishing a public identity *before* the question of nomination arose, later managed to gain some foothold in a local political arena, even if the majority of local actors are striving for a re-interpretation and appropriation of the new legal norms. One has to acknowledge that entering politics in a meaningful way 'overnight' due to some 'mobilization' is highly unlikely. Consequently, the fact that women are elected has to be understood merely as a specific event within a process of politicization which would most appropriately be described as a *political trajectory* (Vianello and Moore, 2000). Within these political trajectories, mobilization by activists may play a role, but not necessarily the most central one, as many women became politically active without one or the other form of 'mobilization'. I would even suggest that 'mobilization' by activists is part of a top-down approach which tends to overlook the complexities of the politicization process, as well as the practices through which politics are socially constructed.

It turned out to be problematic, or even artificial, to single out one of the presented types exclusively as the one and only reason why women enter local politics, or even as an explanation for women's successful carving out of new political spaces. In fact, on the contrary, I argue that those women who can rely on a 'multilayered support-network' consisting at best of representatives from all six types, will have a distinct advantage in achieving local recognition and legitimization. Ideally, this support network crosscuts horizontally and vertically different social spaces, so that different knowledge systems and resources can be accessed and integrated, dependencies attenuated, and thus attempts at co-option held in check.

The question of co-option and possible subtexts to the 'motivation' of those who took it upon themselves to encourage women's political participation lead me to the question raised in the call for papers, whether "current attempts by governments, as well as outside agencies, to encourage 'inclusivity' and 'democracy' [are] bound to be undermined by the very organizational and class forms which are used to propagate these values?" The question, in the context of women and panchayati raj, is relevant to two types of actors discussed in this chapter.

First, in the case of urban feminist activists, it can be argued that, despite the fact that these women usually come from a highly educated middle- or even upper middle-class urban background, they are 'mobilizing' women for local governance, following global discourses on women's rights and gender equity. They may not always succeed in 'speaking the same language' as the village women, because the very discourses they are referring to in order to legitimize their own work as well as the desirability of women's political participation are not commonly available locally. This may also be one reason why feminist activists often fail to transcend caste barriers, but it would be stretching it too far to explain this failure by accusing them of following inconsistent or feigned motives because they are urban elite women themselves.

The same question asked with reference to local bureaucrats might however produce more complex answers. Many of the local officials, if asked in a general sense about the usefulness and desirability of the reservation, would reply, "Of course women should come forward", or that they "try to support the elected women". However, if asked about their personal working relationships with the elected women, many local bureaucrats highlighted 'societal constraints' and 'certain impracticabilities' and the foregoing discussion showed that, in fact, many officials were anything but supportive of women establishing themselves in political institutions. I argue that these inconsistencies have to be understood in the context of the social embeddedness of the bureaucrats, and thus of the local state. The very local bureaucrats who, as representatives of the state that passed the 73rd and 74th Amendments, are supposed to promote the desirability of women's political participation, are entrenched in local communities and participate in the same locally dominant discourses on gender, politics, and the related construction of women as being 'unsuitable' and 'too ignorant' to engage in politics. Therefore, one has to acknowledge that there is at least a latent danger that the inclusivity that was envisioned by the professed democratic ideals of the 73rd and 74th Amendments, and thus claimed by the state, may indeed be undermined by the state's own representatives, that is, the local bureaucrats. However, I argue that the normative bias of 'undermining' tends to turn local bureaucrats into scapegoats, overlooking the fact that new legislation will always be subject to local appropriation and re-interpretation. Local bureaucrats are just one set of actors in the local political arena who are under pressure as representatives of the state to profess ideals which may not be their own.

Following Partha Chatterjee (2002: 176), I would therefore suggest to conceive 'mobilization', in the context of women's political participation, in such a way that we understand the discourse of democratization and its concomitant ideas about equality, rights, and entitlements as a mobilizing force itself. Such a conceptualization would mean giving up the idea that certain actors are mobilizing the 'unenlightened masses' in their own particularistic (class) interests. Whereas a conventional understanding of mobilization primarily refers to a top-down approach of mobilizing masses (or resources) by political parties or organizations with a coherent programme, my material shows that for the case of rural India there is no mobilization that can be disentangled from kinship or caste relations and their particularistic loyalties and identity politics. Prisms of mobilization, conceptualizing mobilization as galvanizing sympathizers into political action along the lines of ideology, interests, and long-term binding political goals, that is, for certain means and ends, do not capture transformations of the self and subtle changes in subjective awareness. Moreover, renegotiations of gender relations, particularly in terms of family relation and conjugal relationships, tend to be overlooked.

The distinctive feature of women activists' programmes in mobilization is empowerment—and not specific goals of action. Empowerment, however, may include unforeseen consequences, because empowerment explicitly aims at enabling women to set their own goals and agendas, and to develop their own strategies how to get there. An example of such unintended dynamics was mentioned earlier in the context of organized and 'empowered' village women who sought to bypass 'unenlightened' women panchayat members to achieve their goals more efficiently.

Making available discourses of democracy, empowerment, gender equity, etc., and thus offering the language around which claims on the resources of the local state can be formulated and legitimized, allows women to participate in wider societal discourses. However, these are open to appropriation and thus are more open and less binding than, for example, party programmes.

Bureaucrats, feminists, or other translocal actors may be seen as catalysts in making the discourse of democracy (as concerns equality, rights and entitlements, self-governance, etc.) more commonly available. They facilitate its diffusion and domestication in the face of other locally dominant discourses and thus are conductive in enlarging the 'multiplicity of discursive fields' (Raheja and Gold, 1994: 3).

Since there is no position strictly outside or inside the state, since the contested terrain is a normative field of competing discourses, any struggle against currently hegemonic configurations of power is necessarily a process of renegotiating meanings of femininity and gendered expectations. The struggle women are currently engaged in is not just against the state or its local representatives over the implementation of the amendments, but in a much broader sense a cultural struggle over meanings and the ways in which 'gender' or 'politics' are socially constructed.

NOTES

1. 'Proxy' is a term widely applied to women who are elected to the panchayat bodies. It assumes that a man (e.g. husband, patron) encourages a woman to be elected and formally take on her office. In most cases even the electorate expects the woman's 'political guardian' to usurp all the women's responsibilities and to run the panchayat. I use the term here, because it dominates the literature on women and panchayati raj and is part of most NGOs' vocabulary as well. I have distanced myself elsewhere from the analytical value of the term (Strulik, 2003).
2. Cf. Strulik (2009).
3. As a form of cultural affirmation in the face of colonial occupation, the panchayat system was 'rediscovered' and glorified, above all by M.K. Gandhi. It was proclaimed that the panchayat system could be seen as the Indian form of primordial democracy and that independent India should hence be ruled 'from below'. Villages were idealized as autarkic units of self-government or so-called 'little republics'. This view was endorsed and further romanticized by the majority of independence leaders (Klimkeit, 1981; Lieten and Srivastava, 1999; Mishra and Dadage, 2002; Parel, 1999). Regarding the 're-invention' and mythical exaggeration of harmonious, autarkic village community, see Béteille (2002: 141–84), Srinivas (1987: 20–59), Madan (2002), and Dumont (1966: 67–89). However, Ambedkar saw any democratization attempt doomed to fail and warned not to endow the panchayats with more self-governing powers, because he saw the Indian village as "a sink of localism, a den of ignorance, narrow-mindedness and communalism" (quoted in Lieten and Srivastava, 1999: 19).
4. In some states the *pradhan* is referred to as *sarpanch*.

5. Other responsibilities are—just to name a few—the identification of appropriate beneficiaries and projects for the available government schemes, application for, and management of the latter, joint management of village resources (e.g. land, forest, water, irrigation, and fisheries), sanitation, rural housing schemes, adult literacy campaigns, electricity, all infrastructure development initiatives, identification of below poverty line (BPL) families, ration cards and ration shops, birth and death registers, issuing of certificates of birth, marriage, death, school, etc., distribution of scholarships, village fairs, Food for Work Programme initiatives, ensuring 'communal harmony', etc. (cf. Gazette of India, Part II, Section I, 20 April 1993 or Government of Himachal Pradesh, 1994).
6. The frequency of *gram sabha* meetings may vary from state to state. There is no complete uniformity in the actual responsibilities of *gram sabha*s and considerable scope for interpretation is left to the respective state governments (Mathew, 1999; Mohanty and Kumar, 2002; Narayanasamy, 1998).
7. The empirical data on which this chapter is based originates from two years of ethnographic fieldwork in India (eastern Uttar Pradesh, Himachal Pradesh, and Maharashtra) between 2000 and 2003. The fieldwork was part of my PhD research project on 'Women's Political Participation in Local Governance and Changing Gender Relations'. Apart from triangulating different qualitative methods, a major emphasis was laid on biographical methods.
8. A village secretary usually looks after one to three *gram* panchayats, keeps all the village registers, is trained in account keeping and administrating governmental schemes, and is the major intermediary between the *gram* panchayat and the block office.
9. This 'blurring' of the line between state and society at the level of local bureaucrats and the latter's re-interpretation of distant state policies "beyond recognition" (Kaviraj, 1991: 91) runs through many studies (Brass, 1997; Fuller and Bénéi, 2000; Gupta, 1995; Manor, 1991) as an explanation for the apparent 'failure of the state' to implement its policies successfully.
10. At the time of my research the BJP was ruling Himachal Pradesh, as well as leading the ruling coalition at the national level.
11. The BDC is the intermediate panchayat institution at the block level.
12. Overall party politics and party support tends to play a lesser role at the *gram* panchayat level. However, to get elected into the panchayat bodies at district or block level party support is important. For one, campaigning without party support is difficult outside one's own panchayat because people may not know the candidate from day-to-day interaction, and to become an integrative candidate identification with certain party ideals and programmes is conducive. Second, people are aware that only a BDC or *jilla parishad* candidate with the right party portfolio (e.g. either from the state's ruling party or the local MLA's party) will succeed in getting a maximum number of schemes and funds sanctioned for his or her constituency.
13. For an example compare the Food and Agriculture Organization's (FAO) eight identified objectives in building women's capacities for panchayati raj institutions (Jain and Polman, 2003). These can be summarized as:

    - To explain the 73rd Constitutional Amendment to newly elected women panchayat members.

- To make women local council representatives aware of laws protecting women's rights.
- To make women council members aware of their roles and responsibilities in local development.
- To enhance participation of women members in development planning within panchayats.
- To develop women's leadership and communication skills for enhancing social mobilization.
- To make them find ways and means to interface with other layers of local self-governance within the state and claim the panchayat's entitlements.
- To familiarize them with rural/women/child development programmes to reduce poverty.
- To empower them to identify and break cultural barriers and improve their social-economic condition.

14. Between March and November 2000.
15. The local women's groups, organized in clusters regularly exchanging 'best practices' and 'experiences', as well as discussing new inputs given by the NGO's field staff, or visiting head-office activists, became in many cases a crucial network for communicating information, as well as for the organization of public protest or supportive clapping during *gram sabha*s etc. In many cases the support structures and networking of the women's group could be interpreted as compensating for the unavailable vertically more varied networks that male politicians can usually rely on. Such positive synergies may overlap with dynamics that will be discussed in the following section.
16. Several NGOs who run capacity-building programmes tend to conceptualize their programmes in terms of what could be called a 'deficiency' approach. Their starting point is women's lack of education, information, economic resources, time, experience, and integration into political networks, etc. But they neglect to build on and encourage women's existing knowledge and strengths. In my view, these approaches, which concentrate only on 'capacity building', are thus dangerously reductive because they fail to take into account the socially constructed nature of gender, as well as of 'knowledge' and 'politics'.
17. A demand occasionally voiced in a similar vein by (purportedly) progressive villagers, as the following quote shows:

    > It is all a question of pressure to stop this *pradhan-pati*-business. If somebody would pressure me, I would send my woman happily to the meetings. But without outside pressure I cannot do it. If I can't say 'Hey listen, I have to send her', people will start talking very bad behind my back.... 'Ohhooo, they have become so much forward now ... they have forgotten what are good manners' (...) Society has to change before I can send her—if I am forced to send her, it would be best if even the villagers themselves would insist. Then people couldn't blame me ... or her ... they then will have asked for it themselves ... or at least the police or whomever.

    In the context of this quote the demand was actually directed to the state that, in people's perception, just had done an inchoate job by passing new legislation. It was felt that a 'responsible state' would ensure that its local representatives (local bureaucrats) would enact the new law, if necessary with disciplinary sanctions, and would provide accompanying measurements to get not only the laws enacted but also the implied values (e.g. equality) transferred.

18. In the following quote Bimla narrates how, after her election, she went about one of her first 'projects' with the help of the women from her group. The particular strategy by which the women sought to draw the MLA into their project illustrates why villagers initially were sceptical about Bimla's 'feminine' way of going about local politics:

    It was on the suggestion by the women of my group that we got a school to our village. We had talked about it often before and the women used to complain that their small children have to go so far to school, that the steep path, especially during the rainy season and in winter, is too dangerous for the small ones. We were discussing how to go about it and how I should raise this point in the next panchayat meeting. We came to the conclusion that it would be difficult to get money sanctioned for the school, but that maybe it would be easier if we first collected some money among ourselves, among the villagers, to get at least the basic structure done. Then—this was our plan—we would ask through the *gram panchayat* for more funds. So we went from house to house and whoever could contributed something, some gave Rs 10 here, some Rs 5 there, some 20 from that house. From the rich people we took Rs 100 and from those who were well-off Rs 50. Those who were very poor we asked to offer us their labour. In this way we got the basic structure ready. Then the MLA came to the village on tour. We approached him as a group and showed him the foundation. We had decided before that we all would have to come to this meeting and that somehow we had to coax him into giving us more money to complete our project. So when he came, we all gathered and we said: 'Listen, we need this school, we have done already this much, but we have no money to complete it. You have to help us. One way or another it is going to happen, but you have to give us the money. We won't let you go from here, until you have promised to get us the money.' He was impressed with our work, but he said he couldn't help. Then we did this small programme for him, with songs and dance and food. Finally he was very impressed and that very day he wrote that our village should get Rs 65,000 to complete the school. Then for three, four months nothing happened. But ultimately the money came to the Block and now the construction work is under way.

19. I exclude local politicians from discussion here as they have been discussed earlier in the section on politicians.
20. *Pahari* ('of the mountains') generally refers to all people from the mountains, their language, culture, or the area. In the area of research, 'pahari' was used for people from higher altitudes in contrast to people from lower altitudes, and particularly to refer to people from the Pathankot-Mandi Highway valley.
21. Many *pahari* villages in Himachal Pradesh are very small and often consist only of a few families. Usually 10 to 15 such 'villages' are combined to make up one *gram* panchayat and each village is taken as a ward represented by one elected

villager in the *gram* panchayat meeting. As a consequence, the ward representative has—compared to what happens in Uttar Pradesh—many more responsibilities. He or she is the main contact person in all ward matters, he or she calls for and presides over the *gaon sabha* (the ward/hamlet's bi-annual assembly), and oversees development work in the ward, and is also the first judicial authority in village fights. Being a panchayat member in Himachal entails many more responsibilities and much more work than in the bigger villages of the plains.

22. Because seats are reserved on a rotating basis, it is impossible to stand for the *pradhan*'s seat a second time. If Ghanshyam Singh was elected *pradhan* on a so-called open seat (no reservation), in the next round of election that seat will be reserved. In the election of 2000 it happened to be an 'open' women's reservation and a Rajput woman (Ghanshyam Singh's sister) was elected.
23. In addition to the cases discussed here, see also Strulik (2008) for another case study from Himachal Pradesh.
24. Or as one woman nicely summed up what is the most important for her is carry ing on her day-to-day life, given the fact that she is economically as well as socially completely dependant on staying an accepted and cared for member in her extended joint family: "If the family is happy, only then can I be happy too.... I mean, whatever my family is happiest with, that I will do [*jis mein mere parivaar kaa sab kaa khushii ho, vahii ham log kare*]".
25. After an initial apprehension about impending changes, but also some palpable excitement about the new opportunities, Manju was hoping to enlarge her own horizon especially by the chance to leave the narrow confines of the domestic domain which hitherto was a male prerogative.
26. I have discussed the limits of the 'proxy' as an analytical category in Strulik (2003). In Manju's case, not only did the rules of *purdah* become a little more open with Manju having access to mixed-gender fictive relatives, she 'acquired a name', had access to political work, and political knowledge systems (manuals, men's discussions, access to block officials, etc.). See also Strulik (2004).

REFERENCES

Béteille, André. 2002 (1965). 'The Distribution of Power', in V. Madan (ed.), *The Village in India*, pp. 227–37. New Delhi: Oxford University Press.

Bierschenk, Thomas and Olivier de Sardan. 2003. 'Powers in the Village: Rural Benin between Democratisation and Decentralization', *Africa*, 73(2): 145–73.

Brass, Paul R. 1997. *Theft of an Idol: Text and Context in the Representation of Collective Violence*. Princeton: Princeton University Press.

Chatterjee, Partha. 2002. 'On Civil and Political Society in Postcolonial Democracies', in S. Kaviraj and S. Khilnani (eds), *Civil Society: History and Possibilities*, pp. 165–78. New Delhi: Cambridge University Press.

Dumont, L. 2000 (1966). 'The "Village Community" from Munro to Maine', in V. Madan (ed.), *The Village in India*, pp. 57–69. New Delhi: Oxford University Press.

Frazer, Elizabeth. 1992. 'Democracy, Citizenship and Gender', in A. Carter and G. Stokes (eds), *Democratic Theory Today*, pp. 73–96. Malden: Blackwell.

Fuller, C.J. and Véronique Bénéi (eds). 2000. *The Everyday State and Society in Modern India*. New Delhi: Social Science Press.

Government of Himachal Pradesh, Rural Development and Panchayati Raj Department. 1994. *The Himachal Pradesh Panchayati Raj Act*. Shimla: Government of Himachal Pradesh.

Girtler, Roland. 1972. 'Ist eine Demokratie "von unten" im Sinne Mahatma Gandhis überhaupt möglich?' [Is democracy "from below" in Mahatma Gandhi's sense even possible?] in Roland Girtler (ed.), *Die 'demokratische' Institution des Panchayat in Indien: Ein Vergleich des 'gesetzlichen' und des 'traditionellen' Panchayat*, pp. 60–75. Wien: Acta Ethnologica et Linguistica.

Gupta, Akhil. 1995. 'Blurred Boundaries: The Discourse of Corruption, the Culture of Politics, and the Imagined State', *American Ethnologist*, 22(2): 375–402.

Jain, S.P. and Wim Polman. 2003. *A Handbook for Trainers on Participatory Local Development: The Panchayati Raj Model in India*. Bangkok: Food and Agriculture Organization.

Kaviraj, Sudipta. 1991. 'On State, Society and Discourse in India', in J. Manor (ed.), *Rethinking Third World Politics*, pp. 72–99. London: Longman.

Klimkeit, Hans Joachim. 1981. *Der Politische Hinduismus: Indische Denker zwischen religiöser Reform und politischem Erwachen* [Political Hinduism: Indian thought between religious reform and political awakening]. Wiesbaden: Harrassowitz.

Kluge, Susann. 1999. *Empirisch begründete Typenbildung* [Empirically based typology-building]. Opladen: Leske and Budrich.

Kuhn, Berthold. 1998. 'Panchayat—Reform lokaler Selbstverwaltung in Indien', *E + Z (Entwicklung und Zusammenarbeit)*, 39(9): 241–43.

Lachenmann, Gudrun. 1996. 'Transformationsprozesse in Westafrika—Widersprüche und Chancen für Frauenpolitik und Wandel der Geschlechterverhältnisse', *Asien Afrika Lateinamerika*, 24: 231–51.

———. 2004. 'Die geschlechtsspezifische Aushandlung von lokalen Entwicklungsprozessen zwischen sozialen Bewegungen, Staat und Nichtregierungsorganisationen im Rahmen von Dezentralisierung und Armutsbekämpfung (Westafrika)', Unpublished Paper, presented at the Jahrestagung der Afrikanisten Deutschlands on 'Afrika im Kontext: Weltbezüge in Geschichte und Gegenwart', 2–6 June 2004, University of Hannover, Germany.

Lieten, G.K. and Ravi Srivastava. 1999. *Unequal Partners: Power Relations, Devolution and Development in Uttar Pradesh*. New Delhi: Sage Publications.

Madan, Vandana (ed.). 2002. *The Village in India*. New Delhi: Oxford University Press.

Manor, J. (ed.). 1991. *Rethinking Third World Politics*. London: Longman.

Mathew, George. 1994. *Panchayati Raj: From Legislation to Movement*. New Delhi: Concept.

———. 1999. 'Gram Sabha and Social Audit', *Kurukshetra*, October: 25–9.

———. 2000. 'Panchayati Raj in India: An Overview', in G. Mathew and G. Buch (eds), *Status of Panchayati Raj in the States and Union Territories of India 2000*, pp. 3–22. New Delhi: Concept.

Mishra, Anil Dutta and Mahade Shivappa Dadage (eds). 2002. *Panchayati Raj: Gandhian Perspective*. New Delhi: Mittal.

Mohanty, Bidyut and Girish Kumar (eds). 2002. *Women and Political Empowerment 2000: Women's Political Empowerment Day Celebrations on Gram Sabha and Women*. New Delhi: Institute of Social Sciences.

Narayanasamy, S. 1998. 'Role of Gram Sabha in the New Panchayati Raj System', *Kurukshetra*, April: 11–16.

Parel, Anthony J. (ed.). 1999. *M.K. Gandhi: Hind Swaraj and other Writings*. New York: Routledge.

Pfaff-Czarnecka, J. 1999. 'Verteilungskoalitionen in Bajhang: Zu einem besonderen Typus von Mittlerstrukturen zwischen Staat und Bürger in (Fernwest-) Nepal' [Distributional coalitions in Bajhang: On a special type of intermediate structure between citizens and the state in (Far West) Nepal], *Peripherie*, 73/74: 77–97.

———. 2008. 'Distributional Coalitions in Nepal: An Essay on Democratization, Capture, and (Lack of) Confidence', in D.N. Gellner and K. Hachhethu (eds), *Local Democracy in South Asia: The Micropolitics of Democratization in Nepal and its Neighbours*, pp. 71–104. New Delhi: SAGE Publications.

Raheja, Gloria Goodwin and Ann Grodzins Gold. 1994. *Listen to the Heron's Words: Reimagining Gender and Kinship in North India*. Berkeley: University of California Press.

Srinivas, M.N. 2002 (1987). 'The Indian Village: Myth and Reality', in V. Madan (ed.), *The Village in India*, pp. 51–70. New Delhi: Oxford University Press.

Strulik, S. 2003. 'Against the Notion of "Proxies": Women Pradhans in Himachal and Uttar Pradesh', in B. Mohanty (ed.), *A Decade of Women's Empowerment through Local Government in India*, pp. 34–40. New Delhi: Institute of Social Sciences.

———. 2004. 'Women Panchayat Members at the Interface of State and Village Politics: Gendered Constructions of the Political Space'. Paper for the 18th European Conference on Modern South Asian Studies at Lund University, Sweden. Available at http://www.sasnet.lu.se/EASASpapers/16StefanieStrulik.pdf (accessed on 13 February 2010).

———. 2008. 'Engendering Local Democracy Research: Panchayati Raj and Changing Gender Relations in India', in D.N. Gellner and K. Hachhethu (eds), *Local Democracy in South Asia: The Micropolitics of Democratization in Nepal and its Neighbours*, pp. 350–79. New Delhi: SAGE Publications.

———. 2009. 'Politics Embedded: Women's Political Participation in Local Governance', PhD thesis, University of Zurich, Zurich, Switzerland.

Vianello, Mino and Gwen Moore (eds). 2000. *Gendering Elites and Political Leadership in 27 Industrialized Societies*. Houndsmill: MacMillan.

Chapter 6

Surveying Activists in Nepal

DAVID N. GELLNER AND MRIGENDRA BAHADUR KARKI

In this chapter we reflect on the process of doing research on activists in Nepal using semi-structured interviews and a questionnaire. Some preliminary results of our work have already been published (Gellner and Karki, 2007, 2008; Karki, 2006) but more is planned.[1] In anthropology, as in all social sciences, there is an intimate and necessary connection between methods and results, and it has for quite some time been conventional to call for more openness about how social science research is actually done. Academic production is slow and considerable time has elapsed already since these materials were gathered. Much has changed in Nepal in the intervening period and the political outlook, though certainly very far from easy, is better than it used to be for many years. We hope that some of these reflections may have value nonetheless, both as a record of how research is done and as an example, though whether an example to be imitated or avoided is for others to judge.

WHY SURVEY ACTIVISTS?

At the time of our research (2003–05) Nepal was in a deep political and social crisis; there was every reason to expect that the crisis would become ever more serious as time passed. Three years later; in 2008, it had—almost miraculously—extracted itself from the morass and is embarked on an unprecedented experiment, the experiment of bringing a successful Maoist revolutionary guerrilla movement 'into the mainstream' and into parliamentary democracy. For all that they provided, the Prime Minister and the bulk of the ministerial positions from August 2008 to May 2009, many Maoists were deeply unhappy at the compromises necessary—and sometimes this seems to include Prime Minister Dahal himself—so it is by no means clear that Nepal has as yet achieved any lasting resolution. Perhaps it never will. Nonetheless, there has been astonishing progress and change.

The immediate cause of the crisis was the very Maoist insurgency, on which there is now a burgeoning literature.[2] Even had this political cataclysm not engulfed Nepal—and we do not believe it was inevitable, but rather that it grew from a series of political decisions or non-decisions—it was certain that the decade of the 1990s was going to lead to considerable political turmoil and the prime reason for this was the great upsurge of activism that followed the introduction of new freedoms after the fall of the Panchayat regime in 1990.[3]

Who were the activists who worked so long and hard to overthrow, or at least reform, the Panchayat regime (and before it, the Rana regime)? Who were the activists who worked within it? What kind of younger generation or new recruits came into activism post 1990? How should the relationship between political and other types of activism be conceptualized? Were there typical pathways and typical backgrounds for different types of activists (ethnic as opposed to political, women's as opposed to Dalit, one generation as opposed to another, and so on)? We pursued these questions in a series of interviews with as many activists of different types as we could get hold of in Kathmandu, Pokhara, and Janakpur in 2003 and 2004.[4] During this period we also considered how we could carry out a questionnaire survey that would reach a larger number of respondents than we could possibly access with open-ended interviews and might, we hoped, throw up some unexpected data.

The study of activists, apart from being interesting in its own right, may also perhaps lead to a deeper understanding both of the social history of the Panchayat period and of the post-1990 era. Before 1990 politics were strictly controlled. Parties were banned and organizations judged 'communal' could not be registered. There have been several critiques of the anthropology of the Panchayat period for being overly focused on traditional aspects of culture and for being insufficiently aware of the social change and political undercurrents that were occurring at the time.[5] Gellner's research in the early 1980s was indeed focused on a kind of 'salvage anthropology', that is, it attempted to understand the Newars' unique form of Tantric Buddhism, a tradition going back in an unbroken line to the now-defunct Buddhism of the Pala dynasty in Bengal (eighth to twelfth centuries) (and which gave the Indian state of Bihar its name, meaning 'monastery'). Despite this past-oriented framework, the published version of the research (Gellner, 1992) included sections on the new Theravada movement and on the decline of Tantric Buddhism.[6] And his first published article derived from the research in Lalitpur (Patan)—impelled by the salience of the topic for his informants—was in fact not on Buddhism at all, but on the Newars' complex, dynamic, and politically charged sense of ethnic identity (Gellner, 1986).

Unlike politics, culture and religion were legitimate fields of activity for Nepalis and of research for foreign anthropologists. They were therefore fields which attracted many activists, both those committed to them in their own terms and those who were using them as a front for more political purposes. And it was precisely in these spheres that foreign anthropologists were likely to come into contact with activists. Krauskopff describes this nexus well—and the relative innocence of the anthropologist at the time:

> One educated Tharu of my field research village, who became a UML [Unified Marxist-Leninist, the main opposition party] nominee to the Upper House after 1990, had devoted much effort in the 1980s to publishing traditional Tharu songs and myths. His excellent texts were based on careful fieldwork, which he valued as a way to make connections with village people. At the same time he supported the idea of writing a Tharu dictionary to promote the Tharu language. When I reminded him of his cultural goals and activities during a private informal chat we had more than ten years later in the 1990s, he smiled.... His cultural activities during the Panchayat period had been the visible tip of an iceberg, that is, of a much more radical movement based on economic and political goals.... But as a female and a novice ethnographer more involved with the elders and the specialists who preserved tradition, I failed to take the opportunity to carry out research on this point. (Krauskopff, 2003: 216–17; first ellipsis in the original)

The innocence of the anthropologist applied also to many ordinary Nepalis, even those who were active in non-political spheres. Political parties, being banned, had to operate underground and observe great secrecy. Even close and trusted friends and family members were often not told of party activities or memberships.[7] It was only in the latter half of the 1980s that the party affiliations of certain public figures became more known and that the parties began to organize more openly, taking advantage of the freedom that necessarily had to be granted to them in order to campaign in the 1980 referendum on whether to continue with the Panchayat system or to allow parties. The claim that is being made is that—as with any authoritarian and controlling regime—a full understanding of it is possible only after it has collapsed or evolved into something else. Paradoxically, only when it is past, only when that which could not be said can be printed openly, can 'how things really were' be understood fully.[8] In short, and at the very least, a study of activists may permit a fuller account of Nepal in the 1960s, 1970s, and 1980s, as well as being of interest on its own account and as contributing to the understanding of the present situation in Nepal.

DEFINING THE FIELD

Although there are activists in rural areas (cf. de Sales and Shneiderman, this volume), and it is important to understand them, there are far greater concentrations in the towns. Even most of those who work in rural areas are based in towns. Furthermore, the largest concentration is in the capital, Kathmandu. In terms of carrying out a survey, the initial idea was to survey 200 in Kathmandu and 200 in a hill centre. This was later increased to 600 respondents, when it was decided to include one Tarai town. Eventually the total of those to be surveyed reached 800 with the final total divided as follows: 200 from each of Pokhara and Janakpur, and 400 from Kathmandu (divided so that 200 would be 'central-level' activists and 200 'local-level'). In this way, both national and regional centres would be covered, and among regional centres, there would be one each from the middle hills and the Tarai, the two main divisions of the country so far as the concentration of population is concerned.[9] The split between Kathmandu and the rest would also roughly correspond to a distinction between 'central-level' and 'district-level' activists. The model here is political parties (see Hachhethu, 2002), to which other organizations correspond only to some degree. Of the 48 national ethnic organizations that were members of the National Federation of Indigenous Nationalities (NEFIN) in 2005, 28 had their head offices in Kathmandu Valley, three in Pokhara, and one in Janakpur.[10] The initial plan was to include 25 per cent of respondents from the central-level organizations, and 75 per cent district-level activists. But it was not possible to stick strictly to these proportions as many organizations lacked distinctions between central and district levels.

The actual survey was planned to be carried out by Mrigendra Karki, Suresh Dhakal, and Basanta Maharjan, all three experienced social science researchers. A pilot questionnaire with 109 respondents was tested by Karki in Janakpur, Pokhara, and Kathmandu in late 2003 and early 2004, and funding was secured from the British Academy in spring 2004. It was decided to put off starting the questionnaire until after the Nepalese festival season, when people are busy and often unavailable; this had the added advantage that Gellner could accompany the three enumerators for two days in Janakpur. Thus, it finally began in December 2004. Surveying was completed in around two weeks in Janakpur. In Pokhara also it took about the same amount of time in January 2005. Generally the enumerators found that they could fill about 6–10 questionnaires per day, though occasionally, with luck, they could do more. Surveying in Kathmandu had just begun when King Gyanendra carried out his coup of 1 February 2005. For a week all phone and Internet access to the outside world was cut off. There was intense lobbying and mobilizing in the outside world, as there were fears that the blackout was being used as a cover for widespread repression. In the end, when communications were restored, it became clear that there had not been widespread bloodshed, just arrests and intimidation.[11]

In this context, it will be easily understood that the following months were a particularly sensitive time to be carrying out research with activists. Many were arrested and many went 'underground' or abroad in order to avoid arrest. The amount of time it took to negotiate access and obtain satisfactory responses was greatly increased. The options 'Maoism' and 'republic' were tippexed out of the questionnaire forms under question 37 in order to protect respondents in case the security forces got hold of them (but the options were still asked and coded for). As time was running out, Suresh Dhakal, who had other commitments, had to drop out and was replaced by Bebi Shrestha. The survey was finally completed in April 2005.

Defining who is an activist was, of course, the key question. There is no commonly accepted criterion and there is no national list that we could have used in order to generate a random sample. The sample was going to be what the experienced Nepali social surveyors call 'purposive', that is, using the snowball method more appropriate for qualitative research. Nonetheless, we had to have a working definition, simply in order to identify whether a particular individual could be included or not. The problem is not helped by the fact that there is no obvious, single, and always valid translation for the English word 'activist' in Nepali. The frequently used *karyakarta* refers especially to the activists of political parties, that is, the party workers or cadres. The much less common *andolankari* means literally 'movement-ist', that is, one who launches or causes a movement. It is has some of the oppositional connotations of 'activist' but is probably more narrowly political. Nepali has a number of different words translating as 'active', such as *sakriya*, *kriyashil*, and *laganshil*, but none give rise to a noun that would refer to a class of people. The same is even more true for more colloquial terms such as *calakh*, with its connotations of 'quick' and 'cunning'. Perhaps this is why the English word is in fact frequently used by Nepalis themselves.

For the sake of the survey—despite the fact that a final definition and analysis of what an activist is in the Nepali context might come only at the end of the study, if then—we had to make a decision and adopt a stipulative definition that could guide the enumerators' work. The definition ran as follows: *An activist is any person belonging either to the district-level or national-level committee of an organization dedicated to ends of a non-economic sort.* Both in Nepal and in English-language usage, there is a tendency to view the type case of an activist as someone oppositional and politically on the left. We thought it better if this bias in the common usage of the word did not over-influence the selection of subjects to be interviewed. In other words, political activists from all sides of the political spectrum should be included (though for practical reasons Maoists were not contacted). Furthermore, Gellner was concerned to insist that organizations whose leaders might not conventionally be thought of as activists, such as Chambers of Commerce and Lions Clubs, should not be excluded from the category of social activists. Although their members might be businessmen (and very occasionally women), and although the aims of the organizations were often economic, the organizations were not to be defined by their pursuit of profit, but rather by other social and charitable ones. Our criterion of membership of the committee of the organization, either at district or national level, was intended to ensure that the person concerned was indeed active, and not simply a subscription member of the organization.

Evidently one category of person was excluded by our criterion, and that is the lone activist. Such people certainly exist in Nepal and some of them are very active and would count as activists by most ordinary criteria. But to include such people would have involved enumerators in making too many subjective decisions about who counts as an activist. (Clearly 'activist' is an evaluative or appraisive term, as anyone who has worked in an organization such as Amnesty International will tell you. Compare also the debates about whether NGO workers can be considered activists, as discussed by Heaton Shrestha, this volume.)

Before proceeding to the field we—the enumerators, plus Gellner and Hachhethu—together decided how to break down the general category of 'activist' into various sub-categories, so that the enumerators would know how to proceed in the field. The initial categories we worked with were: political, caste/ethnic, Dalit, Madhesi, women, religion, human rights, social. Some of these may be seen as very obvious, or universal categories, at least in the modern world. Others are very specific to the Nepali situation, reflecting Nepal's particular history, such as the distinction between caste/ethnic, Dalit, and Madhesi. Later, the complete list that was used in the questionnaire was as follows:

I. Politics
II. Janajati
III. Dalit
IV. Caste group
V. Madhesi
VI. Language/culture
VII. Women
VIII. Religion
IX. Human rights
X. Social reform
XI. Trade union
XII. Business
XIII. Industry
XIV. Other (specify)

Clearly these categories often overlap. Political parties have women, student, peasant, Dalit, and trade union 'front' organizations.[12] Ethnic activists are often simultaneously advocates of language and culture, and may also be active in religion and/or in politics. It was for the respondents to say which was their primary sphere of activity and to rank their subsidiary spheres (up to a maximum of three).

In determining the social background of the respondent we asked for the generally recognized profile of both father and grandfather. In order to estimate the respondent's current social position we asked about current profession, ownership of home, use of car, and (where applicable) the kind of education their children were receiving.

SOME MATERIAL FROM QUALITITATIVE INTERVIEWS

Most of the activists in our sample grew up and had their formative experiences under the Panchayat system (only the very oldest began their activist career under the Ranas). Many of the earliest generation of activists were the sons of men who worked for the Ranas. Their fathers in many cases disagreed with the policies of their own rulers, or in some cases were humiliated or even dismissed by them.[13] In some cases they came from wealthy landowning families, in others from more moderate backgrounds, but never from the poorest, since at that time only the better off had any education.[14]

During the Panchayat era the political parties organized underground. Many activists first became involved in literary activities and through that made contact with political activists. Depending on the generation, the first experience of politics would be through student union politics. Student politics on an organized basis began in the early 1970s and revived particularly from 1978. From that time student identities were tended either to be 'leftist' or 'democrat' (i.e. a Congress supporter); in addition there were some who were supporters of the Panchayat regime, who could be classed as 'royalist'. We have described elsewhere (Gellner and Karki, 2007: 383–8) how progressive ideologies, particularly communism and Maoism, were spread through certain well-known bookshops in Kathmandu, cheaply available literature, and novels such as Gorky's *Mother*.

RESISTING 'SOCIAL EVILS' AND THE ROLE OF EDUCATION

Often administering the questionnaire was the occasion for the recipient to deliver a powerful narrative. In this case, the speaker is a Dalit from Dolakha in the hills east of Kathmandu:

It was 1980 and I was twelve years old and studying in primary school. In my village, the Pradhan Pancha (village head) was a Chhetri, who was sacked from his job as a *subba* [district court non-gazetted officer], because of irregular activities [i.e. corruption]. The punishment was *Hat Kalam*, in other words he was prohibited to give his signature for any social, legal, or political activity. In spite of this he was elected Pradhan Pancha. Our headmaster, who also belonged to the Chhetri community, sent an official letter to the Pradhan Pancha as chairperson of the School *Sanchalak Samiti* [school governing committee]. We—I and a friend named Kumar, who was a Bhujel [a water-acceptable caste]—went to his house to deliver the letter. Outside the house there was a wooden bed frame for sitting on, covered with a wooleen blanket. Even at that age (twelve), I was aware of being a Dalit. My friend sat on the bed but I lifted up the blanket and just leaned against the bed. After a while, the Pradhan Pancha came out of the house. A Brahman priest was preparing to perform a Rudri [a Hindu ritual with a fire sacrifice]. The Pradhan Pancha asked, "Who is this boy?" The priest replied, "He is the grandson of Jangabir Kami [i.e. a Blacksmith]." Suddenly the Pradhan Pancha came towards me with his hand raised and said in a loud voice, "Dangra [an abusive term for blacksmiths]! You [low-grade honorific] dare to sit on my bed! Are you going to go into my house next?" He did not hit me, but his son brought out a straw mat for me to sit on. I was so shocked, I felt the sky was spinning and I did not know where I was. I neither replied nor reacted, but just remained stunned and silent. As a Kami, of lower caste, I thought, it was my mistake. At that time, I had no revolutionary feelings.

However, my grandfather had been a revolutionary Congress Party activist during the 1951 revolution against these very Chhetri families one of whose family members was an army colonel in the Rana regime. My father also had supported his opponent in the elections for village head. He used to oppose social discrimination using logic and reason. I think the Pradhan Pancha was waiting to take revenge for this history of resistance by my family.

In 1982 I was studying in high school and the headmaster was leftist party member, who later was elected as a UML MP. One day, two of my goats ate some wheat in the field of another Chhetri and they captured those goats and announced that they would sell them to get compensation. However, my father disagreed and decided to register a counter application to the ward chief, even though he was also a Chhetri. I wrote the application to the ward chief which was supposed to be signed by an unrelated neighbour as witness. I said to my father, "First get the neighbour to sign it, then submit it." But my father was the only literate person available and ended up signing it in both places himself. Unfortunately our only literate unrelated neighbour (though we have the same name and surname we are not related) was outside the village at the time. Then, the village gathered. All those Chhetris were in a majority. Only my aunt (father's sister), an old woman, was present from our side. The Pradhan Pancha asked me, "Is this your own writing?" I replied yes. Then he ordered to me to write an application saying that it is my writing. I did so and immediately he had that application, he grabbed my hair, which was long because of my young age and slapped on each cheek. Then he ordered my hands to be tied and I was attached to a wooden pillar outside his house. Accusing me of submitting a fake witness signature to the village Panchayat, he decided to send me to the police station near the village. Then they had a long discussion about the goats. They charged five hundred rupees for the damage caused by the two goats in the field, which my father couldn't pay, so he had to borrow the money from a relative of the Pradhan Pancha and give a gold necklace as deposit. They had already planned it like that. We are Sunar [Goldsmiths] so my father always had gold chains.

Ultimately, one of the participants said to my father, "Go and ask the Pradhan Pancha, otherwise your son will have to spend many years in jail on the charge of being a fake witness case. He would be destroyed." So, my father and aunt went up to the Pradhan Pancha and said "We are the dust of your feet, please save my son, etc..." He demanded another thousand rupees, but after some negotiation he accepted five hundred rupees. Again he asked to me to write a formal paper, saying that it was my mistake, I wrote as he instructed. Once he had received the five hundred rupees, he immediately destroyed our previous protest application. He said, "Once forgiven, do not the same mistake again."

Even today, when I remember these events, I cannot control myself. I am overcome by different types of emotion that circulate within my body. After all this had happened, immediately I went to meet the headmaster, who was well known to be opposed to such behaviour. However, I did not get a satisfactory answer from him. He just said, "There are so many Pradhan Panchas in the country. We cannot do anything to him, so we need to start a revolution against its root, the Panchayat system." I returned, disappointed. But later he again sent someone to convince me. Subsequently, I joined the communist movement. After 1990, I won the election defeating that very Pradhan Pancha as chair of the Village Development Committee, and I celebrated at the exact place where he used to hold his own celebrations and I did same what he had done to us. I gave him a taste of his own medicine.[15]

This respondent rose through the UML organization. For many others, education in India was a formative experience. Educational facilities have always been much more advanced in India than in Nepal and many Nepalis have taken advantage of the open border to access them. In the case of the Dalit activists interviewed, it is striking that education in India was often a key part of their personal development, in fact the only way in which they could survive in education to the end of high school:

> When my father was young he was a *hali* (ploughman) for a Bahun. Then he went to India for more than 15 years, to Agra, Delhi, and Haryana. Later on the whole family, my elder brother and sister and me, went with him. If I hadn't gone to India, I wouldn't be here now. My mother and father were not educated, though my mother now knows [how to read]. I went to school in Agra. The schooling was in Hindi and English, up to third class. [Then I returned to school in the hills of Nepal.] At that time my elder brother was (politically) conscious (*sacet*). In the village there was a Chhetri-Bahun majority. There were no Damai, but there were Magars in the hills around. [On one occasion] it was the school's *barsik diwas*, an annual function. I was a little forward as a speaker, so I was one of the speakers. [When tea was served] they discriminated: the ward chairman (*adhyaksha*) forced me [to wash my cup]. I thought: There cannot be discrimination in a line of teachers. I opposed it right there. "Rather than wash it, I'll break it" [I said]. They threatened me, so I ran away. My grandfather came and took away the glass [and cleaned it]. [On normal days as well] at school the peon used to discriminate. He would have to pour water for us [rather than let us get it for ourselves]. I just didn't go for water. (30-year-old Dalit activist)

> My father was working in Gonda, UP, not far from Banaras... I had no experience of untouchability in India. When I came back to visit Nepal, there was. Once I went to a friend's house. I was stopped at the door: "Don't come in here!" (*yahan na au*). My friend was sprinkled with water and taken inside. I went to my father and asked, "Why do they do this?" He said, "Nepal's customs are like that." It was very unpleasant, very painful for me. So I joined the anti-untouchability campaign. (70-year-old Congress Dalit activist)

In a less dramatic way, India's more developed education system and more conscious political environment had a significant impact on other (non-Dalit) Nepalis as well. Of those who lived in the Tarai, some were sent to boarding schools in Lucknow, Darjeeling, or Kurseong. Others went to more ordinary Indian schools and stayed in hostels or lodgings nearby. Many of those closely associated with the Congress Party received their education in India, because they were in exile. Others were drawn to the party while studying in Banaras because they then had contact with B.P. Koirala and his followers and family. In at least one case we interviewed, the activist was drawn into leftist politics via contacts with members of the Communist Party of India while studying just over the border in Bihar.

Even for those who did not study in India, simply moving to the Tarai was often the occasion to acquire a better education than would have been available in the hills and to receive exposure to radical ideas at the same time. This was the case both for Gore Bahadur Khapangi, President of the Nepal Magar Sangh from 1990 to 2002, but an underground communist activist before 1990, and for Narayan Man Bijukchhe (Rohit), President of the Nepal Workers and Peasants Party. Bijukchhe's father had been a tax collector for the Ranas in the Tarai and stayed on there as a civil servant after 1951. Bijukchhe spent two years studying there in school, where he was impressed by the application of his teachers and by the extreme poverty of those afflicted by the floods he witnessed there.

CONCLUSIONS

We hoped that the questionnaire would turn up some unexpected findings, but so far we have not been able to analyse the data with sufficient rigour to discover any such. One correlation which is interesting, though not perhaps unexpected, is that, among those activists who are politically aligned, the further to left they are ideologically, the less likely they are to perform any daily ritual or meditation. Thus, at one extreme, 76 per cent of Rastriya Prajatantrik Party (RPP) members, 62 per cent of Sadbhavana members, and 58 per cent of Congress members either pray or meditate. By contrast, only 20 per cent of UML members do so, and none of 12 recorded members of the Ekta Kendra.[16] Far more, we are sure, could be done both on this and on other questions to reveal further interesting correlations.[17]

On the question of personal histories, we mentioned earlier the unexpected significance of Gorky's novel *Mother*, a fact that we discovered in the course of very loosely structured interviews and not as part of the survey. However, when asked directly and simply about motivations for activism, it was rare that a book was cited as the main influence, and likewise only a minority of respondents said that a single individual had influenced them (see Tables 6.1 and 6.2). Rather, it frequently seemed to be the case that some intermediary institution was responsible for drawing the person in—whether kin, club, school, or college. There was an interesting contrast between Janakpur, where, for young men, socio-religious clubs seem to play a very important role, with Pokhara, in the hills, where women's associations (*ama samuha*) are very prominent.

Table 6.1
Factors Inspiring to Join Organization (Q5)—1st Response

	Number	*Per cent*
Opposition to social evils	172	21.5
Family	136	17.0
Ideology	100	12.5
Person	73	9.1
Events	47	5.9
Ethnic cause	43	5.4
Self awareness	45	5.5
Social service	39	4.9
Promotion of own professional/group interest	34	4.3
Peer association	16	2.0
Book(s)	15	1.9
Preservation of art, religion, and culture	14	1.8
Reaction to activism of others	13	1.6
Others	12	1.5
Educational institute	9	1.1
Social environment	9	1.1
Historical tradition	9	1.1
Social exclusion	8	1.0
Political party	6	0.8
Total	800	100.0

Opposition to existing (unequal) social conditions was revealed to be a major motivation for activism, as the single biggest first response (21.6 per cent) to the direct question on this matter, going up to

Table 6.2
Factors Inspiring to Join Organization (Q5)—Combined Responses

	Number	*Per cent*
Opposition to social evils	286	35.8
Ideology	272	34.0
Family	177	22.1
Person	170	21.3
Event(s)	118	14.8
Book(s)	68	8.5
Ethnic cause	58	7.3
Self awareness	56	6.9
Social service	54	6.8
Promotion of own professional/group interest	38	4.8
Peer association	29	3.6
Reaction to activism of others	21	2.6
Others	20	2.5
Preservation of art, religion, and culture	20	2.5
Social environment	19	2.4
Historical tradition	12	1.5
Social exclusion	11	1.4
Educational institute	9	1.1
Political party	8	1.1
Total	800 (people)	180.8

Note: Percentages are based on multiple responses.

35.3 per cent when up to three responses are allowed. 'Ideology' is given as a first response by only 12.5 per cent, though this increases to 34 per cent when up to three responses are included. Once the responses are broken down by type of activist (Table 6.3) some perhaps predictable regularities can be observed: political activists are much more likely to have been influenced by an ideology or a text than others; Janajati, women, and Dalit activists are much more likely to be influenced by a desire to resist social evils or by events than others; and business or commercial activists are influenced by neither, with over 50 per cent saying that the advancement of their professional interests was their motivation.

This stark contrast between types of activism deserves to be explored further. But it certainly suggests one reason—the fact that they are quite straightforwardly aiming to advance their own professional interest—why commercial activists are not seen as typical activists. Thus, despite widespread cynicism about activists' motives and the benefits they derive from their activities, it seems that

Table 6.3
Factors Inspiring Various Activisms by Type of Activist
(simplified version: less commonly chosen responses are excluded)

	Political		*Janajati*		*Dalit*		*Women*		*Members of Chambers of Commerce and Industry*	
Inspired by	N	%	N	%	N	%	N	%	N	%
Ideology	57	51.8	24	22	17	25.8	14	20.6	12	25.5
Books	19	17.3	4	3.7	6	9.1	2	2.9	1	2.1
Events	26	23.6	9	8.3	20	30.3	11	16.2	3	6.4
Person	51	46.4	12	11	7	10.6	13	19.1	4	8.5
Family	25	22.7	22	20.2	8	12.1	21	30.9	6	12.8
Opposition to social evils	15	13.6	52	47.7	50	75.8	36	52.9	6	12.8
Total respondents	110	175.4	109	112.9	66	163.7	68	142.6	47	68.1

Note: N totals give number of activists, not total of all respondents; because of multiple responses the percentage totals sum to more than 100. The total number of respondents was 800, but not all have been included here.

nonetheless the popular image of activists in Nepal allows that they should have, or paradigmatically do have, non-economic interests and that they are pursuing other-directed goals.

APPENDIX 1: QUESTIONNAIRE AND TABLES

Nepali Activists Questionnaire
(English translation)

A. Organization/Institution

1. Name of the organization/institution of your present affiliation
2. Your designation (1. executive member from chair to treasurer, central commitee, 2. executive member from chair to treasurer, district, 3. committee member, central, 4. committee member, district)
3. Were you involved in activities connected to the aims of the present organization /institution before you joined it?

   I. Yes
   II. No (If no, skip to question 5)

4. If yes, since when (year): (1. before 1951, 2. 1952–60, 3. 1961–80, 4. 1981–90, 5. 1991 onwards)
5. Please specify the three major factors (in rank order) which inspired you to join the above-mentioned organization?

   I. Ideology
   II. Book/literature
   III. Event(s)
   IV. An individual
   V. Family
   VI. Resistance to existing social evils (*kuriti*)
   VII. Other (specify)

6. Have you worked for any student organization?

   I. Yes
   II. No (if no, skip to question 9)

7. If yes, which organization did you/do you belong to?

   I. Akhil Nepal Rastriya Swatantra Vidyarthi Union (Fifth Convention) [UML]
   II. Akhil Nepal Rastriya Swatantra Vidyarthi Union (Sixth Convention) [Jan Morcha]
   III. Nepal Vidyarthi Manch [Sadbhavana]
   IV. Nepal Vidyarthi Sangha [NC]
   V. Nepal Rastriya Vidyarthi Federation [pro-Russian CPN]
   VI. Rastriya Prajatantrik Vidyarthi Union [RPP]
   VII. Nepal Krantikari Vidyarthi Union [NWPP]
   VIII. Others (specify)

8. Please specify your position in the student organization:

   I. General member
   II. Active member
   III. Official (portfolio in the free student union or particular student organizational unit)

9. Which of the following areas of activism are you involved in? (Please rank answers with 'A' being the most important.)

   I. Politics
   II. Janajati
   III. Dalit
   IV. Caste group (*anya jatiya*)
   V. Madhesi
   VI. Language/culture
   VII. Women
   VIII. Religion

IX. Human Rights
X. Social Reform
XI. Trade Union (*majdur*)
XII. Business
XIII. Industry
XIV. Other (specify)

10. Are you associated with any political party?

I. Yes
II. No (if no, skip to question 14)

11. If yes, which one?

I. Ekata Kendra Masal (Jan Morcha)
II. Communist Party of Nepal (Unified Marxist-Leninist, UML)
III. Communist Party of Nepal (Marxist-Leninist, ML)
IV. Nepali Congress
V. Nepali Congress (Democratic)
VI. Nepal Majdur Kishan Party (NWPP)
VII. Nepal Sadbhavana Party (Mandal)
VIII. Nepal Sadbhavana Party (Anandadevi)
IX. Rastriya Prajatantra Party (RPP)
X. Other (specify)

12. If you have changed party or grouping (*dal/samuha*), in which party/group did you start your career?

I. Nepal Communist Party (1949–62)
II. Fourth Convention (CPN *Chautho Mahadhibesan*)
III. Nepal Communist Party (Marxist-Leninist)
IV. Nepal Communist Party (Unified Marxist-Leninist)
V. Nepal Communist Party (Masal)
VI. Nepal Communist Party (Mashal)
VII. Nepal Communist Party (Marxist)
VIII. Nepal Communist Party (Pushpa Lal)
IX. Praja Parisad
X. Gorkha Parisad
XI. Nepali Congress
XII. Nepal Majdoor Kishan Party (NWPP)
XIII. Nepal Sadbhavana Party (NSP)
XIV. Rastriya Prajatantra Party (RPP)
XV. None
XVI. Other (specify)

13. When did you join politics?
Year: (1. before 1951, 2. 1952–60, 3. 1961–80, 4. 1981–90, 5. 1991 onwards)

B. Personal Information

14. Year of birth:
15. Place of birth:

    I. Geographic region (1. Mountain, 2. Hill, 3. Tarai)
    II. Development region (1. Ktm Valley, 2. Eastern, 3. Central, 4. Western, 5. Mid Western, 6. Far Western)
    III. Rural/urban:
    VDC or Municipality
    IV. 1. India, 2. Other foreign

16. Education:

    I. Illiterate
    II. Literate (without any formal education)
    III. School level (1. 1–5, 2. 6–7, 3. 8–10, 4. SLC)
    IV. IA or equivalent
    V. Bachelor level
    VI. Master level
    VII. PhD

17. Religion (no options; coding to be done later):
18. Sex

    I. Male
    II. Female

19. Marital status

    I. Unmarried
    II. Married
    III. Divorced
    IV. Widow/widower
    V. Other (specify)

20. Marriage

    I. Within same caste/same ethnic group
    II. Inter caste/inter ethnic group

21. Do you perform ritual, meditation, prayers, worship, or other religious acts daily?

    I. Yes
    II. No (if no, skip to question 24)

22. If yes,

    I. At which time(s): (1. morning, 2. daytime, 3. evening, 4. morning and evening, 5. night, 6. at any time)

II. Duration: (1. up to 10 minutes, 2. 11–30 minutes, 3. 31–60 minutes, 4. over 1 hour)

23. Caste/ethnicity (*jati*):
24. Which languages are used among the members of your family? (specify for each of four generations: parents, siblings, wife/husband, children)

    I. Nepali (only one or main)
    II. ... (only one or main) (specify)
    III. Nepali and ...
    IV. Nepali, English, and ... (specify)
    V. Other

25. Besides Nepali and English, how many other languages of Nepal do you know? (1. one, 2. two, 3. many, 4. none)
26. For Nepali, your best other language of Nepal (if applicable), and English, please specify your level (very good, good, some, none) at each of the skills of understanding, speaking, reading, and writing.
27. Main occupation or source of income:

    I. Teaching
       School
       Campus/university
    II. Lawyer
    III. Professional
    IV. Ex-police/army
       UK
       India
       Nepal
       Other (specify)
    V. Business/industry
    VI. Service (incl. pension)
    VII. Traditional (caste/ethnic) occupation
    VIII. Agriculture
    IX. Housewife
    X. Student
    XI. Other (specify)

28. Since when are you living in Kathmandu Valley/Dhanusa/Kaski? [depending on site: Kathmandu/Janakpur/Pokhara]
29. In what kind of accommodation do you live in Kathmandu/Dhanusha/Kaski?

    I. Own house
    II. Rented house
    III. Lodge/hotel
    IV. Friend's house
    V. Relatives' house

VI. Hostel
VII. Other (specify)

30. Do you have your own vehicle?

I. Yes
II. No

31. Do you use your office's vehicle?

I. Yes
II. Sometimes
III. No

C. Family Background

32. What is your father's and grandfather's social status? (more than one answer possible)

I. Elite (*thalu/mukhiya/jimmawal*)
II. Merchant/trader
III. Priest/astrologer
IV. Social worker/reformist
V. Religious reformert
VI. Caste/ethnic leader
VII. Political leader
VIII. Office holder/teacher
IX. Ex-police/army
X. Member of public
XI. Other (specify)

33. Among your relatives is there anyone in an elite position (*thulo ohada*) (as defined in question 34)?

I. Yes
II. No (if no, skip to question 35)

34. If yes, in which field?

I. Politics (MP, Minister, DDC Chair, Mayor)
II. Government office (gazetted officer or above)
III. Army/police (officer level or above)
IV. Industrialist/trader
V. Professions
VI. International service
VII. Other (specify)

35. Where are your children being educated?

I. State school/college/university
II. Private school/college/university
III. International school/college/university (specify country)
IV. Not of school age
V. Other (specify)
VI. None

D. Ideological Information

36. Which is your preferred liked ideology (*siddhanta*)? (Please rank up to three, with 'A' being most liked.)

I. Active Monarchy
II. Constitutional Monarchy
III. Republic
IV. Democracy (*prajatantra*)
V. Socialism
VI. Communism
VII. Maoism
VIII. Gandhism
IX. Liberalism
X. Multiculturalism
XI. Capitalism
XII. Other (specify)
XIII. Don't know/don't wish to answer (in which case skip questions 37 and 38)

37. During which period of your life were you inspired to your most preferred ideology?

I. From schooling/childhood
II. From campus, university/youth
III. From entry into profession/service
IV. From retirement
V. Other (specify)

38. Which factors motivated you to be committed to your most preferred ideology? (Please rank up to three answers with 'A' being the most important.)

I. The ideology itself
II. Book/literature

III. Event(s)
IV. Family
V. Resistance to existing social evils
VI. Other (specify)

NOTES

1. Karki will submit his doctorate to Kwansei Gakuin University, Nishinomiya, Japan, in 2010. It will include statistical analysis of the questionnaire results. Gellner has two papers in press that also draw on this research (Gellner forthcoming a, b).
2. See Thapa (2003), Thapa and Sijapati (2004), Hutt (2004), Karki and Seddon (2003), Gellner (2003), Fujikura (2003), de Sales (2003), Gersony (2003), Whelpton (2004), Onesto (2005), Riaz and Basu (2007), Ogura (2007, 2008), Shah and Pettigrew (2008), and Lawoti and Pahari (2010). For the numerous reports and books produced in Nepal, up to 2005, see Simkhada and Oliva (2005).
3. For discussions of the impact of the new ethnic activism in Nepal, post 1990, see Gellner et al. (1997), Lecomte-Tilouine and Dollfus (2003), Fisher (2001), Guneratne (2002), Krauskopff (2003), Hangen (2007), and Lawoti (2005).
4. Krishna Hachhethu was also a part of this project and carried out some of the interviews with Gellner. His expertise was indispensable, both in designing the questionnaire and in dealing with political activists.
5. See Mikesell (1993) and Hachhethu (2007) for critiques of Levy (1990) along these lines. Several ethnographic monographs have been produced since 1990 that are not susceptible to the same criticisms. An innovative ethnography of urban middle-class consumption patterns, which perhaps goes too far in ignoring 'traditional' culture, not to mention modernizing forms of religion, is Liechty (2003). For a critique of history-writing in the same vein, see Onta (1994). For monographs that did pay attention to the political context under the Panchayat regime, and therefore are honourable exceptions to the charge of politics-blindness, see Caplan (1975) and Borgström (1980).
6. He also stressed in the introductory chapter that the Kathmandu Valley "is changing rapidly" (Gellner, 1992: 20). For a monograph on the modernizing and revitalizing Theravada movement in Nepal, see LeVine and Gellner (2005).
7. For an autobiography that vividly conveys the atmosphere of the time, as well as the great suffering experienced by those who were politically active, and the negative consequences for relatives, see Pokhrel and Willett (1996).
8. For a study of censorship in Nepal at a later period, see Hutt (2006).
9. This omits the Himalayan region of the country, but only 7 per cent of the population is to be found there.
10. By 2008 NEFIN membership had risen to 54 of the 59 officially recognized Janajati groups. Twenty-nine had their headquarters in the Kathmandu Valley, and the rest were in districts where the Janajati groups are concentrated.
11. There had long been serious human rights abuses, documented by Amnesty and others, both on the part of the 'security forces' and the Maoists. The army is alleged to have intensified such abuses following the king's dismissal of the

government in September 2002 and the breakdown of the subsequent ceasefire in August 2003 (see, for example, the Office of the High Commissioner for Human Rights (OHCHR) report, 2006, on the Bhairavnath Barracks).

12. On student politics, see Snellinger (2007).
13. This happened for instance to the father of K.P. Malla and Malla K. Sundar, both well-known intellectuals and activists: like all high-level government servants, he arrived one year for the annual *pajani* ceremony to find that he was not to receive a turban. He had to walk home without one, a public and humiliating form of dismissal. He refused government employment under the Ranas forever after (Gellner, 1996: 39–40). For a similar humiliation at the hands of the Ranas for Tanka Prasad Acharya's father, and its radicalizing effect on Tanka Prasad, see Fisher (1997: 50–1).
14. This is very clear among the Tharus. The early activists who set up the Tharu Kalyankarini Sabha in 1949–50 were the sons of landlords. Only in a much later generation, in the 1990s, did those from poorer backgrounds set up other mass organizations, notably Dilli Chaudhuri's BASE or Backward Society Education (see Guneratne, 2002, and Krauskopff, 2003, on the different social bases of these two leading Tharu organizations).
15. As told to Karki on 13 April 2005. Compare the relations between Chhetris and Thangmis in the same district as described by Shneiderman (this volume). Compare also Vasily (2009).
16. 442 out of the 800 respondents were members of a political party.
17. One wonders who the four UML members are who claim to do more than an hour of ritual every day (equivalent numbers were 16, 3, and 10 for NC, Sadbhavana, and RPP respectively—amalgamating the two NCs and two Sadbhavana parties). As noted earlier, many more statistical results, with a different method of categorizing influences on activists, will appear in Karki's future work. It will also show significant differences between the generations.

REFERENCES

Borgström, B.E. 1980. *The Patron and the Pancha: Village Values and Panchayat Democracy in Nepal*. New Delhi: Vikas.

Caplan, L. 1975. *Administration and Politics in a Nepalese Town: The Study of a District Captial and its Environs*. London: Oxford University Press.

de Sales, A. 2003. 'The Kham Magar Country: Between Ethnic Claims and Maoism', in D.N. Gellner (ed.), *Resistance and the State*, pp. 326–57. New Delhi: Social Science Press. (Also published 2000 in *European Bulletin of Himalayan Research* 19: 41–71; D. Thapa, D. (ed.). 2003. *Understanding the Maoist Movement of Nepal*. Kathmandu: Martin Chautari; and in French in 2003 in *Purusartha* 22: 271–301.)

Fisher, J.F. 1997. *Living Martyrs: Individuals and Revolution in Nepal*. New Delhi: Oxford University Press.

Fisher, W.F. 2001. *Fluid Boundaries: Forming and Transforming Identity in Nepal*. New York: Columbia University Press.

Fujikura, T. 2003. 'The Role of Collective Imagination in the Maoist Conflict in Nepal', *Himalaya: The Journal of the Association for Nepal and Himalayan Studies*, 22(1): 21–30.

Gellner, D.N. 1986. 'Language, Caste, Religion, and Territory: Newar Identity Ancient and Modern', *European Journal of Sociology*, 27(1): 102–48.

———. 1992. *Monk, Householder, and Tantric Priest: Newar Buddhism and its Hierarchy of Ritual*. Cambridge: Cambridge University Press.

Gellner, D.N. 1996. 'From Literature to Linguistics to Culture: An Interview with K.P. Malla', *European Bulletin of Himalayan Research*, 11: 37–52.

——— (ed.). 2003. *Resistance and the State: Nepalese Experiences*. New Delhi: Social Science Press.

———. forthcoming a. 'Rituals of Democracy and Development in Nepal', in S. Hettige (ed.), *Governance and Development in South Asia*. New Delhi: SAGE Publications.

———. forthcoming b. 'Belonging, Indigeneity, Rights, and Rites: The Newar Case', in J. Pfaff-Czarnecka and G. Toffin (eds), *Citizenship, Democracy, and Belonging in the Himalayas*. New Delhi: Sage Publications.

Gellner, D.N. and M.B. Karki. 2007. 'The Sociology of Activism in Nepal: Some Preliminary Considerations', in H. Ishii, D.N. Gellner, and K. Nawa (eds), *Northern South Asia: Political and Social Transformations*, pp. 361–97. New Delhi: Manohar.

———. 2008. 'Democracy and Ethnic Organizations in Nepal', in D.N. Gellner and K. Hachhethu (eds), *Local Democracy in Nepal and South Asia*, pp. 105–27. New Delhi: SAGE Publications.

Gellner, D.N., J. Pfaff-Czarnecka, and J. Whelpton (eds). 1997. *Nationalism and Ethnicity in a Hindu Kingdom: The Politics of Culture in Contemporary Nepal*. Amsterdam: Harwood. (New edition, 2008, Vajra Books, Kathmandu, as *Nationalism and Ethnicity in Nepal*.)

Gersony, R. 2003. 'Sowing the Wind… History and Dynamics of the Maoist Revolt in Nepal's Rapti Hills'. Mercy Corps International. Available at www.un.org.np (accessed on 17 December 2008).

Gorky, M. n.d. *Mother (A Novel in Two Parts)*, translated by M. Wettlin. Moscow: Foreign Languages Publishing House.

Guneratne, A. 2002. *Many Tongues, One People: The Making of Tharu Identity in Nepal*. Ithaca and London: Cornell University Press.

Hachhethu, K. 2002. *Party Building in Nepal: Organisation, Leadership and People: A Comparative of the Nepali Congress and the Communist Party of Nepal (United Marxist-Leninist)*. Kathmandu: Mandala Book Point.

Hachhethu, K. 2007. 'Social Change and Leadership: A Case Study of Bhaktapur City', in H. Ishii, D.N. Gellner, and K. Nawa (eds), *Northern South Asia: Political and Social Transformations*, pp. 63–89. New Delhi: Manohar.

Hangen, S.I. 2007. *Creating a 'New Nepal': The Ethnic Dimension*. Washington: East-West Center.

Hutt, M. (ed.). 2004. *Himalayan 'People's War': Nepal's Maoist Rebellion*. London: Hurst & Co.

———. 2006. 'Things that Should not be Said: Censorship and Self-censorship in the Nepali Press Media, 2001–2', *Journal of Asian Studies*, 65(2): 361–92.

Karki, A. and D. Seddon (eds). 2003. *The People's War in Nepal: Left Perspectives*. New Delhi: Adroit.

Karki, M.B. 2006. 'Social Networking and the Recruitment Process among Activists in Nepal', *Contributions to Nepalese Studies*, 36(1): 33–72.

Krauskopff, G. 2003. 'An "Indigenous Minority" in a Border Area: Tharu Ethnic Associations, NGOs, and the Nepalese State', in Gellner (ed.), *Resistance and the State: Nepalese Experiences*, pp. 199–243. New Delhi: Social Science Press.

Lawoti, M. 2005. *Towards a Democratic Nepal: Inclusive Political Institutions for a Multicultural Society*. New Delhi: SAGE Publications.

Lawoti, M. and A.K. Pahari (eds). 2010. *The Maoist Insurgency in Nepal: Revolution in the Twenty-First Century*. London and New York: Routledge.

Lecomte-Tilouine, M. and P. Dollfus (eds). 2003. *Ethnic Revival and Religious Turmoil: Identities and Representations in the Himalayas*. New Delhi: Oxford University Press.

LeVine, S. and D. Gellner. 2005. *Rebuilding Buddhism: The Theravada Movement in Twentieth-Century Nepal*. Cambridge: Harvard University Press.

Levy, Robert I. 1990. *Mesocosm: Hinduism and the Organization of a Traditional Newar City*. New Delhi: Motilal Banarsidass.

Liechty, M. 2003. *Suitably Modern: Making Middle-Class Culture in a New Consumer Society*. Princeton, NJ: Princeton University Press.

Mikesell, S.L. 1993. 'A Critique of Levy's Theory of the Urban Mesocosm', *Contributions to Nepalese Studies*, 20(2): 231–54.

Ogura, K. 2007. 'Maoists, People, and the State as seen from Rolpa and Rukum', in H. Ishii, D. Gellner, and K. Nawa (eds), *Political and Social Transformations in North India and Nepal: Social Dynamics in Northern South Asia*, Volume 2, pp. 435–75. New Delhi: Manohar.

———. 2008. 'Maoist People's Governments, 2001–05: The Power in Wartime', in D.N. Gellner and K. Hachhethu (eds), *Local Democracy in South Asia: Microprocesses of Democratization in Nepal and its Neighbours*, pp. 175–231. New Delhi: SAGE Publications.

OHCHR. 2006. 'Report of Investigation into Arbitrary Detention, Torture and Disappearances at Maharajgunj RNA Barracks, Kathmandu, in 2003–2004', Office of the High Commissioner for Human Rights. Available at http://nepal.ohchr.org/en/Torture.html (accessed on 16 December 2008).

Onesto, L. 2005. *Dispatches from the People's War in Nepal*. London: Pluto; California: Insight.

Onta, P. 1994. 'Rich Possibilities: Notes on Social History in Nepal', *Contributions to Nepalese Studies*, 21(1): 1–43.

Pokhrel, D. and D. Willett. 1996. *Shadow over Shangrila: A Woman's Quest for Freedom*. Washington DC: Brassey's.

Riaz, A. and S. Basu. 2007. *Paradise Lost? State Failure in Nepal*. Lanham, MD: Lexington Books.

Shah, A. and J. Pettigrew (eds). 2008. *Windows into a Revolution: Ethnographies of Maoism in India and Nepal*. London: Hurst.

Simkhada, S.R. and F. Oliva. 2005. *The Maoist Insurgency in Nepal: A Comprehensive Annotated Bibliography*. Geneva and Kathmandu: PSIO. Available at http://graduateinstitute.ch/corporate/nepal_en.html.

Snellinger, A. 2007. 'Student Movements in Nepal: Their Parameters and their Idealized Forms', in M. Lawoti (ed.), *Contentious Politics and Democratization in Nepal*, pp. 273–98. Los Angeles: SAGE Publications.

Thapa, D. (ed.). 2003. *Understanding the Maoist Movement of Nepal*. Kathmandu: Martin Chautari.

Thapa, D. and B. Sijapati. 2004. *Kingdom under Siege: Nepal's Maoist Insurgency, 1996–2004*. London: Zed.

Vasily, L. 2009. 'Struggles against Domination: Forms of Nepali Dalit Activism', in D.N. Gellner (ed.), *Ethnic Activism and Civil Society in South Asia*, pp. 215–38. New Delhi: SAGE Publications.

Whelpton, J. 2004. *A History of Nepal*. Cambridge: Cambridge University Press.

DEVELOPMENT

Chapter 7

Disciplined Activists, Unruly Brokers? Exploring the Boundaries between Non-governmental Organizations (NGOs), Donors, and the State in Bangladesh

DAVID LEWIS

INTRODUCTION

This chapter explores the subjects of activism and non-governmental organizations (NGOs) within the context of Bangladesh. In particular, it revisits a troubled episode from 2002 to 2004 in the difficult relationship that has long existed between Bangladesh's NGO sector and the government, and it then goes on to explore some of the ways in which events during this period connect with current conceptual issues in the anthropology of development policy. Bangladesh's extensive NGO sector has been widely documented from perspectives which have both celebrated and critiqued NGOs' various roles in development, democracy, and poverty reduction (Blair, 2005; DFID, 2000; Karim, 2001; Lewis, 2004; Stiles, 2002; White, 1999).[1] This chapter is not primarily concerned with these types of issues, but instead explores the ways in which boundaries between activism, NGOs, and government are articulated.

The chapter draws on observations made during regular research visits to Bangladesh since the mid-1980s, and on ethnographic data collected during a recent research project on the life histories of policy activists and professionals who have crossed between the state and non-state sectors (Lewis, 2008). Building upon an approach taken by Mosse (2005a) it argues that an important way in which policy is secured and maintained is through the establishment and protection of definitions and models of non-governmental action which must be continually negotiated by a range of actors, including international donors.

The chapter first introduces and discusses the so-called 'three sector' policy model which underpins current international donor frameworks of good governance, and explores the ways in which it has taken root in Bangladesh. It then analyses recent events in the NGO sector which have led first to a rupture of the model, and then to efforts towards its restoration, through the attempt by government to establish a new set of rules and limits around non-governmental public action. The argument aims to go beyond conventional accounts of NGO–government relations that tend to emphasize the 'opening up' or the 'narrowing down' of space for NGO work to argue that we must also consider the important role played by the construction and maintenance policy representations, and the various histories in which such representations are embedded.

ACTIVISM IN BANGLADESH

The discourse of activism in Bangladesh, as it is anywhere, is wide-ranging and one that can be unpacked in several different ways. The broad historical importance of the activist tradition in East Bengal among peasant, student, and women's organizations is well documented. For example, the language movement was an activist response to the imposition of the Urdu language by the Pakistani authorities on the Bengali-speakers of the east. Five Dhaka university student protesters were killed by the Pakistani army on 21 February 1952, an event that is still commemorated each year in Bangladesh. This movement was a crucial component of the resistance that ultimately led to the liberation war of 1971 in which Bangladesh emerged as a separate independent nation.

Today, to be 'active' (*shocriyo*) may imply taking part in some kind of public action or movement (*andolon*), as for example a woman activist (*shocriyo nari andolan kormi*) or an environmental activist (*poribesh andolon kormi*). Political activism in the sense of working for a particular party (*party kori*) has slowly moved from having positive social connotations to one which has become more negatively associated with the problem of confrontational politics and deadlock that characterized political life since the democratic period that began in 1991. It also speaks of a perception among many sections of the community of the essentially predatory relationship between the two main political blocs and the rest of society, one that led to the cautious welcoming of the unelected Caretaker Government that assumed power in December 2006 after a period of prolonged political tension and uncertainty over plans for the next national election process.

Outside the framework of party politics, individual independent activists, motivated by secular or religious values, can also be seen working through routes which intersect with activities normally associated with understandings of charity or religious duty. On a plane journey to Dhaka in 2004, I met two young British Bangladeshi men who were travelling to their original home district in Sylhet to assist people, using their own savings, with grants to rebuild houses damaged in a recent flood. They were not part of any particular organization, nor were they going back to work with family, but were driven apparently by a sense of transnational cultural solidarity. Religious activism has also become more topical in recent years. This tends to be associated—at least by more secular observers—with radical or marginal groups pursuing agendas within 'uncivil society'. Examples would be the current campaign of intimidation against the minority Ahmadiyya Muslim sect, the criminal 'Bangla bhai' gang in the north-west of the country engaged in vigilante violence against so-called anti-religious elements and *sarbahara* leftists,[2] or the Islamic Chhatra Shibir student wing of the Jamaat-i-Islami political party which has long been associated with intimidation and extreme violence within student politics.

In a society strongly dominated by the institutions and discourses of international aid, one important reading of the activist identity has always been an 'oppositional' one, in the sense that an activist is usually one who steps outside the business of international aid and the NGO world in particular, in favour of a less compromised, 'purer' form of political or social action. In this perspective, a social activist in Bangladesh may in one sense be understood as a person who is in politics, research, or manages an NGO but who crucially seeks to operate, or present a view of operating, outside the formal framework of development agency funding. But activism has also long had meaning within the NGO sector itself. To be an activist is also to be an organizer (*sangathan kori*), which is also how some people within NGOs engaged in grassroots organizational work—building grassroots groups (*samitys*) for example—may describe themselves.

The war of liberation created an independent Bangladesh, but in the subsequent decades periods of democracy have been interrupted by periods of authoritarian rule. During the periods of intense nation-building, catastrophic natural disaster, and increasing authoritarianism that followed 1971, a concept of the 'non-governmental organization' emerged, influenced both by international agencies and the resources they brought to the newly formed country and by local activists. One important component of the idea of the NGO was as a means by which young idealists from student politics, as well as some from sections of business and academia (e.g. F.H. Abed and M. Yunus respectively), could connect their work to the challenges of national reconstruction and poverty reduction (Lewis, 2004; Seabrook, 2001).

For example, recent work on understanding the life histories of activists and professionals within the NGO sector in Bangladesh and their relations with government provide insights into some of the trajectories taken during this period and subsequently, and a few brief ethnographic sketches from this work can serve to illustrate some of the archetypal trajectories of such individuals (Lewis, 2008). One informant described growing up during the 1960s in southern Bangladesh: he was active in local village associations and later became a freedom fighter during the 1971 war. After graduating from university soon afterwards with a degree in commerce, he nevertheless joined first an international NGO as a volunteer and then later helped establish a small rural development organization where he has subsequently remained, though he has also spent periods of his career working on government placements within foreign-funded projects in order to support his family. The balance of engaging in social change activity within the NGO sector is often combined with periods of work within other, better-resourced sectors. Another informant, who began as an activist within a left political party while a student in the mid-1960s, subsequently drifted into the civil service. He spoke of the "noble examples" of "serious activists who had turned into first-class administrators". He went on to play an important role in building the government's social welfare capacity during the 1970s before ending up towards the end of his career back in the NGO sector as executive director of a legal aid organization. For a younger generation coming from the middle classes, NGOs and civil society have provided a relatively professionalized arena for activism which can also serve as a space in which a person can gain experience and knowledge for careers in other sectors. For example, another informant had spent several years working with a human rights network before she went on to build a career in the public sector judiciary as a human rights lawyer with an activist agenda around gender issues (see also Strulik, this volume, for comparisons with India).

Today, the vast majority of NGOs are providers of credit and other developmental services to local communities. In some ways this resembles the view of NGOs as the depoliticized end-points of once-vibrant social movements that have lost their radical edge and evolved into professionalized organizations (Kaldor, 2003: 94). But the NGO sector in Bangladesh still contains some diversity, with some organizations remaining outside the 'mainstream NGO sector' and within a sub-sector of 'activist NGOs'. For example, Samata has evolved from origins in small-scale grassroots activist work to seek influence over the allocation and use of government *khas* land to landless rural people.[3] Nijera Kori has set out to build the 'collective capabilities' of women and men as citizens as opposed to the individualized identities of 'beneficiaries', 'clients', or 'customers' (Kabeer, 2003). There are also pockets of activist activity within more mainstream development agencies, such as individuals who claim to be carrying forward activist reform agendas internally. One such person was a social development adviser at the World Bank who had been recruited from the women's NGO sector, and who presented herself within the agency as an outsider/insider playing an 'activist' role in relation to gender and civil society.

THE 2002–04 RIFT

In 2001, an important section of the NGO community entered a period of crisis after the election of the Bangladesh Nationalist Party (BNP)-led coalition government in October. Five well-established NGOs were accused by the new government of both financial irregularities and politically partisan behaviour. In particular, it was alleged that certain NGOs had lent assistance to the electoral campaign of the ruling Awami League party, which some felt had unexpectedly lost the election. The best known of these NGOs was

Proshika, a national-level organization engaged in a wide range of development activities across Bangladesh (and the second-largest NGO in the country), including a range of service delivery and campaigning work.[4] As we have seen, leftist student activists in the 1970s had been inspired by the recent liberation of the country from Pakistan, but felt constrained in the pursuit of their style of progressive politics under the increasingly authoritarian style of government of Sheikh Mujib Rahman. When Proshika was established in 1976, it provided a way of linking of activist and developmental objectives. In the words of Smillie and Hailey (2001: 8), "Proshika grew out of a donor project which was also staffed, and later taken over, by young social activists." Led by its founder Q.F. Ahmed, Proshika had always tried to set itself apart from the mainstream development NGO community by seeking to maintain and project a strong 'activist' public profile.

As discussed earlier, while it has been usual for many of Bangladesh's NGOs to claim and display their radical roots—Paulo Freire's *Pedagogy of the Oppressed* was a formative text for several founder leaders and supporters in the 1970s—much of the sector by the 1990s had followed organizations such as Grameen Bank and the Association for Social Advancement (ASA) into work which had microfinance service provision at its centre in place of 'social mobilization' strategies. Proshika, on the other hand, while it also operated an extensive national-level programme of credit provision in both rural and urban areas, had also gradually expanded its campaigning and activism, establishing a dedicated research and advocacy centre, and is seeking to build what it termed a 'civil society movement' that could help link together other like-minded NGOs, women's organizations, trade unions, and newspapers in support of issues such as women's rights, environmental issues, and democratic governance.[5]

By the end of the 1990s, the space available for this type of work appeared to have narrowed, due to a combination of both internal and external factors. One important set of internal factors was undoubtedly organizational. Favoured by international donors to a high degree, many NGOs had expanded very rapidly and this growth had placed a considerable strain on their administrative systems and overall coherence.[6] At the external level, several types of macro factors have operated, including the changing priorities of international donors, the increased flow of private finance alongside development initiatives, and a set of Islamizing processes within national politics. NGOs in Bangladesh had been subject to changing priorities within the international donor community, where an earlier and somewhat uncritical pro-NGO position was hardening into one in which more emphasis was being placed on performance and accountability issues, in which the measurable targets of the millennium development goals were gaining in priority. The government too, always somewhat wary of the NGOs but having reached an effective accommodation with them around service delivery partnerships and common interests in expanding microfinance provision, was also changing its position.[7]

The key for activist development NGOs going about their work in South Asia has generally involved "keeping politically neutral and negotiating with whoever is in power", as Appadurai (2001: 23) has put it, in connection with his work with the Society for the Promotion of Area Resource Centres (SPARC) in India. But by 2002 the difficulty of maintaining such an approach, and the political hazards of grassroots organizing work, began to become more starkly apparent for Proshika and the other NGOs. What were the reasons for the subsequent rupture that took place, and what are its implications for our understandings of the ways in which governance relationships are negotiated and secured within the current complex policy framework of international development assistance (cf. Mosse, 2005b) and within the Bangladesh state's own fragile systems, strategies, and structures?

Since the fall of General Ershad in 1990, the new system of parliamentary democracy has produced regular general elections and a BNP-led government from 1991 to 1996, an Awami League government in 1996–2001, and the subsequent BNP-led alliance government that continued until 2006. Despite this democratic process, as Kochanek (2003: 1) puts it,

> Formal democratic institutions have proven to be weak and there persists an informal political process that has failed to instil or support equality of access to core political institutions, an adequate popular voice, effective governmental performance and full protection of citizen's rights.

Frequent *hartals* (politically organized enforced stoppages that originally evolved as a form of resistance to British colonial rule), increasing political violence, and frequent boycotts of parliament have each come to characterize political life, alienating many citizens from any trust in formal political processes. Some sections of the NGO community have responded to increasingly confrontational and gridlocked parliamentary politics with a more activist style and approach. A wide range of mass demonstrations and civil society alliances were effectively coordinated by Proshika and the Association of Development Agencies in Bangladesh (ADAB) during the second half of the 1990s. Karim (2001) in my view exaggerates when she suggests that at this time a section of the NGO community—led by Proshika—had actually 'taken over' oppositional political processes in the name of 'non-party politics', but the higher political profile of such NGOs had clearly begun to rattle some nerves.

Like many of the development NGOs, Proshika was broadly identified with the secular nationalist vision of a democratic Bangladesh, and one that was loosely associated with the Awami League party. But its leadership had also long been vocal in its criticisms of what it saw as extremist and unpatriotic religious elements in the public sphere, such as the Jamaat-i-Islami party, elements of which are believed to have collaborated with the Pakistani army in the killing of thousands of citizens during the liberation war in 1971. As Riaz (2003: 301–2) has argued, there has indeed been a "conservative Islamization process" underway in Bangladesh for the past few decades.[8] But it would be a mistake to interpret this as driven by the "reassertion of a dormant Muslim identity". Rather, it is encouraged primarily by the "crises of hegemony" of the ruling elites and by a "politics of expediency" on the part of the secularist political parties. As a result, there have been cases of violence in some parts of the country by religious activists against Proshika and other NGO offices and fieldworkers and Proshika's president himself became the target of several *fatwa* by local religious leaders. The increasing profile and voice of Islamist political interests, which had for some time been hostile to the development NGO community in relation to their foreign funding and discourses of women's empowerment, was another factor that disturbed the uneasy equilibrium between NGOs and government.

After the 2001 election, the Jamaat-i-Islami political party for the first time gained significant electoral ground within the ruling coalition formed by the BNP. Both parties saw an opportunity to settle old scores with Proshika and other NGOs which they regarded as unruly. The government began in 2002 by blocking around US$50 million donor funds which were due to Proshika on the basis of alleged 'financial irregularities', after an audit of Proshika was ordered by the prime minister. This action led the European Union, one of Proshika's main funders, to intervene and raise concerns with the government about the lack of accountability of its investigation, suggesting that an international audit of Proshika's accounts should be undertaken, but this appeal was ignored by the government. Meanwhile, harassment of Proshika staff and looting of local offices by ruling party activists was reported around the country. This continued at a low level until in May 2004 the President and the Vice-President of Proshika—along with some other staff—were arrested and held in custody for several weeks, without clear charges being brought, triggering an Urgent Action appeal from Amnesty International. This time, the government announced that it had clear evidence that Proshika had assisted the opposition party in its election campaign and had diverted donor funds for political purposes, pointing in particular to its work with voter education and its funding of small local NGOs in certain parts of the country. The final straw for the government, according to *The New York Times* (25 May 2004), was the Awami League's statement earlier in 2004 that it would undertake a mass campaign to bring down the government by the end of April, and allegations that Proshika would lend its support to such a movement.[9]

At the same time, the government quickly moved to reassert its control over the NGO sector more generally. It began efforts to amend a 1978 Ordinance that regulates donations to NGOs from foreign sources through a new 'NGO Bill'—currently said to be stalled—which would give the government new powers to intervene in any NGO that it suspected of misusing funds or transgressing the sectoral rules and expectations around NGO participation in politics or business.[10] The government also set about sidelining ADAB which had, since its foundation in 1974, acted as the NGO umbrella coordinating organization. In practice, ADAB had by the 1990s moved well beyond this coordination role and was now running its own projects and, as in the case of some of the other larger NGOs, funding many small local NGOs around the country. Some argued that ADAB had become less effective by the accumulation of these new roles, and by the emergence of political tensions and wider patronage relations within the NGO sector. In the government's view, ADAB had ceased to act as a neutral NGO apex body with an ability to coordinate NGO work effectively and it regarded ADAB as a politicized obstacle to building an effective regulatory environment for NGOs. In early 2003, an invitation from the government was issued to development NGOs to attend a meeting intended to create a new alternative NGO forum with which the government could work. This new forum took the form of a brand new organization—the Federation of NGOs in Bangladesh (FNB). As a result, a new 'government-friendly' national NGO network was established, with a comprehensively laid out organizational structure that was specifically designed to promote clearer lines of accountability than had previously existed, and with strong barriers to deter party politicization.[11] The Memorandum of Association for the FNB states clearly that "no organization shall be recognised as an NGO if it or any of its office bearers is aligned or associated with any political party in any form whatsoever" (p. 16).[12] This issue was given particular prominence because the Proshika President, a known Awami League sympathiser, had himself previously occupied the position of ADAB chair for more than one term.

CHANGING POLICY FRAMEWORKS FOR NON-GOVERNMENTAL ORGANIZATIONS

What is the significance of these events, and what do they tell us about the changing forms of activism and the nature of civil society in Bangladesh? The subject of NGOs and development has now generated a considerable research literature, but one which has generally been theoretically weakened by its overwhelming focus on normative agendas (Fisher, 1997; Igoe and Kelsall, 2005; Lewis, 2005). Among a set of diverse themes and issues in this literature, two broad theoretical frameworks can be seen to have entered research and policy debates in relation to NGOs and their operation.

The first is the 'three sector' idea which sets out a tripartite institutional model of organized social action based on state, market, and a 'third' category of non-state, not-for-profit actors. The concept of the third sector has its roots in organizational theory and draws on Etzioni's (1961) analysis of three different kinds of power relationships or 'compliance' in the determination of organizational forms.[13] Najam (1996) shows how Etzioni's framework is used to argue that essential differences exist between the three institutional 'sectors', namely coercion and legitimate authority (the state), negotiated exchange in markets (business), and shared values in consensus-based systems (voluntary organizations). Within policy circles the discovery of the 'third sector' idea has been seen as having several possible purposes: as another potential delivery system for services, as an area of 'private' activity into which government can shift responsibilities, and as a public arena in which individuals can organize social action. The concept of the 'third sector' can therefore be seen as a guiding metaphor (Wuthnow, 1991) or as a Weberian 'ideal type', which at the policy level in particular has provided a framework for structuring organizational and institutional relationships. Despite this, the 'three sector' framework is unlikely to correspond closely with political and organizational realities on the ground, as I shall show in the following.

The three sector model underpins the 'good governance' agenda that emerged among international development donors in the 1990s. This centred on the promotion of positive synergies between the state, the market, and the third sector and which, while appearing to bring the state more firmly into development policy, remained essentially a "market-driven, competitive model which favours the strong in every area—technical, educational, political, economic, financial" (Archer, 1994: 8). In Bangladesh, the three sector model achieved particular prominence during the mid-1990s through the World Bank and the Asian Development Bank's (ADB) explicit interest in promoting partnership between government and NGOs (White, 1999).

By overstating the firmness of the boundaries, the three sector model serves to obscure important historical differences between diverse organizations and contrasting historical contexts, feeding a functionalist policy view of NGO–government complementarity based on comparative advantage (Tvedt, 1998). It also overlooks the private or personal connections that cross sectoral boundaries and may help structure NGO–government relations. One could cite examples such as the college cohort links of the first NGO Affairs Director with various NGO leaders (Lewis and Sobhan, 1999) or the family relationship that links the director of one major NGO with the current opposition through a brother who is an opposition MP (Siraj, 2004), or the director of another leading radical NGO connected to the current BNP cabinet through a brother-in-law.

The shortcomings of the model are also illustrated by the fact that NGO structures and processes are now firmly embedded in the strategies of local rural elites' livelihood strategies. NGOs are now intertwined with the pursuit of patronage, networking with kin, and bargaining for government resources as powerful rural families seek to diversify their power base far beyond the traditional foundation of landownership. In Hilhorst's (2003) phrase, "the practice of NGO-ing" has become an important strategy for some powerful households. In one village in Faridpur district, a local NGO called Polli Bandhu (meaning 'Village Friends') was established in 1994 by a graduate from a well-established rural family, suggested by two uncles who were mid-level civil servants in Dhaka (Lewis and Hossain, 2008). They suggested starting an NGO as a way of improving his social and economic position, and to get him started, one of them within the Environment Ministry provided him with government start-up funds for a 'fake' project concerned with pollution awareness. Despite the lack of priority of this issue in the area, he held some public meetings, carried out some activities and soon the organization had built a 'real' profile. Before long, the NGO had attracted other funders to support a range of activities which included credit, education, health, and land rights. Out of seven persons involved in the governance of the NGO, four were family members and the others were close friends.

In 2001, with the NGO doing well, the founder became involved with the activist NGO Samata and received funding for *khas* land work. Before starting, he first went to the local Union chairman[14] in order to get him on his side in challenging powerful interests at the sub-district level who were supporting illegal land occupations in the area, and to remove potential opposition from the chairman, who had been highly critical of local NGOs previously in relation to their micro-credit work. Since the chairman knew these interests were supporters of his political rival (the previous chairman) he agreed to back the NGO with the result that 114 acres of *khas* land was recovered from local business interests and, despite an ongoing legal challenge, are being redistributed to Samata members. Although this founder initially used 'corrupt' connections to establish the NGO, he later negotiated effectively with government and NGO actors to undertake potentially transformative redistributive work.

Nevertheless, in Bangladesh the three sector model remains firmly embedded among donors and government. For example, the World Bank's policy framework is analysed by White (1999: 308), who deconstructs the politics of representation within an influential

World Bank report published in Bangladesh in 1996 entitled *Pursuing Common Goals*. This set out the challenges of guiding government and NGOs towards a higher level of complementarity and partnership:

> The image on the report's front cover ... aptly expresses the vision contained within it. It shows the two parallel rails of a train-track, in perfect harmony and perfect complementarity, seeming to converge as they lead off into the middle distance, with the beams that support them appearing like the rungs of a ladder, leading onward and ever upward.
>
> Despite its central position as a simple policy map, the model's loose fit with the institutional and political realities requires constant effort of maintenance to ensure that it remains in place.[15]

While NGOs today are perhaps no longer the favoured children of the development industry that they once were, civil society is still a key part of the good governance agenda (Lewis, 2005). There has been some disappointment with emerging evidence about NGO performance and accountability, and there has been a subsequent shift in policy discourse. As disillusionment with NGOs has set in, NGOs as an idea within development policy became subsumed beneath continuing but broader versions of the good governance model based increasingly on wider—though often conceptually vague—ideas about 'civil society'. The long and complex philosophical roots of the concept of civil society are less relevant for our discussion here than the fact that two basic understandings of the term can be identified: the 'liberal' and the 'radical' (Lewis, 2002). In the liberal view, which is generally favoured by governments and donors, civil society is an arena of organized citizens that balances state and market. It has, as Howell and Pearce (2000) have argued, been associated with initiatives seeking to 'build' civil society along externally determined lines much of which has in the end, perhaps ironically, led back to the NGOs again as the most visible and recognizable proxies for civil society in non-Western contexts. In the radical view of civil society, derived mainly from Gramsci, there is—in place of harmony and synergy—an emphasis on conflict, on struggles for power among different interest groups, and on unclear boundaries with the state (see also Fisher, this volume).

In Bangladesh, where as we have seen, there is an unusually diverse and extensive NGO sector, and as much as a third of the population receives some form of service from non-governmental sources, the concept of civil society has been widely debated by activists and academics. While the historical importance of organized action by citizens in Bangladesh (such as the historical role of the language movement and the importance of cultural activists, professionals, and other citizen groups in the construction of national identities in the 1950s and 1960s) provides a counter-narrative to current discourses of civil society generated among contemporary NGO actors, there were signs (as we have seen) that the NGO-centred civil society activity was becoming more political by the mid-1990s. For example, ADAB's Democracy Awareness Programme coordinated the activities of 15,000 trainers across the country thereby substantially increasing turnout and other NGOs promoted landless candidates in local government elections, sometimes meeting with violent resistance by established interests (Ashman, 1997: 31).

Although there have long been criticisms by government of the ways the NGO sector has conducted itself, and a set of long-running tensions between NGOs, government, and other sections of society, the events of 2004 represented a 'sea change'. Government was able to make it clear that a significant part of the 'NGO community' had crossed the line, moving beyond what is defined as the acceptable limits of complementary development work on poverty reduction. In the words of the Director of the FNB, whom I interviewed in 2005, action had been necessary because elements of the NGO sector had become "infected with politics".

The dominant paradigm—shared by government and some, though not all, of the donors[16]—of a distinct developmental 'NGO sector', which is largely set apart from politics and confined to a safe sphere of developmental activities away from the messy realities of politics and patronage, had broken down. The new government saw itself as instituting a process of reform and discipline for troublesome or transgressive non-governmental individuals and actors. On one level, this failure to maintain a coherent set of representations and explanations in relation to the NGO sector is reminiscent of Mosse's (2005a) arguments, which draw from Latour's work within science studies, about the need to understand the workings of development projects in relation to the imperatives of project actors to maintain coherent explanations and social representations of their actions. In this case, the prevailing equilibrium within a negotiated set of shared meanings about what NGOs are and what they do became untenable and unsustainable within the context of wider political changes. The unruliness of activists within a significant section of the NGO 'community' prompted a set of realignments among both government and NGOs, and to a certain extent, donors. This failure was also partly an outcome of the Bangladesh state's increasingly troubled efforts to stabilize an acceptable representation of its own role and legitimacy. After military rule ended in 1990, what had emerged was a period of confrontational politics and increasingly uncertain democracy. This 'evolving institutions' argument is made against a comparatively recent authoritarian past, the history of Liberation, and the more distant experience of colonialism from which ongoing tensions over power and identity are still derived.

ASSERTING PARADIGMS, DISCIPLINING ACTIVISTS?

If the three sector model has been re-asserted, what then has happened to the policy discourse around 'civil society'? The neo-Tocquevillian 'liberal' model of self-regulating stability can be seen to have been ruptured by the intrusion of organizations and events embodying the 'radical' civil society tradition of Gramsci, in which struggle and conflict triumph over harmony and balance. By taking action against a significant section of the NGO sector, the government has acted to restore order through the deployment of the mutually reinforcing orders of the three sector model and the liberal civil society paradigm. This restoration can be considered in the light of Foucaultian ideas about 'governmentality', that is, the changes need to be viewed in the context of Bangladesh's relatively recent transition to democracy from an authoritarian past, and as part of a process of institutional adaptation and adjustment to changing local and global realities. In other words, these events can be seen as part of the ongoing and essentially 'failing' project of the 'governmentalization of the state', part of which is the process through which government is operationalized by co-opting what it does not control (Rose and Miller, 1992). This is in part achieved through the direct curbing of NGO action, but also works more subtly by presenting and shaping a definition of self-identity to which NGOs must subscribe.

Beyond the Proshika story, the way in which this process operates can also be seen in other areas of the NGO sector, such as the Manusher Jonno (MJ) project.[17] Manusher Jonno—which means 'for the people'—is a large-scale (£13.5m) local fund established in

2002 by DFID to fund innovative human rights work. Its progress to date illustrates the ways in which the more activist approaches to development work have been both facilitated but also constrained by recent political events. Designed to promote and support a wide range of civil society partners through a decentralized locally controlled funding mechanism, MJ, once constituted, was immediately faced with the practical problem of gaining government approval via the NGO Affairs Bureau, particularly since it aimed for projects and partners interested in pushing at the boundaries of mainstream work. Fearing that government approval would be difficult or impossible to secure for sensitive activities such as voter awareness or the rights of religious minorities (likely to be considered 'political' after the recent tensions), the project managers opted for a more 'softly softly' approach to governance and human rights which emphasized the less contentious—though still very relevant—issues of child rights, violence against women, and local government accountability.

What of the donors' role in the crisis? Hossain (2004) shows how donors successfully backed the NGO sector against government hostility to the NGOs in the early 1990s. However, the reality today is that donors no longer carry the same level of influence they once did in Bangladesh, since the role of foreign aid has been overtaken within the overall economy by the growth of export income and remittances.[18] The imperatives of the millennium development goals (MDGs) and the more intrusive mechanisms of aid that link donors more directly to government (such as Poverty Reduction Strategy Papers) have both led donors away from NGOs as mechanisms for stabilizing governance indirectly towards a more direct relationships with government (Mosse, 2005b). This can be seen in the changing attitude of DFID since the original design of the MJ project five years ago as a 'flagship process project' to a situation in which it is now seen as a project that must generate measurable impacts. By contrast, its initial brief had given it considerable leeway to experiment and learn from the process of building a set of new approaches to human rights and governance work. Even the 'blueprint' tools of development management have become flexible and shifted during this process of realignment. The original project design documents stated clearly that only 50 per cent of MJ's partner projects needed be 'successful' in terms of meeting their objectives and that the others would still be valued, since even if they did not succeed on their own terms they would generate useful 'lessons and learning'.

At a meeting with local DFID staff in April 2005 I was surprised to find that the logical framework[19] for the project that stated this clearly—normally the foundation blueprint for any bilateral project to which donors make usually explicit reference at points of debate or crisis—was waved aside as being unimportant in this case. In the way that development donors are always moving forward, erasing history and promising a next phase of this time 'getting it right' (Mosse, 2005a), governance and rights work in this case appeared to have been sacrificed to the wider and more tangible priorities of growth promotion and measurable poverty impacts.

CONCLUSION: NON-GOVERNMENTAL ORGANIZATIONS AND ACTIVISM

Normative assumptions about NGOs and civil society can be analysed using an anthropological perspective in order to better understand how the organization and practices of civil society are shaped by state and international aid agencies. The conventional 'story' of the relationship between activists and NGOs is one in which NGOs serve to tame or domesticate the unruliness of the activist. An activist, already mobilized by some earlier engagement within the political arena (such as within the student movement or environmental campaigning), comes into contact with international development agencies and eventually sees an opportunity or is persuaded to establish his or her own NGO. In setting up an NGO, the 'activist impulse' then becomes contained within this more formal vehicle, and begins to lose its radical edge and, for many other activists, its legitimacy. The activist becomes constrained within the apparatus of the international development industry where, depending on one's point of view, a person either becomes an 'activist insider' working to subvert neo-liberal development policies from within, or alternatively, is fatally co-opted within 'the system' by foreign aid, its associated managerialism, and the wider workings of Ferguson's 'anti-politics machine'.

Activists—particularly those in senior leadership roles within NGOs in the case discussed here—can therefore be seen as brokers or intermediaries operating at the interfaces between the organized worlds of NGOs and a wider set of informal arenas, relationships, and resources that lie beyond civil society, closer to government and donors. Such activists can provide useful insights into the fault-lines and ambiguous boundaries between the worlds of state and non-state, national and international actors. The construction of the three sector model, and the ways in which it may be simultaneously both maintained and undermined, forms part of the regulation process of the overall organization of neo-liberal aid and governance. As Mosse and Lewis (2006: 7) put it,

> ... we should be far less confident about the *a priori* existence of social and institutional realms. All actors (and not just sociologists) produce interpretations, and powerful actors offer scripts into which others can be recruited for a period...

The three sectors may be illusory, but the model serves a set of policy interests and has powerful effects in terms of resource allocation. In this sense, the three sector model exists in the realm of Mitchell's (2002: 15) "politics of techno-science", as part of a primarily managerialist logic of governance.

An important aspect of the NGO sector that therefore needs further exploration is its role—within the wider context of the power of international development—in containing or 'disciplining' activists seeking to challenge or redefine governability. NGOs may act as organizational spaces for activism, but they also present spaces into which governmental power can be projected. In this chapter, the 'rupture' between the BNP coalition government and a section of the NGO sector in the period after the 2001 elections has provided an entry point to the analysis of NGOs, government, and activism in the distinctive context of Bangladesh. Analysis of these events helps to illustrate the ways in which the liberal definitions of 'civil society' favoured by donors tend to obscure tensions and conflicts among non-state actors. It also throws light on the ways in which the 'three sector model' (government, market, and civil society), that helps to frame current 'governance' policies, oversimplifies dramatically the ways in which power operates among institutions. As part of its negotiation with the overall imperatives of neo-liberal policy, the government of Bangladesh has attempted to reassert the three sector and the liberal civil society models and place them at the centre of policy. Nevertheless, these policy models remain very thinly stretched over complex local realities of NGO patronage, kinship and conflict, and local traditions of activism.

NOTES

1. My thanks are due to M. Shameem Siddiqi and Abul Hossain for earlier discussion on the topic of activism. I also wish to thank David Mosse for extremely useful discussant comments on the earlier conference draft of this chapter. It has been estimated that there may be more than 20,000 NGOs in Bangladesh. These are mainly small, local organizations with only a dozen or so large-scale national NGOs on the scale of the internationally known agencies such as Grameen Bank, Proshika, or Bangladesh Rural Advancement Committee (BRAC).
2. The Purba Banglar Sarbahara Party (PBSP) was a pro-China faction of the Bengali left. It was active militarily against Pakistan and Jamaat-i-Islami during the liberation war, and later opposed the Awami League after 1971. Contemporary offshoots still operate underground in small numbers in some parts of the country, with long-standing political scores and new struggles over resources still occasionally being settled by force.
3. The allocation of *khas* land, which is unowned land that emerges from river and coastal realignments, is supposed to be made by government to landless households, but plots are frequently seized by force by local landowners. See Devine (2002).
4. The other organizations were smaller, more specialized NGOs: PRIP Trust, Bangladesh Nari Pragati Sangha (BNPS), and the Centre for Development Services (CDS).
5. This is illustrated by several initiatives, including the establishment of the Institute for Development Policy Analysis and Advocacy (IDPAA) in 1994 as a semi-autonomous research, advocacy, and training institution. Its activities included coordinating the Pro-Poor National Budget campaign to promote participatory budgeting approaches and the Structural Adjustment Participatory Research Initiative (SAPRI) which brought a range of non-state actors together to debate and challenge the World Bank's structural adjustment programme.
6. One high profile earlier casualty of this had been Gonoshahajjo Sangstha (GSS), one of the largest NGOs in the country which had been funded by European Union, DFID, and Sida, among others. GSS was taken over by the government in June 1999 amidst allegations of financial mismanagement of international aid funds. This severely disrupted GSS's national-level network of innovative non-formal village schools. At the same time, GSS's origins had been in radical Freirean social mobilization, it had resisted the microfinance agenda and its founder had had a long history of activism on the political left.
7. An earlier period of confrontation with the BNP government in the early 1990s, which led to the establishment of an NGO Affairs Bureau to improve the regulation of NGOs' use of international funds, was in the end resolved in favour of the NGOs largely through the intervention of donors (Hashemi, 1995).
8. The state principle of secularism was removed from the Constitution in 1977 and Islam was declared to be the state religion in 1988.
9. Q.F. Ahmed was released on 25 July 2004 without any charges having been brought.
10. Another area of controversy in relation to the 'three sectors' (a concept explored more fully in the next section of the chapter) has been the issue of whether NGOs such as BRAC, which has an extensive network of not-for-profit businesses,

should pay taxes on earnings. Some in the private sector have argued the case of unfair competition.

11. Some suggested that this was open invitation; others that certain NGOs unpopular with the government for their more 'political' stance were deliberately excluded from this meeting.
12. *Memorandum of Association and Articles of Association*, FNB, Dhaka, 30 April 2003.
13. Power relations differ in terms of the means used to achieve compliance. They are either *coercive*, which is the application or threat of physical sanctions (such as pain or restrictions on the freedom of movement); *remunerative*, which is based on control over material resources and rewards (such as wages or benefits); or *normative*, which is based on the manipulation of symbolic rewards and deprivations, the use of the power of persuasion, and on appeals to shared values and idealism.
14. Union is the lowest tier of local government, with an elected chairman.
15. Wade's idea of the 'art of paradigm maintenance' is comparable, although his analysis goes well beyond the role of NGOs (Wade, 1996).
16. In recent years, a division has opened up between a 'mainstream' large donor grouping composed of the UK Department for International Development (DFID), ADB, USAID, and Japan—who provide the bulk of Bangladesh's foreign aid—and a smaller grouping of bilateral donors including the Scandinavians, the Dutch, and the Canadians who tend to take a more politically radical stance in relation to policy advocacy and civil society campaigning. There were suggestions in diplomatic circles and in the press in 2005 that the government might follow India's example and expel this group of small-scale but inconveniently 'shrill' donor group (sometimes referred to disparagingly by government officials as the 'five taka donors').
17. I was involved as a consultant with another colleague to document this project in order to generate lessons and learning. More detail of the initiative can be found in Beall (2005). MJ became an independent local trust in 2007.
18. In 1993–97 aid was 71 per cent of total development expenditure, but this had fallen to 51 per cent by 1998–2002 (Hossain, 2004).
19. The logical framework is the dominant planning tool used by many donors and NGOs for projects design, and takes the form of a grid setting out project objectives, purposes, indicators, and assumptions.

REFERENCES

Appadurai, A. 2001. 'Deep Democracy: Urban Governmentality and the Horizon of Politics', *Environment and Urbanization*, 13(2): 23–43.

Archer, R. 1994. 'Markets and Good Government', in A. Clayton (ed.), *Governance, Democracy and Conditionality: What Role for NGOs?*, pp. 7–34. Oxford: International NGO Research and Training Centre (INTRAC).

Ashman, D. 1997. 'The Democracy Awareness Education Program of the Association of Development Agencies in Bangladesh (ADAB)', *Discourse: A Journal of Policy Studies*. Dhaka: Institute for Development Policy Analysis and Advocacy (IDPAA), Proshika.

Beall, J. 2005. *Local Funds for Local Governance*. London: ITDG Publications.

Blair, H. 2005. 'Civil Society and Propoor Initiatives in Rural Bangladesh: Finding a Workable Strategy', *World Development*, 33(6): 921–36.

Devine, J. 2002. 'Ethnography of a Policy Process: A Case Study of Land Redistribution in Bangladesh', *Public Administration and Development*, 22(5): 403–14.

DFID. 2000. *Partners in Development: A Review of Big NGOs in Bangladesh*. Dhaka: UK Department for International Development (DFID).

Etzioni, A. 1961. *A Comparative Analysis of Complex Organizations: On Power, Involvement and their Correlates*. New York: The Free Press of Glencoe.

Fisher, W.F. 1997. 'Doing Good? The Politics and Anti-politics of NGO Practices', *Annual Review of Anthropology*, 26: 439–64.

Hashemi, S.M. 1995. 'NGO Accountability in Bangladesh: NGOs, State and Donors', in M. Edwards and D. Hulme (eds), *NGO Performance and Accountability: Beyond the Magic Bullet*, pp. 103–10. London: Earthscan.

Hilhorst, D. 2003. *The Real World of NGOs: Discourses, Diversity and Development*. London: Zed Books.

Hossain, N. 2004. 'The Real-life Relationship between Donors and Recipients in Bangladesh: Exploratory Research into the Sociology of Aid Relations'. IDS, mimeo.

Howell, J. and J. Pearce. 2000. 'Civil Society: Technical Instrument or Force for Change?' in D. Lewis and T. Wallace (eds), *New Roles and Relevance: Development NGOs and the Challenge of Change*, pp. 75–88. Hartford: Kumarian Press.

Igoe, J. and T. Kelsall (eds). 2005. *Between a Rock and a Hard Place: African NGOs, Donors and the State*. Durham, NC: Carolina Academic Press.

Kabeer, N. 2003. 'Making Rights Work for the Poor: Nijera Kori and the Construction of "Collective Capabilities" in Rural Bangladesh', IDS Working Paper 200. Brighton: Institute of Development Studies, Sussex. (www.research4development.info)

Kaldor, M. 2003. *Global Civil Society: An Answer to War*. Cambridge: Polity Press.

Karim, L. 2001. 'Politics of the Poor? NGOs and Grassroots Political Mobilisation in Bangladesh', *Political and Legal Anthropology Review (PoLAR)*, 24(1): 92–107.

Kochanek, S. 2003. *Policy Process in Bangladesh*. Dhaka, Bangladesh: UK Department for International Development.

Lewis, D. 2002. 'Civil Society in African Contexts: Reflections on the "Usefulness" of a Concept', *Development and Change*, 33(4): 569–86.

———. 2004. 'On the Difficulty of Studying "Civil Society": Reflections on NGOs, State and Democracy in Bangladesh', *Contributions to Indian Sociology*, 38(3): 299–322.

———. 2005. 'Actors, Ideas and Networks: Trajectories of the Non-governmental in Development Studies', in U. Kothari (ed.), *A Radical History of Development Studies*, pp. 200–21. London: Zed Books.

———. 2008. 'Crossing the Boundaries between 'Third Sector' and State: Life-work Histories from Philippines, Bangladesh and the UK', *Third World Quarterly*, 29(1): 125–42.

Lewis, D. and A. Hossain. 2008. *Understanding the Local Power Structure in Rural Bangladesh*. Sida Studies No. 22, Stockholm: Swedish International Development Agency.

Lewis, D. and B. Sobhan. 1999. 'Routes of Funding, Roots of Trust? Northern NGOs, Southern NGOs, Donors, and the Rise of Direct Funding', *Development in Practice*, 9(1 and 2): 117–29.

Mitchell, T. 2002. *Rule of Experts: Egypt, Techno-politics, Modernity*. Berkeley: University of California Press.

Mosse, D. 2005a. *Cultivating Development: An Ethnography of Aid Policy and Practice*. London: Pluto Press.

———. 2005b. 'Global Governance and the Ethnography of International Aid', in D. Mosse and D. Lewis (eds), *The Aid Effect: Giving and Governing in International Development*, pp. 1–36. London: Pluto Press.

Mosse, D. and D. Lewis. 2006. 'Introduction', in D. Lewis and D. Mosse (eds), *Development Brokers and Translators: The Ethnography of Aid and Agencies*, pp. 1–26. Bloomfield, CT: Kumarian.

Najam, A. 1996. 'Understanding the Third Sector: Revisiting the Prince, the Merchant and the Citizen', *Nonprofit Management and Leadership*, 7(2): 203–19.

Riaz, A. 2003. '"God Willing": The Politics and Ideology of Islamism in Bangladesh', *Comparative Studies of South Asia, Africa and the Middle East*, 23(1–2): 301–20.

Rose, N. and P. Miller. 1992. 'Political Power beyond the State: Problematics of Government', *The British Journal of Sociology*, 43(2): 173–205.

Seabrook, J. 2001. *Freedom Unfinished: Fundamentalism and Popular Resistance in Bangladesh Today*. London: Zed Books.

Siraj, S.M.B. 2004. 'Good Governance as a Policy Agenda in EU Development Assistance: Conditionality and Effectiveness', Paper to European Studies Association (ECSA) Conference, University of Southern Denmark, Odense, 24–25 September.

Smillie, I. and J. Hailey. 2001. *Managing for Change: Leadership, Strategy and Management*. London: Earthscan.

Stiles, K. 2002. 'International Support for NGOs in Bangladesh: Some Unintended Consequences', *World Development*, 30(5): 835–46.

Tvedt, T. 1998. *Angels of Mercy or Development Diplomats? NGOs and Foreign Aid*. Oxford: James Currey.

Wade, R. 1996. 'Japan, the World Bank and the Art of Paradigm Maintenance: The East Asian Miracle in Political Perspective', *New Left Review*, 217: 3–36.

White, S.C. 1999. 'NGOs, Civil Society, and the State in Bangladesh: The Politics of Representing the Poor', *Development and Change*, 30(3): 307–26.

Wuthnow, R. 1991. *Between States and Markets: The Voluntary Sector in Comparative Perspective*. Princeton: Princeton University Press.

Chapter 8

Activists and Development in Nepal

CELAYNE HEATON SHRESTHA

After several months of unrest in Nepal's major urban centres, the 30-year ban on political parties was finally lifted on 8 April 1990 and fundamental rights such as the right to organize were restored.[1] This laid the grounds for the effervescence of non-governmental activity: the number of NGOs soared in the years that followed, growing from a mere 250 in 1989 to over 12,000 NGOs in 2001.[2] For NGO leaders,[3] this growth not only provided the opportunity to realize their aspirations for Nepal, but also served as a boon for the country's nascent multi-party democracy: NGOs would, in one NGO activist's words, "function as a catalyst: as mobilisers, facilitators, analysts, and advocates of the people" (Tuladhar, 1991, quoted in Rademacher and Tamang, 1993: 21). Reportedly, during this early period, "a plethora of literature was churned out by members of the NGO sector, asserting that NGOs are central to both the process of democratization and to the effective working of any established democracy" (Rademacher and Tamang, 1993: 21). A decade later, NGO leaders still saw an important political role for NGOs, classifying these mostly development-oriented organizations on a par with trade unions and human rights organizations (e.g. Chand, 2000; Dahal, 2001). Not everyone shared this conviction, however. Giving vent to a wide-spread sentiment regarding NGOs, Chintan Siwakoti, a lawyer and human rights activist, wrote:

> Campaigns and movements [that existed before 1990] ... have been converted into NGOs. Their attitude and working style has been dominated by NGO culture. Their activities cannot be sustained without foreign funds. Even people with a good track record and political commitment such as intellectuals and academics have become

> part of NGOism leading to a great loss for the nation. Moreover, NGO culture is giving birth to a new and highly luxurious and corrupt class of people. It is diverting the strength of youth away from socio-political and anti-imperialist movements. The people who could be the leaders in these movements are running away with excuses of political corruption, poverty and unemployment. They have been smart enough to define NGOs as parallel to social work and that NGOs offer them name, fame, wealth, and even political gain. This has been spreading all over the country as a chronic disease. The process of mushrooming of NGOs as well as their death is also rampant. ('Chintan' Siwakoti, 2000: 136)

Many (including some donors) saw in NGOs little more than 'service-delivery organizations', a part of the private sector rather than the space of civil society (e.g. Gyawali, 2001); while ethnic activists and feminist activists were reportedly keeping their distance from these organizations described by one scholar and activist as an 'infection' (Bhattachan, 2000: 76). A Nepali activist expressed surprise at the inclusion of a paper on NGOs in a workshop on activism in South Asia: "They are service-delivery organizations, not activists," he objected. Although NGO leaders in Nepal would express some difficulty in identifying with certain elements of the description of 'activist' (as defined by Gellner and Karki, Chapter 5, p. 136)—in particular, with the political, oppositional character of activism[4]—there is no doubt that many NGO leaders in Nepal would recognize in themselves some other elements of the definition. Specifically, they would not dispute that they belong to an organization whose ends are non-economic, public, and which aim to change some aspect of the world. The same applies to some (albeit not all) staff employed by these organizations.

These contrary perspectives on NGO activity indicate that 'activism' is just as contested and contentious a term as 'civil society'. They also raise a series of questions concerning the nature of relations between political, ethnic, and feminist activists and NGOs, and about the complex relation between movements and NGOs (broached by Fisher, 1997 and this volume), as well as on the effects of professionalization on activists (Hulme and Edwards, 1997), including the 'blunting' of radicalism. Furthermore, questions regarding the meaning of NGO activity arise, on how it is positioned in relation to the spheres of the market on the one hand, and of government and politics on the other; and how NGOs negotiate these boundaries. Elsewhere (Heaton Shrestha, 2002), I have explored the ways in which 'elite' NGOs in the 1990s defined themselves against 'the market', or the private, for-profit sector. The aim of this chapter is to contribute ethnographically to an understanding of the way in which NGO workers negotiate the boundary between the spheres of government and politics, on the one hand, and the 'third sector' of non-state or not-for-profit actors, on the other.

I use material from ethnographic work on NGOs in Nepal carried out in the 1990s (1996–97), and from interviews with government officials in various positions within the state apparatus. I describe the attempts of NGOs to emerge as a sector distinct from the sphere of power and politics, and their enduring imbrication with this sphere, both socially and culturally. Socially, because of the close ties, professional and familial, of senior NGO personnel with members of the state elite;[5] and culturally, as the social background and experience of many NGO workers in the public sector continues to inform these agencies' and their staff's modes of working and orientations.

This is set against a background of considerable political turmoil, a time of 'disintegration', brought about by the loss of a legitimate central ultimate power following the revolution of 1990 (Lecomte-Tilouine and Dollfus, 2003). The chapter documents, also, the considerable uncertainties and doubts in this period surrounding *(a)* NGO–GO relations,[6] *(b)* GOs' own power and authority, *(c)* the proffered GO benevolence and desire to include NGOs in the national development process, and *(d)* the capacity of the highly politicized post-1990 state to work constructively with the NGO sector.

The third section of the chapter explores the continuities and discontinuities between NGOs' visions and programmes and those of the state. It is shown that NGOs programmatically differ very little from the state, appropriating many of the development themes and priorities of the latter. However, they have introduced changes in how these are put into practice, drawing heavily on the resources of, and connections within, international agencies, as well as their experience within international development settings.

Finally, it considers the relation of NGOs to political parties, which is, too, characterized by the ambivalence noted in NGO–GO relations: a realization of the real material benefits that can accrue to both NGO and political parties from this relationship, but also the symbolic costs to NGOs, in terms of the latter's credibility and the quality of their relations with project beneficiaries. The concluding part of the chapter returns to the issue of 'activism' and the implications of the ethnographic data presented here for our understanding of this domain of activity.

But, first, we take a brief look at these organizations, their characteristics and objectives.

NON-GOVERNMENTAL ORGANIZATIONS IN NEPAL: OFFICIAL DEFINITIONS AND CHARACTERISTICS

> When I was at university, I used to write. Welfare for humanity, social concern, all those were really there... I thought of setting up a consultancy firm, but my wife said I could always do my own business, but a greater challenge would be to start an NGO... a consultancy firm is like a shop, it's only to earn money. People can get money from any source, but not a reputation (*nam*). (NGO founder)

> I don't want to live in a country where half the population is backward. (NGO Junior Technical Assistant, explaining his enthusiasm for teaching women's literacy classes)

Officially, three main criteria distinguish NGOs from other types of non-state organizations: according to the main act regulating NGOs, the SWC (Social Welfare Council) Act 1992, NGOs are non-profit, non-political organizations, founded for the purpose of carrying out social service (*seva*) and to "improve the economic and social capacities of society's backward groups". Their legal existence depends on a 'three window' registration and approval process: they are required to register, first of all, with the Chief District Officer (CDO) of the District Administration Office in the district in which their central office is situated. Then, those organizations seeking foreign funding are required to register with the SWC. The SWC is a semi-governmental body with representation from the NGO sector based in Kathmandu, in the Ministry for Women and Social Welfare. Affiliation with the SWC is only compulsory for NGOs seeking foreign financial support. SWC affiliation also allows for tax exemption on equipment imported for projects, visas for foreign nationals to work with the NGO, government funding for NGO projects, and training in subjects such as project formulation, account keeping, orientation on NGO formation, and management. Finally, NGOs are required to seek approval for their individual projects from relevant line ministries and the National Planning

Commission (NPC); these are then forwarded to the Ministry of Finance and copied to the SWC. The NPC, based in Singha Durbar in Kathmandu, is in charge of the design and implementation of Nepal's development plans. It gives direction to government policy towards the non-governmental sector, and, together with line ministries, the NPC is responsible for ensuring the compatibility of NGO activities with government policies.

At sub-regional level, another GO with a stake in NGO activity is the Village Development Committee (VDC), the smallest of local government bodies. The two main functions of this elected body are to implement development plans formulated in consultation with the NPC (National Planning Commission in Kathmandu) and settle local disputes. The VDC Act of 1991 envisages that VDCs will *(a)* encourage NGOs to identify, plan, operate, monitor, maintain, and evaluate the programmes within their given area; *(b)* implement their projects through NGOs; and *(c)* procure resources for NGOs to run projects. NGOs, in turn, are expected to 'coordinate' with the VDCs and submit their detailed project proposals to VDCs.

In practice, the types of organizations covered by the label 'NGO' varied tremendously. Some were no more than 'pocket NGOs' while others were multi-sited organizations employing hundreds of workers. The NGOs of which I write in this chapter are what have been termed 'national NGOs'. By this was meant middle-class, 'non-membership' organizations, very often with their central office (CO) in Kathmandu and field offices (FO) and projects in several districts across the country. They were few in number but exerted considerable influence on the sector[7] and a vast majority were dependent financially on foreign donors. Unlike 'local' NGOs, very few national NGOs generated resources internally. Riddell, in a 1994 report, placed the percentage of foreign funds in the overall NGO budget at 88 per cent, and the contributions from local and governmental sources at 8 and 4 per cent respectively (Riddell, 1994: 10). There was little to indicate that the situation was any different in 1996/97.

While small NGOs would often be manned solely by volunteers, this was not the case for larger, national NGOs. In the latter, only the board of directors and members of the organizations' general assembly were unremunerated for their work with the organizations. Besides giving their time voluntarily, board members in the NGOs in this research would, not uncommonly, make material or financial contributions to the organization. In this case, board members would commonly make a living from employment in GOs or as consultants to INGOs and multilateral agencies such as Food and Agriculture Organization (FAO) or United Nations Development Programme (UNDP). The majority of female board members were unsalaried, working as housewives. Neither salaried nor unsalaried board members were engaged full time in the NGO's affairs. Day-to-day operations, on the other hand, would be run by a core of well-paid permanent staff and, at the field level, a number of fieldworkers on fixed-term contracts. FO staff were frequently assisted by a range of locally recruited 'paid volunteers', so called because of their very low rates of pay, such as Non-formal Education Facilitators or Community Health Volunteers. Generally, wages for these volunteers ranged from Rs 250 to Rs 450 in the NGOs studied, while staff salaries ranged from Rs 1,600 for an office messenger to Rs 6,000 or even Rs 8,000 for a technician, and up to Rs 20,000 for a field coordinator.[8] This does not impugn an NGO's non-profit status in the eyes of the law, since, according to the SWC Act 1992, it is sufficient for the board members to work without receiving a salary from the organization for it to be 'non-profit'. It did, however, put into question its non-profit status in the eyes of the general public, many of whom felt that the symbolic rewards of heading an NGO (increase in reputation; distribution of patronage) meant that NGO activity hardly qualified as 'disinterested' (see Heaton Shrestha, 2002).

The formal objectives of these NGOs were mostly developmental; very few were involved in advocacy alone or even primarily.[9] In keeping with international development priorities, NGOs in the study stressed the development and strengthening of 'civil society' and included non-formal education, microfinance, and the promotion of income-generating activities and various construction activities (drinking and irrigation water tanks and pipelines, latrine construction) as the means to this end. Alongside these official objectives, day-to-day NGO activity at field level followed a strong social reformist agenda. Staff saw their contribution to local development as lying in their role as educators: they would seek to improve people's 'habits and behaviour', imparting basic literacy and numeracy skills, as well as 'good habits' such as thrift and cleanliness. In project areas, gambling or alcohol drinking, and the suspected ill-treatment of women were the object of fieldworkers' reprimand. Further, and in keeping with NGO values of openness and non-discrimination, as well as with the new 'gender' agenda in development, and a conviction—internalized over decades of development education—that caste was 'anti-developmental' (see Pigg, 1992; Tuladhar, 1994), many fieldworkers actively sought to question local caste and gender practices. They castigated beneficiaries for their religious orthodoxy and sought to break caste norms of commensality. They would, for example, ridicule the custom of not farming chickens near temples for fear of angering deities; they would also forcibly obtain food from low castes, or enter by ruse kitchens from which their own caste status would have barred them. Male staff would verbally challenge beneficiary men's strict control over women's movements, insisting on women's attendance at project events. Male and female fieldworkers would walk to the field together and eat together, in deliberate defiance of local practices of gender segregation.

These activities were not dissimilar from those of caste reform movements in India and Nepal, such as the Arya Samaj,[10] or welfare organizations which define their role as the upliftment of particular castes or ethnic groups (such as the Tharu Kalyan Karini Sabha described by Krauskopff, 2003), and whose goals included the spread of education, the abolition of seclusion of women, the reduction of expenditures (e.g. lavish wedding parties or dowries, gambling), dancing, and drinking. This 'unofficial' programme was similar, too, to the kinds of activities sponsored by the state in the 1970s through a kind of youth civic service, the National Development Service (NDS). Under the NDS, launched in 1974, all postgraduate students at Tribhuvan University were required to spend one year in service in a rural community, teaching in the village school, and taking part in development work. Volunteer activities included campaigns against usury, child marriage, bonded labour, drinking, and gambling, among other 'social evils'.[11] We will return to continuities with governmental practice in the following. For now, it suffices to note that the intention to bring about social change was present as a motivation for NGO activity, even if it existed alongside motives of a personal, economic nature or, as the opening quote by the founder of a national NGO suggested, of a symbolic nature.

SOCIAL BACKGROUND OF NGO WORKERS AND RELATIONS WITH THE STATE ELITE[12]

As has been noted for intermediary NGOs in other parts of the world (Arellano-Lopez and Petras, 1994; Carroll, 1992), NGOs in Nepal have drawn most of their staff from the middle classes—or, at least, the majority of their 'core' staff and a number of fieldworkers (Heaton Shrestha, 2002, 2004).[13] This middle class, whose members also tend to be of high-caste status and urban origins, has largely grown with the influx of aid and the development industry (Seddon, 1987). It has been stimulated by the increased educational and employment opportunities in the bureaucracy, funded by foreign aid during the years of Panchayat democracy (Blaikie et al., 1980) as well as the rapidly proliferating private consultancy firms providing services to international donor agencies from the mid 1980s. Their predominance among the personnel of development NGOs is, therefore, hardly surprising. Their involvement with the development industry has allowed them to build the contacts and familiarity with the language and modus operandi of international development that are key to the successful establishment and running of an NGO.

Dr Sharma,[14] the founder of a national NGO, was not untypical. By then in his mid forties, he was born in a hill district north of Kathmandu. He studied in the Tarai from class eight. He was trained in agriculture in India to bachelor degree level with the support of an international scholarship. Back in Nepal, he went on to work in various GOs, first in the Tarai and then the hills, for the best part of 10 years. This was followed by a nomination to study abroad and four years of studying which resulted in him being awarded a PhD. He rejoined government services, but this time began 'moonlighting', taking on various consultancy jobs on projects funded by foreign government agencies and international foundations while on leave from his government post. He soon became dissatisfied with this arrangement and, in the early 1990s, finally quit his government job and began working as a consultant to the international sector on a full-time basis. It is during this period, he recalled, that the idea of founding an NGO first occurred to him. Eventually, with the support of friends, his own resources, and research contracts, he finally established his own NGO. Through his career Dr Sharma has become part of a transnational network of relations that is continuing to benefit the NGO: indeed, many of the donors funding the NGO's projects were at first employers of the founder himself.[15]

The early professional training of senior NGO staff and founders among the corps of 'modern bureaucrats' that emerged during the years of Panchayat democracy, also proved a valuable asset for NGOs. Mr Dhungana, a member of the general assembly of the same NGO, worked in a relatively elevated position in a government department. He described his relation with the NGO as one of mutual benefit: he was called upon by the NGO to provide expert opinion on specific matters, while he was able to glean ideas from the NGO's work and feed these back into his department's work in technology development. Another general assembly member, working at the time of research in a private consultancy firm, also used to work in the same department. He explained that the main benefit of this experience was that it had given him an insight into governmental procedures and modes of working, and this had, in turn, facilitated negotiations with government officials at different levels:

> I realize that it [working in government] has given me some sort of exposure that was very valuable for my career as well, having known how the government system works. For example, you know what people are there, most of your friends are there—not in terms of influencing them in other activities, but at least you know how that bureaucracy works and within that, how you fit in our activities given these norms and everything.

But NGOs were not, of course, socially homogeneous. There was, in particular, a marked difference between field staff and 'core' or CO staff in terms of their educational and occupational histories, their area of origin, and their ethnicity. For the most part, 'core staff' belonged to the urban middle classes and field staff to well-to-do rural families.[16]

Raju was a fieldworker in the same NGO. His curriculum vitae read rather differently. At the time of research, Raju was around 30 years old. His early school years were spent in his home village in the hills of the mid-western region. After class 7, he left for a larger city, where he studied until class 10, and obtained his School Leaving Certificate. He returned to his village, and taught in his school village for one and a half years, at first without pay, and then for the sum of Rs 1,200 per month. He described his teaching stint as a period of "volunteer service in village" (sic). He then returned to full-time education, moving to Kathmandu to study geography, economics, and Nepali at college. He obtained a BA in the same college in geography and economics, and then a Master's degree from Tribhuvan University. The next 18 months were spent working as a research assistant in a private research organization in Kathmandu and were followed by yet another bout of studying, this time for a Bachelors in Education. His intention then was to become a headmaster or teacher at a higher secondary school. He did not, however, complete the course: always on the lookout for job openings, he had decided to drop by NGO Z's CO and enquire about possible vacancies. He left his C.V. and was called for a meeting with the organization's president. He was formally appointed as field officer a few days later, and decided to defer his studies.

Unlike Raju, most of the CO staff were Kathmandu residents. Some had themselves migrated to Kathmandu, others were the children of migrants from districts in the central and eastern regions. FO staff, on the other hand, came from very different areas, mostly rural, from the eastern Tarai to the far-western hills. CO staff tended to be drawn from higher-status castes, while at the FO level, 'local' or 'ethnic' staff was given preference. FO staff had also studied in less prestigious institutions than CO staff: their formal education usually began in local schools, and was followed by a period of study in one of the various government institutes (Institute of Engineering, Institute of Forestry, Institute of Agriculture), Kathmandu's Tribhuvan University, or one of the technical schools run by the CTEVT.[17] None had attended, like many CO staff, exclusive Kathmandu schools such as St Mary's or St Xavier's, nor establishments of higher education abroad. Field and core staff also differed in terms of their occupational history. Field staff spent much of their time either unemployed, or engaged in teaching in local private and state schools. The staff of the national NGOs in the study had entered the NGO either straight after finishing their studies, or while studying part-time, or had worked on projects in government and NGOs, international and national, usually as fieldworkers (rather than consultants as was the case with senior staff). Unlike CO staff, many FO staff had practised agriculture, although none had done so as their primary occupation. Rather, FO staff who had not been able to secure work in GOs or NGO projects in their home area, nor migrated in search of work, had for the most part held teaching jobs in local schools. Most staff had come from families with a history of government work or were former *jamindar*s (landlords) in Nepal's Tarai districts.

The staff of FOs and COs also displayed significant disparities along gender lines. Women were most likely to gain employment where the job was marked as 'women's work'. In gender-unmarked jobs, men were generally given preference over women, and official explanations were couched in terms of the lower educational achievements of women. Men, on the other hand, were either poorly represented or not represented at all among women development assistants (WDAs), nurses, assistant nurse midwife (ANMs), receptionists, and secretaries. Women staff made up a minority of the total number of employees, from around one-third to one-eighth in the NGOs in the study, and were generally found in field positions.

There was also an interesting contrast between the backgrounds of the young NGO employees and the more senior ones. We saw earlier that many senior members of staff had once been government employees; in all likelihood, they had also been socially similar to other GO staff.[18] On the other hand, while some of the junior staff had had some experience of work in GOs—some were actually permanent government employees on leave from their government jobs—the profile of the younger staff was rather different from that of their counterparts within GOs. They differed principally in terms of the subject area of their studies: many NGO employees are qualified in 'modern subjects' such as zoology or microbiology and environmental science; the government sector, on the other hand, has long privileged qualifications in subjects such as commerce or administration. Many of the younger staff, moreover, could not conceive of themselves as working within the governmental sector. Shraddha, a member of CO staff, was taken aback by my question over her choice of sector of employment: "I never thought about it! It was just expected that I would work with an NGO or INGO". Another member of staff explained, after a similar reaction, his choice: "The NGO sector is modern; in government everything is delayed; and people who think broadly go outside of Nepal". The Nepali NGO sector was increasingly seen as a viable source of employment and career option by young middle-class people: indeed, in the early to the mid-1990s, the private community and social services sectors had one of the fastest growing labour forces (Guru-Gharana, 1996).

This rootedness in and movement away from the state noted here in sociological terms was also to be found culturally in NGOs and GOs. In the next section, we consider the continuities and discontinuities of NGO and governmental development practice.

RE-APPROPRIATING DEVELOPMENT: CONTINUITIES AND DISCONTINUITIES IN GO AND NGO PRACTICE

> We three women wanted to do something for our community to do with waste disposal ... difficult because we didn't have any authority; it got easier after we got the backing of [NGO X] because we were able to say "we are an organization". We arranged for drums to be placed every few houses and someone to collect rubbish from there.... We did it for our *nam*, for the feeling of pride, being able to say 'we housewives have done something'. We got students and women sitting at home out of their houses and got them to do something, we formed this organization. (Kripa, NGO board member)

> Working in government, I had this conviction that "we can do better". (Ram, NGO founder)

From her early experience with a project to manage waste in her neighbourhood, Kripa went on to become a member of the board of a national NGO. For her, like Ram, this involvement with an NGO was born out of a desire to take 'development' in her own hands and the view, not uncommon among Nepal's intellectual and professional classes, that the state had largely failed to better the lot of people in Nepal. The unequal nature of state-led development was also a matter of concern, leaving swathes of the country 'backward' (e.g. Guru-Gharana, 2000; B.K. Shrestha, 2001). Some have attributed the failure of governmental attempts to reach these groups to the attitude of officials towards the rural poor.[19]

NGO workers recounted numerous instances of government workers' reluctance to leave their headquarters, requiring, instead, that beneficiaries call upon them; or of government offices left empty as a result of their incumbents being busy lobbying the central administration for a transfer to an urban or peri-urban post. Nor was the following scenario, recounted by beneficiaries in one of the projects in the study, atypical: although many low castes (men and women) had worked as labourers on governmental construction projects, not a single government official had ever set foot in their ward. "*Sarkar* (the state or government) does not see us; does not touch ward number 3", they commented. What's more, their letters to the district headquarters requesting the installation of water stands and electricity had never been answered.

More charitably, an NGO leader and former government official explained that this was due to the limited resources at the disposal of GOs:

> Service and sub-service centres have been provided but not well managed. Governmental services are only available at a certain place or a certain time, so only people who are conscious or with political connections can access these services.

Dahal (2001) and B.K. Shrestha (2001) concur, putting the lack of impact down to a weak institutional capacity and limited resources, and also pointing to the deleterious effects of corruption within the state system, specifically, the use of personal connections to access state resources.[20] Some have argued for development alternatives: for instance, Bhattachan (2000) has called for a development model that acknowledges the relationship between ethnicity and (lack of) development. On the whole, however, NGOs have not sought to propose an alternative to the paradigm that has informed state-led development activity. Rather, they have adopted many of the models and the language of government. The way they have embraced the notion of *seva* is a case in point. *Seva* has a long history in governmental discourse where it has been associated with the idea of 'nation-building', of *deshprem* or 'love of the country' (Adhikari, 1996). Until 1990, as Burghart (1994) observed, *seva* was very much the preserve of the state. The public could only legitimately engage in *seva* as individuals; political and other interest groups were not seen as having a legitimate part to play in the process and attempts to engage in public acts of *seva* by such groups were invariably repressed (Burghart, 1994). Now, like the state and erstwhile Panchayat leaders (Ramirez, 2000), NGOs were claiming to be serving people across the country.

Similarly, in adopting the language of 'participation' and 'people-centred' development, NGOs did not depart from governmental praxis. Indeed, the idea of grassroots participation in development had long been employed by the state: Panchayat democracy itself was officially defined as a 'grassroots' or 'village' democracy. Nepal's Small Farmers' Development Programme (SFDP), a governmental programme that has been hailed as one of the best models in participatory rural development in Asia, was launched in 1976. The language of 'mass participation' in development activities already featured prominently in the 6th Five Year Plan of the early 1980s.

But if NGOs were taking on these models of development seemingly uncritically, they were also calling for a profound transformation at the level of practice. They are, in other words, challenging not so much the model of development that has informed development interventions in the 1980s, but the ways in which the models were put into practice.

> NGOs and GOs have a different attitude: what sort of orientation you have, *are you really interested in working with people.* (NGO board member)

NGOs have sought to transform practice, first of all by replacing the field at the centre of their work. In most aspects of organizational practice and in their identity as development organizations, 'the field' occupied a central and elevated place. In terms of day-to-day practice, re-committing to the field meant organizing NGO work around the tempo and rhythms of the field: setting the date and time for monthly meetings by beneficiaries' schedules; travelling on foot, rather than in an air-conditioned 4×4, as many INGO employees do; spending more time in individual sites; having more contact with beneficiaries, including the low-caste and non-caste groups than government workers; seeking to engage with, and even seeking out, the most recalcitrant members of the rural population, from whom government workers (purportedly) remained aloof. For staff in the CO, it meant also setting their visits to FOs by fieldworkers' schedules. Repositioning the field at the centre of NGO praxis has also required a re-valuation of fieldwork by acknowledging its demands and complexity. Both managers and fieldworkers recognized the existence of skills and competencies particular to fieldwork—although most were as yet uncodified and did not form part of an explicit body of teaching. Training in 'fieldwork skills' was limited to PRA or gender-in-development training. Other competencies, such as knowing how to talk, how to convince or 'mobilize' people, and how to negotiate the physical terrain of the field, were rather inculcated through prolonged field presence and the teachings of other members of staff and local people. To be sure, not all NGO members were enthusiastic participants in this overhaul of development practice. Unofficially, FOs were seen as less enviable places of work and—some fieldworkers hoped—only a temporary phase in their progression towards desk jobs. The profile of staff also indicated that the hierarchies of field/office and rural/urban continued to inform non-governmental practice. Still, their role as 'specialist organizations', brokers between rural Nepal and those urban dwellers—whether Nepali (such as students wishing to do some field research for their dissertations) or foreigner (including actual or potential donors)—who lacked the social connections and the *savoir faire* that would give them access to rural areas and populations, was guarded jealously.

This new way of practising development was also to be realized through the professionalization of development work. This involved levels of incentives and rewards sufficient to ensure quality of service. Management claimed high wages were necessary in order to attract competent, qualified staff and prevent them from looking for 'other opportunities' to make ends meet while carrying out the NGO's work—as was the case for staff in GOs. Professionalism also involved developing the systematization and efficiency seen to be lacking in GOs. For many of the more senior staff, moving into the non-governmental sector had been prompted by what they perceived to be the shortcomings of work in GOs: its proceduralism, the practice of promotion via political connections, and the paucity of opportunities for training, compounded by a general 'disinterest in learning'. Governmental services and the work environment in GOs, NGO staff expressed, was plagued by "hypocrisy", "a sense of wasting your time", and a "lack of discipline".

> I got involved in the beginning with [NGO X] mostly out of a concern for my own professional development ... there are limitations within government for professional advancement; government norms mean one is in a certain position and you are constrained within that limit working in government. (A senior member of the NGO)

Hulme and Edwards (1997) have deplored the increasing managerialism of NGOs and the fact that

> a little under ten years ago, Charles Eliott ... wrote of NGO personnel informed by Freire and Alinsky: talk with field managers nowadays and you are much less likely to hear of ideas of mobilising the poor. North American management gurus such as Stephen Covey and Peters and Waterman are more likely sources of inspiration, despite the fact that their writings are more about making profits and organizational survival. (Hulme and Edwards, 1997: 280)

But for staff, and even junior staff whose experience of government would have been as consumers of its services alone, the NGO's systematization—its planning and reporting procedures, the hierarchical organizational structure, the job descriptions, the deadlines and strict time-management—did not represent a corruption of their values and modes of working. On the contrary, it constituted an opportunity to realize their aspirations, whether it is related to their personal development or that of the broader society. What's more, as far as NGO leaders were concerned, this professionalism and their commitment to 'the field' were not contradictory but actually reinforced one another. As one NGO director explained:

> [Going to the field] adds to our professional ability ... by going to the field we get exposed to tools and our writing ability can be developed, skills can be refined ... with regular work, they do not.

The response of GOs to the arrival of these new development players, which both questioned and affirmed, as they took forward, the state's programme, was ambivalent. It is to these complex relations that we now turn.

THE UNCERTAINTY OF THE NGO–GO BALANCE OF POWER

During the 30 years preceding 1990, non-governmental activity in Nepal had been relatively muted, a function, primarily, of the strict control the Panchayat regime sought to exercise over public life. Under this system of 'guided democracy', introduced by King Mahendra in 1960, all political parties were banned, and any formal organization independent of the state was regarded with suspicion by the authorities. With the Organization and Associations (Control) Act of 1962, the state sought to ensure that no organization would be set up without the prior authorization of the government. The Act principally targeted political parties, but also resulted in the dissolution of all organizations capable of competing with official organizations, and of all organizations with objectives that could be regarded as political, such as peasant and workers' unions and other non-governmental students' and women's associations. The bureaucratic trammels imposed by the Social Service National Coordination Council (SSNCC), established in 1977, further discouraged non-governmental initiatives, as well as ensured tight surveillance of their activities. The few organizations with a more public remit that operated openly during this period were generally those blessed with official connections and patronage. Among these were a number of government-organized NGOs (GONGOs), such as the Nepal Family Planning Association (NFPA) set up in 1959, the Nepal Red Cross Society in 1960, and the Nepal Children's Organization founded in 1964. After 1990, GO attitudes towards NGOs changed radically. In June 1992, Prime Minister Koirala sought to reassure social workers, whom 30 years of strict governmental control had rendered wary of the state, that:

> The government does not wish to control the functioning of social organizations; rather it wishes to encourage them. However, it does wish to acquire information regarding their works [sic]. (quoted in Rademacher and Tamang, 1993: 21)

The legal framework was considerably liberalized and, for the first time, the contribution of NGOs to national development was acknowledged—even sought—in the national Five Year Plan:

> Considering the fact that NGOs and community organizations have been effectively involved in rural development over the past several years, such organizations will be involved in development activities to the maximum possible extent during the eighth plan. For this purpose, the government will remove obstacles presently facing these organizations and support policies ... laws and regulations concerning the regulation and structure of NGOs will be simplified while legal provisions relating to taxation will be improved to make them capable of better mobilising internal resources. In order to understand their difficulties and provide necessary back up, communication and contacts will be enhanced among the NGOs. NGOs will be granted full autonomy to work in areas accorded priority by the government. (8th Five Year Plan (1992–97), NPC, July 1991)

The desire for a new relationship was also evident in the sensitivity, expressed by GOs in interviews conducted in 1996 and 1997, towards NGO claims of excessive control and interference in NGO affairs:

> They [NGOs] will say that there's too much control from government, but they are *so* free, they can do whatever they like, the only thing is that if they want to take foreign loan, or involve with INGOs, they have to go to the SWC and ask permission and also... the minister of finance and concerned ministry ... that is the simplest thing! (senior staff, National Planning Commission)

The response of GOs to the changes was mixed: there was, in all of the interviews with GO representatives, a certain feeling of disempowerment in relation to the NGO sector, a loss of authority, and a difficulty in controlling a body of organizations felt to have become 'arrogant'.

> The SWC ... should be in a position to *say* to the NGO ... why haven't you given your report on time, or why haven't you adhered to the format which we gave you. Even the SWC is not doing its job properly ... maybe because it's a transitional period, we are having our democracy, and it is very new, and so many NGOs, they are interpreting it like they do not need to give it regularly, [thinking] "We don't need to report, we are independent, why should we be under one umbrella?"... before democracy they would think that this was a strong regulatory body, a controlling ... because ... the head of this institution was the Queen ... now it's under the Ministry so they don't take it as seriously. (Giri, senior staff, SWC)[21]

At local (village and district) levels, the same sentiments were expressed by government officials:

> No NGO or INGO has so far put a link with the VDC.... [T]hey just do their own work ...We should not allow NGOs ... to work in the VDC if they don't put a link with us. ... [INGO A], [NGO B] have been here. [NGO B] has finished its work and gone. We can't say how much benefit the local community has obtained because these organizations don't put a link with us. [They] don't tell us how many have taken part, in what project, and so we have no idea ... they say "we did this" but I have been there and not seen anything.... (Mr Bhattarai, VDC chairperson)

> NGOs do not come to the meetings, only two or three NGOs turn up. ... We've asked for reports ... [but] we don't get reports. Only the CDO has a control mechanism over NGOs and that is to cancel their registration. This has never occurred in this district to my knowledge. NGOs submit audit and reports to the CDO, but we don't find out about these ... we even have no idea what the programme budget is—not overheads and admin—but if an NGO is giving tubewells we should know too so that we don't give in the same area. ... NGOs are becoming a parallel government. The DDC has a control mechanism by the Ministry of Finance, but NGOs have none. Before 1990, there was an SSNCC and NGOs *had* to tell it what their budget was, and the Ministry would tell the district of the programme budget. Now NGOs may have told the Ministry, but the latter doesn't report to us at district level, so we don't know. (Mrs Dahal, Local Development Officer, district Z)

NGO leaders saw the situation somewhat differently, namely, as a failure of the state in its responsibilities towards NGOs:

> There is such a bias against NGOs that ... when you talk about the development need, when they [GOs] hold a development meeting they make it a point that the NGOs are not called, even if they are physically present, they are not called in developmental discussions.... They say "We don't know what you are doing." I said *you* are to be blamed. When I do my registration with the CDO office, he has every right to ask what I'm doing ... just one page database could be developed ... incorporated in the registration procedure and just request them to fill that form ... so if you can't monitor the activities of 15 NGOs, if you remain arrogant yourself, saying "You come and see us, we should not go to them," then who is to be blamed? ... if I pollute ... the environment and the department of industry doesn't know about it, *I* am not to be blamed only! (Hari, NGO leader)

> The SWC is not doing its job; it's supposed to coordinate, but it's not coordinating ... it should know which NGO is working where, so that it can tell other NGOs not to go, so as to avoid duplication. (Anita, NGO director)

The loss of authority was attributed by many to the recent political changes, change in leadership of various institutions, a weakening of the means of coercion at their disposal, and the fragmentation of the state system.

> HMG is not very clear ... in the Eighth Five Year Plan, there is mention of NGOs but nowhere of the SWC. I drafted and sent a paper to the NPC, the plan came out and nothing! [there was no mention of his contribution]. HMG is institutionally biased [towards particular institutions] ... because now [the chairperson] is a minister and ministers are political animals ... HMG doesn't give attention to the infrastructure needed to coordinate activities within the SWC ... and there hasn't been an increase in the budget in 6 years! (Mr Shrestha, senior staff, SWC)

Similarly:

> The SWC has not been able to perform as expected...[because of] recent political changes and because there are a lot of people with vested interests.... (Kamal, senior staff, SWC)

The 'neglect' from central government was attributed, in part, to the 'politicization' of the state apparatus, and to the transfers of senior personnel and their staff that would normally result from a change in government. Kamal further clarified that, like other GOs, the SWC had become "a hotbed for political parties to recruit their own personnel". Among the staff of the NGOs in the study were several individuals who had left government service fearing that they would be appointed elsewhere with the next change of government.[22]

The loss of authority may also have had its source in the greater resources, material and symbolic (development knowledge, foreign contacts), at the disposal of NGOs. This was clearly a source of tension between GO and NGO workers, and, according to Mayhew (2005: 741), also perceived by GOs as a threat. In a four-country study that included Nepal, she found that

> Government officials ... felt frustrated at their comparative weakness and perceived some threat to their hegemony. ... Governments in Bangladesh, Cambodia and Nepal all faced the dilemma of wishing to maintain supremacy over the public sector, but recognising that government alone was not sufficient to provide adequate health services and NGOs were needed to help fill the gap. (Mayhew, 2005: 741)

The relative 'weakness' of local government officials was palpable in trainings organized by NGOs for the benefit of district and village-level government officials in project areas: acting as subordinates, willingly following the instructions of NGO staff. I was struck by this strange reversal of roles, but cannot, unfortunately, comment on the NGOs' nor the government officials' take on these kinds of events. But what is certain is that despite expressions of a desire to cooperate with each other both on the part of GOs and of NGOs, there was a sense, expressed by some government officials, that NGOs were *intruding* on GO remit. Memorably, a senior member of staff at the SWC, interrupting a question about the role of Kathmandu-based NGOs in national development, exclaimed: "Encroaching! They're encroaching on our [i.e. the government's] area!"

Generally, then, political, moral (i.e., tied to a concern about losing legitimacy in the new democratic set-up), as well as logistical factors were undermining the capacity of GOs to work with NGOs. This lack of 'capacity' was not, however, perceived as absolute. Contradicting their own assertions of powerlessness, government officials would occasionally make remarks such as the following:

> This concept of NGOs as parallel institution to the government is slowly being talked over here, even in Kathmandu ... but I don't think that's the right approach. ... NGOs should really understand and appreciate that the government is making an effort in providing them with this opportunity to really work as partner to the government. Because if the government takes out a policy, saying that we'll not let any NGO work, what can the NGO do? Of course that situation won't come, but NGOs should appreciate this.... (senior staff, SWC)[23]

It may be the case that certain NGOs sought to bypass local GOs. One NGO worker claimed: "The programme *can* run without ... a paper [from the VDC], but it's useful in case other organizations come and want to work in that area. The one with the paper can show it and say it has been given the right to work there" (Ram, NGO fieldworker and social worker). This may have been bravado on Ram's part: he was, indeed, later obliged to comply with the very same VDC chairman's demand for a formal letter outlining the organization's purpose, in order to be granted a plot of land on which to build a new FO. On the whole, NGO workers emphasized the need to work with government officials:

> Some NGOs think that the government message is useless, deformed; some workers in NGOs create that kind of antagonism, but we should be cautious not to hurt GOs. The government has laws and rules in their hands and we should work with them, as well as draw on their resources and infrastructure. (Anil, NGO director)

> We need to work with government agencies because the people will respect whichever VDC chief is there in the VDC. People already have a link with government offices, but not NGOs, because there were no NGOs here until recently. (Krishna, NGO fieldworker)

In day-to-day life, NGOs seemed to have much more interaction, and interaction of a much more cordial nature, than the GO characterization of NGOs suggested. NGOs in the study would cultivate relations with GOs at different levels, occasionally receiving ministers at NGO headquarters, or inviting these to NGO conferences; senior management paid courtesy visits to government officials in project areas. NGOs would not infrequently include government officials, and, in one instance, a police post among their beneficiaries.

Courtesy went hand in hand with an enduring suspicion of GOs and the newly established SWC, as noted in the early 1990s by Rademacher and Tamang (1993). Many NGO workers still doubted both the state's benevolence towards, and desire to work with, NGOs.

> [NGOs are a parallel government] on paper, not in reality. When government says this, it's a warning that some NGOs are trying to get out of their control, [and] to become independent. [There are] criticisms of NGOs, [such as] ... they are trying to impose alien values, Christianity, women's empowerment, [and these criticisms are meted out] by GOs to NGOs that are independent, or trying to establish their identity, that want to be heard. (Jeevan, NGO director)

The sense that GO liberalism was a veneer was also expressed by Meena Acharya (2000: 96), a well-known NGO leader, when she stated that the state 'preferred' that NGOs limit themselves to service delivery, rather than take up advocacy roles. Another NGO leader regretted the attitude of a former colleague, still in government service: "[He always says] 'Ramjyu, have you come to talk about NGOs? Please let's not talk about it'. They [GOs] don't even want *to hear* about NGOs".

What stood out from discussions with NGO leaders and government officials was a sense of uncertainty about the extent of power that NGOs, on the one hand, and the state, on the other, had. While NGOs were recognized as significant new players in national life in the 1990s, just how powerful they were was still moot seven years after the restoration of multi-party democracy. GO's loss of authority, fragmentation, and doubts over the willingness and capacity of the state to work with NGOs were also evident. Like NGOs, government officials, many of whom occupied similar positions during the previous regime, were having to adapt to the new democratic set-up, the changed relations between state and citizens, and the redefinition of spheres of government, voluntary activity ('service'), and the realm of private, self-interested activity.

RELATIONS WITH POLITICAL PARTIES AND POLITICIANS

Relations with political parties were equally contradictory. The benefits of being 'associated' with a political figure were widely acknowledged. In the specific case of NGOs, the benefits of being affiliated to a political party or belonging to a given political circle were felt to give privileged access to valuable information, especially concerning sources of funding. An NGO leader explained:

> For example, there is a rural development project to be implemented by some foreign government in Dhankuta: you have that piece of information with you, and this information is shared within the political circle. ... Whosoever is the ruling party that information is given, is shared with the DDC, or DDC shares it with the social worker there. ... What they tell you is OK, you register your NGO and through that NGO the entire delivery process takes place. This has become common in most districts.

The flow of benefits seemed to work the other way, too. Numerous NGO workers told of pressure on the part of politicians on the NGO at various levels, from directors to fieldworkers. One NGO worker recalled his experience on a project in the mid hills:

> At one point a group of Maoists came to the office and said to [the project director] "You will not be able to hire any staff if you don't take them from Gorkha", meaning they were told to recruit staff form the Samyukta Jana Morcha group. [The project director] refused: "We are not a political organization", [he replied], and the next day they came and raided the field office, they tore up papers and broke furniture.

Another benefit for politicians of being affiliated with an NGO was felt to be that they could help secure votes or 'enter the community' where the politician did not have strong links, as for instance in a new area or ethnic group. In one 'ethnic' organization, obtaining membership for persons from another ethnic group required the applicant to donate the sum of Rs 100,000 to the organization. A senior member justified this ruling: "Very few people will do things without benefit, by joining an organization one gets the political benefit of being introduced to the community and speaking with them".

Most NGOs were suspected of being 'politically coloured'. In interviews, NGO directors and workers would readily volunteer information about the political sympathies of other organizations' leaders. This information was gleaned from countless clues: NGO 'slogans', the terminology used in naming the NGO—"*sangathan* is communist; *samiti* is Rastriya Prajatantra Party [RPP], and *sangh* is Nepali Congress [NC]", an NGO worker explained[24]—or family connections with one or the other political figure. Political affiliation can also be deduced, people believe, by observing which party was in power when the individual happened to occupy a post in GO. Some NGO leaders acknowledged the significance of political 'colour' for their own organization:

> The government looks at the political colour of persons and so relationship with government will depend on the colour of the people in the committee [of this NGO]; so what the committee does is get people from the organization with the same colour as the party in power to link between the committee and the government. ... Full time must be devoted to making links, thinking who to meet, what links to make, and how. (Ananda, NGO board member)

However, most NGO leaders denied that political contacts played a significant role for their own organization, and emphasized instead the professional nature of their relations with government officials:

> [The recent elections] do not matter for [our NGO] because...political persons ... are here three months and then there'll be different persons in power. If we follow these persons, we will end up like them. We try to work with the community whether party A or B is in power. (Bikas, NGO director)

> In the committees, [our NGO] does not remove [government officials]: the government persons are kept because they are professionals. They are valued because of their professionalism and because they have clout within the ministry. (Kamal, NGO director)

Rivals were frequently accused of 'politicization'. The costs for NGOs of being identified with a political party were many. Not only did this place the NGO in direct contravention of SWC regulations, the suspicion that an NGO was in some way involved in party politics would mean missing out on project opportunities or compromising the quality of relations with project beneficiaries.

> We had a networking seminar at Himalayan Hotel, about six months back. It so happened that from the floor a question came, and it went: "The present president of [NGO network], we want his identity". The said president was to present a paper and I was to present a paper and I said it would be appropriate for the gentleman to answer for himself.

> And it so happened that he was chairman of the DDC and he was president of the [NGO network], so it was quite embarrassing and I was also not aware of the fact ... if you are chairman of the DDC your priority is definitely towards your political party rather than towards the service of the beneficiary. (Sunil, NGO leader)

Another NGO director recalled:

> We were the members of the executive committee of UNDP; ... at one point there were proposals that we had to assess and evaluate and give our verdict. There was a proposal from the women's organizations of the Congress faction ... and the member secretary of the SWC [a political appointee] who was also member of the committee brought up the proposal. Very vocally I said that if we award the project to the women's organization of the Congress Party, we would be obliged to award a project [also] to the women's organization of the Communist Party, the women's organization of RPP, the women's organization of Sadbhavana. The whole issue became politicized. It's better for us to remain aloof from politics. The project was not awarded.

NGO leaders not only denied their own involvement in party politics, they also expected NGO workers to act accordingly. Wherever the NGO is recognized, I was told,

> [S]taff should not put a link with political persons, nor engage in PP (political practice) which means to advertise for a party, give a speech for that party. Staff can vote, that is their constitutional right, but wherever [this NGO] is not recognized, [the NGO] does not care what PP staff engages in there.

NGO fieldworkers developed public 'avoidance strategies' in a bid to emphasize the non-party political nature of the NGO. At the field level, 'strategies of avoidance' were visibly played out in day-to-day life. Staff refrained from 'talking politics', lest their words be overheard by some local person who might then conclude that the entire organization supported a particular party. In the days running up to elections, avoidance strategies were stepped up: staff would visibly keep away from 'election work' as mere proximity to representatives of one or another party was deemed sufficient for locals to identify the NGO with that party. When they had to hold project meetings in public places, the locus of most political activities, staff would sit away from any gathering comprising known political figures. When invited to join the group and listen while beneficiaries made their way to the project meeting, they would decline, for fear that the politicians "may claim he himself had called them [this NGO]". Project activity slowed down during this period, some staff taking advantage of the lull to take a brief holiday home. "It's not a good idea to form savings groups now, because of the coming election people will extract another meaning, i.e. that [this NGO] is trying to mobilize people politically". Finally, on the day of the election, staff who were still in the project area steered clear of voting booths, observing the proceedings from a hilltop or the office balcony. Several took a trip to another city.

However, while NGO staff were generally encouraged to 'overlook' the political affiliations of beneficiaries by management, it was as important for fieldworkers to know the political affiliation of beneficiaries as it was for managers to know that of other NGO leaders. Indeed, it enabled staff to "know what kind of work they [beneficiaries] will do", whether they would cooperate or not. For instance, during my stay, a water project had come to a halt when the chairman of one VDC had refused to let the water pipe feed water into another VDC, ruled by a different party, across his own VDC. Almost every NGO worker had a similar tale to tell; and, like their managers, they would disparage the political motives of others—just as they kept silent about their own political convictions and connections.

CONCLUSION

This chapter began as a reflection on the activist credentials of NGOs in Nepal. These are, of course, contested: for the most part, by activists whose associational style and approach to social transformation are very different. The public, political relevance of NGO activity was contested on the grounds that the relation of NGOs to the market (their handsome remuneration and well-equipped offices), and to power (their lack of 'radicalism' and oppositional tenor), were too close in the first instance, and too remote on the other. I then took a closer look at the relations of NGOs to the sphere of government, power, and politics, the relations between NGOs and GO actors, and between NGO ideology and culture and that of the state.

It emerged that socially and culturally, in 1996–97, NGOs and GOs shared much; meaning that a view of NGOs as autonomous and independent from the state was untenable (a point made by Lewis, this volume, in relation to Bangladesh). The personal networks of members of national NGOs frequently cut across the 'state–civil society' boundary—to the benefit of both NGOs and the state. In many respects, GO and NGOs differed little in terms of the vision of 'the good life' that guided their work. This state of affairs prevailed for the best part of the decade that followed. However, the Constituent Assembly elections of April 2008, which saw an overwhelming victory for the Communist Party of Nepal-Maoist (CPN-M) and the formation, in August that year, of a coalition government dominated by CPN-M have introduced a wild card in GO–NGO relations. The CPN-M is no longer stridently opposed to NGOs (referred to as "agents of imperialism" in the CPN-M's 40-point demand of February 1996 with which they launched their 'People's War').[25] A recent interview with a central committee member of CPN-M described the party's stance towards NGOs as:

> ...not negative. We said that [referring to item 9 of the 40-point demand] because we are against the corruption that goes on in the name of NGOs and INGOs; resources don't go where they should and certain interests come with INGO/NGOs. We have to distinguish among NGOs, those who are in true spirit, those who come with interests in the name of NGOs. (Interview, Dinanath Sharma, 4 February 2008)

By all accounts, however, to date CPN-M members' personal networks do not—unlike, in particular, CPN-UML—include NGO leaders. Besides bestowing all manner of practical benefits to both party and NGO, these close connections are generally suspected of underpinning the selective response of NGOs to government policies: UML-affiliated NGOs are less likely to oppose government policy when the government is UML-led and contrariwise when the government is led by the Nepali Congress party. Given the lack of such connections between the NGO sector and CPN-M cadres, the question arises of whether we may in future witness a more consistent and unified opposition to the government on the part of NGOs—increased 'activism'—accompanied by a more radical divergence in terms of their agendas and visions for change. As the CPN-M began consultations with NGOs in mid-2007, another scenario was put forward by observers of the NGO sector: that CPN-M might become 'NGO-ized' and, like the UML before it, lose its radical edge. The only certainty at present is that NGO and CPN-M relations will undergo some interesting transformations in the coming years and these will leave neither the NGO sector nor the CPN-M unchanged.

A second point to emerge from the material present in this chapter was that NGOs were not necessarily 'accommodating' for power: indeed the motivation for NGO work often originated out of a lack of confidence in the state, a desire to 'do better'. That it was made political by its implicit critique of the state has been argued by many in Nepal, *inter alia* by Panday (1993). Besides, it could be noted that what is considered 'oppositional' in one period might not be in the next: in a manner reminiscent of the pre-1990 era, it seems (and particularly after the royal coup of 1 February 2005) government became wary of the political potential of NGOs once again. Reportedly, local government bodies began to 'advise' NGOs to refrain from using terminology such as 'empowerment', and to drop any 'civil-society building' activities from their programmes. In the wake of the coup of 2005, Arjun Karki, chairperson of the NGO Federation of Nepal (NFN, a network of over 2,000 NGOs across the country), was placed on a travel ban and arrest list, together with political party leaders and eminent human rights activists. And, in September 2005, the government issued a draft code of conduct for NGOs, which stipulated that that NGO personnel "should not get involved in activities that undermine social harmony", and empowered the government to dissolve, without recourse, NGOs which do not abide by the code.[26]

Third, we saw that as well as trying to maintain good relations with GOs, NGOs sought to distance themselves from governmental practice and keep political parties at arm's length, firstly in a bid to distinguish themselves from past development failures (Heaton Shrestha, 2001, 2002) and secondly in order to obviate charges of 'profiteering'. Public office was widely seen at the time as a platform for personal, material gain; the 'three sphere' model often collapsed into a 'two sphere' model of disinterested action versus profit-motivated action that cut across the public/private and state/non-state boundaries.

The situation seemed little changed 10 years later. In June 2007 the newly established daily newspaper *Naya Patrika* ran a series of news items condemning the close relation of party members and NGOs. For instance, in the article 'Netaharu parti kam NGO badhi calaunchan',[27] senior political party members who were known to run NGOs were listed and challenged by the *Naya Patrika* to account for their involvement in the NGO sector. The journalists' questioning were met with denials or, exceptionally, shrugged off. A *Naya Patrika* journalist (prompt to point out the interviewee's former membership of the Commission for the Investigation of the Abuse of Authority) recalled one such instance: when probed, the then Minister on Development of Water Resources retorted: "I am running an NGO, I don't drink [alcohol], I don't play cards, why do you blame me?"

Fourth, I have sought to bring out how, within a single organization, different modalities of action prevailed, so that a 'service delivery' approach coexisted with a 'social reform' approach. Following the more conventional definitions of 'activism', this meant that a single organization could be both 'activist' and 'non-activist'. A further point could be added: many NGO workers, who took forward this social reformist agenda would not, in all probability, have otherwise been engaged in 'activism'. While an enthusiasm for social reform was not lacking—many had been involved in *seva* in their own communities in the past and were speaking of doing so once again in the future—their fuller engagement in *seva* would have been hampered by their own life-projects at the time: indeed, many fieldworkers were young, newly wed, and their priority was to acquire the means to support a married life.

These points are lent further support by the developments of 2005–06, and the role that NGOs played in the movement for democracy and peace. With the exception of human rights NGOs, which raised their voice immediately after the coup of 2005, NGOs rarely opposed the King's regime overtly *qua* NGOs. Only two instances stand out: in 2004, the NFN had acted as the secretariat of a Citizens' Campaign for Democracy and Social Transformation, an alliance of NGOs and professional associations founded to create public pressure for peace and democracy. But apart from a string of activities during December 2004 (rallies, interactions, submitting a memorandum to the Speaker of the House on Human Rights Day), the campaign never seemed to attract much media attention or public support. Openly oppositional action by NGOs became significant again after the regime directly threatened NGO interests, through introducing the aforementioned code of conduct in November 2005. The NFN again led series of protests, which included handing over a memorandum to the then Minister for Children, Women, Social Welfare; organizing a special meeting of national NGOs in Kathmandu to express opposition to the code; requesting members across the country to burn copies of the code of conduct; organizing a petition and handing it over to the Supreme Court; raising black flags in front of offices of NGOs across the country and work in their offices with black bands tied on their hands for one week; conducting a protest on Human Rights Day 2005. Apart from these two instances, the activities of NGOs remained somewhat muted and where they did exist, unreported.

However, focusing on activities carried out under an organization's 'banner', so to speak, detracts from the significance of NGOs for the movement for the restoration of democracy and peace that rose up from July 2005. This movement, which culminated in the King reinstating the Nepal House of Representatives on 24 April 2006, drew heavily on the resources of NGOs—computers, faxes, printers, phones, social networks. This was done unofficially, sometimes unbeknownst to, sometimes with the full knowledge and tacit support of, NGO managers. Without these resources, as well as the relative security that the international connections of key persons of the movement (connections, again, developed through years of involvement in the NGO sector) afforded, it is moot whether the movement would have been as effective.

The foregoing suggests that, rather than simply 'routinizing' activists (as often claimed), or even 'disciplining' activists (as Lewis, this volume, argues in the case of Bangladesh), NGOs also 'enable' activism and 'create' activists. While routinization certainly does occur, it neither does so 'invariably' nor 'irreversibly'. A more historical perspective shows individuals and organizations moving across the non-activist/activist boundary over time and lifetimes. Detailed attention to everyday life in NGO settings further brings to light the complex relation of NGO to governmental power: at times disciplining, at times producing the activists that (in Lewis' terms, this volume) seek to redefine governability.

Thus, the material presented here holds implications for our understanding of 'activism': it shows that 'activism' is just as contested as 'civil society'; and indicates that as well as moving between 'spheres', actors (individual and organizational) also move in and out of 'activism' or 'activist modes'. I suggest that exploring how 'activist modes' articulate with 'non-activist' modes—the 'backstage' of 'activism'—will considerably enrich this promising area of inquiry.

A final point to emerge concerns the role of state and non-state actors in maintaining the boundaries between different spheres: the picture that emerged from interviews with government officials during 1996 and 1997 was of a weakened and fragmented state, unsure of its ability (moral and logistical) to 'discipline activists' and to secure the boundaries between spheres in contrast with the situation in Bangladesh (Lewis, this volume). In the reproduction of the dominant paradigm of distinct spheres, NGOs played a much more central role than in Bangladesh, where, it seems, the state was the key player: they did so through their efforts to develop a culture clearly unlike that of GOs, denying or disguising the nature of their relations with government officials, and keeping a distance from political parties and political figures—in other words, by defining themselves in opposition to the sphere of government and politics.

NOTES

1. The chapter is based on research carried out among development NGOs in Nepal between October 1996 and December 1997. It involved fieldwork in the headquarters and field sites of two national non-governmental development organizations (NGDOs) in Nepal. Research spanned 18 field sites across three districts for the first NGO and 20 field sites across two districts for the second. Observations were also carried out in the two NGOs' central offices, which I attended during normal working hours, in the field offices, as well as in project sites, which I visited alongside field staff during their scheduled visits. I spent a considerable amount of time with staff outside of 'work hours' in field offices, taking meals and spending the best part of my leisure time with them. During this time, I also held discussions with representatives of a total of 30 NGOs, both local and national, government officials, beneficiaries, and other 'locals' as well as nine donor organizations, and I attended numerous international non-governmental organization (INGO)/NGO seminars and workshops. All prices are in Nepalese rupees. At the time of fieldwork one US dollar was approximately equivalent to Rs 50 and one pound sterling to about Rs 80.
2. This number refers to NGOs registered with the Social Welfare Council (SWC). The number of organizations registered in the District Administration Office (the minimal legal requirement) was estimated at 30,000 across the country.
3. In the text, I use the terms 'NGO leader', 'NGO founder', and 'NGO director' to refer to, respectively, the founder of an NGO who is still acting as chairperson or president of the NGO board, the founder of an NGO who is no longer acting as chairperson or president, and an employee of the NGO who directs day-to-day operations. The term 'leader' was not used by NGOs, and is used here as it provides a convenient shorthand.

4. Although, and in contradistinction with views of NGOs as part of the spread of neo-liberal values (e.g. Wallace, 2004), many NGO workers recalled that under the Panchayat regime, a desire to work with the poor was widely seen as 'communist'. The same was the case for NGO activity in the early 1990s. What's more, by the early 2000s, it was widely held that the vast majority of NGOs had close links with the Communist Party of Nepal (Unified Marxist-Leninist) (CPN-UML). Affiliation to other political parties was seen as a more rare occurrence. Explanations given for this state of affairs ranged from the coincidental (people with the skills necessary to run NGOs in the early 1990s as international funding started to pour in happened to be CPN-UML supporters) to the conspiratorial (this was a deliberate move by the US to co-opt an emerging communist leadership).
5. A. Cohen (1981) describes a 'state elite' as comprising the professionals in the bureaucracy and in occupations related to state services. Here it is used loosely to refer to the middle-level and senior staff in government organizations.
6. GO stands for government organization.
7. The research also included regional NGOs; socially, such organizations are very different from the national NGOs described here, as are their origins, and, to some extent, their relations with donors. These are not given consideration here.
8. In contrast, in the project areas of these NGOs, in 1997, a senior officer in a local government office could expect no more than Rs 5,000 per month. In 2001, Dahal reports that the monthly wages of NGO and GO workers, on average, ranged between US$600–2,500 and US$80–120, respectively (Dahal, 2001).
9. At the time of research, human rights organizations did not call themselves NGOs.
10. Hindu revivalist movement founded by Swami Danayand Sarasvati in India in 1875. It made significant contributions to education, offering a curriculum based on Western education, as well as Indian lore and politics, taking part in the freedom struggle against the British. Its social reform programme included activities such as *suddhi* ('purification') or the reconversion to Hinduism of former Hindus who had become Muslims or Christians. Some Arya Samajists, feeling that the Swami's views on caste were not radical enough, founded the Jat Pat Torak Mandal or the Association for Breaking Caste, in 1922 in Lahore, which sponsored inter-caste dinners and marriages (Llewelyn, 1993). It was introduced into Nepal by Madhav Raj Joshi in 1895. This, comments Chand (2000: 66), "can be safely considered as one of the first processes of institutionalising voluntary action to socially and spiritually liberate the community by generating awareness against the cruelty being imposed in the name of religion".
11. See Messerschmidt and Yadama (2004) for an account of the NDS and an argument concerning the role it has played in opening up the space of civil society in Nepal. See Dhungel (1986) for a less positive view of the scheme.
12. The data that follows is based on the NGOs in the study. However, there is evidence to suggest that this profile applies to most national NGOs. A study by PACT in 1988 found that the staff of service-type NGOs and nationally registered organizations were highly educated (65 per cent with tertiary education) and predominantly 'middle class'. While there is no quantified data for the non-governmental sector as a whole, it was little disputed that the larger, donor-funded NGOs were run and staffed by high castes and Newars (Bhattachan, 2000).

13. Liechty (2003) defines the middle class less by its material standards than its 'mindset' and consumption patterns. The middle class is described as characterized by a sense of being 'in between', and by an uneasy relation with modernity. Seddon (1987) defines this group in terms of occupation, and includes university and college teachers, self-employed professionals such as journalists, teachers, lawyers, and doctors, persons almost completely separated from substantial land-owning employment. The persons described as 'middle class' here belonged for the most part to these occupational groups.
14. This, like other personal names in this chapter, is a pseudonym.
15. A similar pattern of employment in GOs, training abroad, and eventual shift to the NGO and INGO sectors is described in K.M. Shakya's autobiographical piece in Gellner and Hachhethu (2008).
16. There were of course exceptions: for many less well-connected and educated middle-class individuals, a stint as a fieldworker was inevitable, as a prelude to their securing a desk job.
17. Council for Technical Education and Vocational Training. Established in 1989, the CTEVT describes itself as a national autonomous body committed to the growth and development of basic and middle-level workforce for Nepal. It has an assembly with 24 members and a governing board of seven members. The Assembly and the Council are both chaired by Minister of Education. The Council has a full time Vice-Chairman and a Member-Secretary appointed by government. (source: http://www.logos-net.net/ilo/195_base/en/init/nep_4.htm#Introduction accessed 21 July 2006).
18. This is certainly the case in terms of caste or ethnicity. The judiciary, army, civil service, and the majority of senior political posts are still today overwhelmingly occupied by high castes (Bahun and Chhetri) (see Lawoti, 2005: 104–5). In the absence of other recent sociological data on civil servants, I am unable to comment further on their similarities.
19. See, for example, Brown (1996) for an account of the Back to the Village National Campaign scheme launched by King Mahendra in 1967 and which lasted into the mid-1980s. That state-led programmes were not totally ineffective at reaching the poorest groups, however, is highlighted by Messerschmidt and Yamada's (2004) account of the National Development Service programme of the 1970s. This programme was closed, they suggest, because it was *too successful* at reaching and mobilizing the poor.
20. See Bista (1991), Kondos (1987), and Adams (1998) on the institution of *aphno manche* ('one's own people') in Nepal, and its widespread condemnation.
21. There are provisions, in law, for the monitoring of NGO activity through annual reports and audits.
22. The period covered by the fieldwork was particularly unstable, seeing no fewer than three different coalition governments in the space of 15 months.
23. The SWC Act 1992 makes a provision for the unilateral dissolution, by government, of NGOs deemed to be engaging in activities 'against the national interest' or in breach of the latter's own constitutions.
24. *Sangh* and *sangathan* are synonyms meaning association; *samiti* is usually translated 'committee', but can equally be used to designate local organizations.
25. Item 9 of the 40-point demand read: "The invasion of colonial and imperial elements in the name of NGOs and INGOs should be stopped".

26. Open Letter to the Proposed Code of Conduct, 7 November 2005, accessible from www.amnestynepal.org drafted by Amnesty International and the International Commission of Jurists.
27. ('Political leaders spend more time running NGOs than they do on the party') *Naya Patrika* 1(72) Sunday 10 asar 2064 (24 June 2007).

REFERENCES

Acharya, M. 2000. 'Non-governmental Organisation (NGO)-led Development Strategy in Nepal', in K.B. Bhattachan and C. Mishra (eds), *Developmental Practices in Nepal*, pp. 69–99. Kathmandu: Central Department of Sociology and Anthropology, Tribhuvan University.

Adams, V. 1998. *Doctors for Democracy: Health Professionals in the Nepal Revolution*. Cambridge: Cambridge University Press.

Adhikari, K.R. 1996. 'Naming Ceremonies as Rituals of Development', *Studies in Nepali History and Society*, 1(2): 345–64.

Arellano-Lopez, S. and F.J. Petras. 1994. 'Non-governmental Organisations and Poverty Alleviation in Bolivia', *Development and Change*, 25(3): 555–68.

Bhattachan, K.B. 2000. 'People/Community-based Development Strategy in Nepal', in K.B. Bhattachan and C. Mishra (eds), *Developmental Practices in Nepal*, pp. 100–48. Kathmandu: Central Department of Sociology and Anthropology, Tribhuvan University.

Bista, D.B. 1991. *Fatalism and Development: Nepal's Struggle for Modernization*. Calcutta: Orient Longman Ltd.

Blaikie, P., J. Cameron, and D. Seddon. 1980. *Nepal in Crisis: Growth and Stagnation at the Periphery*. London: Routledge.

Brown, L.T. 1996. *The Challenge to Democracy in Nepal: A Political History*. London and New York: Routledge.

Burghart, R. 1994. 'The Political Culture of Panchayat Democracy', in M. Hutt (ed.), *Nepal in the Nineties: Versions of the Past, Visions of the Future*, pp. 1–13. New Delhi: Oxford University Press.

Carroll, T. 1992. *Intermediary NGOs: The Supporting Link in Grassroots Development*. West Hartford: Kumarian.

Chand, D. 2000. 'Understanding Voluntary Action in Nepal', in J. Vartola, M. Ulvila, F. Hossain, and T.N. Dhakal (eds), *Development NGOs Facing the 21st Century: Perspectives from South Asia*, pp. 65–73. Kathmandu: Institute for Human Development.

'Chintan' Siwakoti, G. 2000. 'Foreign Intervention in Politics through NGOs: A Case of the Left in Nepal', in J. Vartola, M. Ulvila, F. Hossain, and T.N. Dhakal (eds), *Development NGOs Facing the 21st Century: Perspectives from South Asia*, pp. 134–43. Kathmandu: Institute for Human Development.

Cohen, A. 1981. *The Politics of Elite Culture: Explorations in the Dramaturgy of Power in a Modern Society*. Berkeley, Los Angeles, and London: University of California Press.

Dahal, D.R. 2001. *Civil Society in Nepal: Opening the Ground for Questions*. Kathmandu: Center for Development and Governance.

Dhungel. D.P. 1986. 'The People's Movement and Experiment in Nepal', *Community Development Journal*, 21(3): 217–25.

Fisher, W.F. 1997. 'Doing Good? The Politics and Antipolitics of NGO Practices', *Annual Reviews in Anthropology*, 26: 439–64.

Guru-Gharana, K. 1996. 'Economic Reforms, Employment and Labour Markets in Nepal', *The Indian Journal of Labour Economics*, 39(3): 625–44.

———. 2000. 'State-led Development Strategy in Nepal', in K.B. Bhattachan and C. Mishra (eds), *Developmental Practices in Nepal*, pp. 16–43. Kathmandu: Central Department of Sociology and Anthropology, Tribhuvan University.

Gyawali, D. 2001. 'Are NGOs in Nepal Old Wine or New Bottle? A Cultural Theory Perspective on Nepal's Contested Terrain', in K.B. Bhattachan, D.R. Dahal, S. Rana, J. Gyawali, M.B. Basnet, K.R. Bhusal, and R.R. Pokharel (eds), *NGO, Civil Society and Government in Nepal: Critical Examination of their Roles and Responsibilities*, pp. 13–33. Kathmandu: Central Department of Sociology and Anthropology and FES.

Heaton, C. 2001. '"Our Differences Don't Make a Difference": Practising Civil Society in Nepal's Non-governmental Sector', PhD dissertation, SOAS, University of London.

Heaton Shrestha, C. 2002. 'NGOs as *Thekadar* or *Sevak*: Identity Crisis in Nepal's Non-governmental Sector', *European Bulletin of Himalayan Research*, 22: 5–36.

———. 2004. 'The Ambiguities of Practising *Jat* in 1990s Nepal: Elites, Caste and Everyday Life in Development NGOs', *South Asia*, 27(1): 39–85.

Hulme, D. and M. Edwards. 1997. 'Conclusion: Too Close to the Powerful, Too Far from the Powerless?' in M. Edwards and D. Hulme (eds), *NGOs, States and Donors: Too Close for Comfort?*, pp. 275–84. New York: St. Martin's Press/Save the Children.

Kondos, A. 1987. 'The Question of "Corruption" in Nepal', *Mankind*, 17(1): 15–29.

Krauskopff, G. 2003. 'An Indigenous Minority in a Border Area: Tharu Ethnic Associations, NGOs, and the Nepalese State', in D.N. Gellner (ed.), ***Resistance and the** State: Nepalese Experiences*, pp. 199–243. New Delhi: Social Science Press.

Lawoti, M. 2005. *Towards a Democratic Nepal: Inclusive Political Institutions for a Multicultural Society*. London: Sage Publications.

Lecomte-Tilouine, M. and P. Dollfus (eds). 2003. *Ethnic Revival and Religious Turmoil: Identities and Representations in the Himalayas*. New Delhi: Oxford University Press.

Liechty, M. 2003. *Suitably Modern: Making Middle-Class Culture in a New Consumer Society*. Princeton and Oxford: Princeton University Press.

Llewelyn, J.E. 1993. *The Arya Samaj as a Fundamentalist Movement: A Study in Comparative Fundamentalism*. Delhi: Manohar.

Mayhew, S. 2005. 'Hegemony, Politics and Ideology: The Role of Legislation in NGO-Government Relations in Asia', *The Journal of Development Studies*, 41(5): 727–58.

Messerschmidt, D. and G.N. Yadama. 2004. 'Civic Service in South Asia: A Case Study of Nepal', *Nonprofit and Voluntary Sector Quarterly*, 33(4) (supplement): 98–126.

National Planning Commission (NPC). 1991. *8th Five Year Plan*. Kathmandu: NPC, HMG.

Panday, D.R. 1993. 'Development: NGOs at the Grassroots', *The Rising Nepal*, volume 22.

Pigg, S.L. 1992. 'Inventing Social Categories through Place: Social Representations and Development in Nepal', *Comparative Studies in Society and History*, 34(3): 491–513.

Rademacher, A. and D. Tamang. 1993. *Democracy, Development and NGOs*. Kathmandu: SEARCH.

Ramirez, P. 2000. *De la disparition des chefs: Une anthropologie politique Népalaise* [On the disappearance of chiefs: A political anthropology]. Paris: CNRS.

Ridell, R. 1994. *Strengthening the Partnership: Evaluation of the Finnish NGO Support Programme—Country Case Study Nepal*. London: ODI.

Shakya, K.M. 2008. 'Foreign Aid, Democracy, and Development: Personal Experiences', in D.N. Gellner and K. Hachhethu (eds), *Local Democracy in South Asia: The Micropolitics of Democratization in Nepal and its Neighbours*, pp. 258–75. New Delhi: SAGE Publications.

Seddon, D. 1987. *Nepal: A State of Poverty*. New Delhi: Vikas.

Shrestha, B.K. 2001. 'The Sociological Context of (I)NGO Work in Nepal', in K.B. Bhattachan, D.R. Dahal, S. Rana, J. Gyawali, M.B. Basnet, K.R. Bhusal, and R.R. Pokharel (eds), *NGO, Civil Society and Government in Nepal: Critical Examination of their Roles and Responsibilities*, pp. 41–63. Kathmandu: Central Department of Sociology and Anthropology and FES.

Tuladhar, J. 1991. 'The Growth and Development of NGOs in the 1990s', paper presented at the seminar 'National NGO conference 1991', Kathmandu, 23–25 September 1991.

Tuladhar, A.R. 1994. 'Naming Anti-developmental Attitudes', *Contributions to Nepalese Studies*, 21(2): 191–212.

Wallace, T. 2004. 'NGO Dilemmas: Trojan Horses for Global Neo-liberalism?' in L. Panitch and C. Leys (eds), *The New Imperial Challenge*, pp. 202–19. New York: New York University Press.

Chapter 9

From Big Game to Biodiversity

Middle-class Environmental Activists and Wildlife Conservation in Sri Lanka

ARJUN GUNERATNE

INTRODUCTION

Sri Lankan environmentalists like to point to the record of edicts promulgated by various kings of the past, such as Devanampiya Tissa, in whose reign Buddhism was introduced to Sri Lanka, and Nissanka Malla, the last great king of the Polonnaruwa period, to argue that the conservation of wildlife has a long tradition in Sri Lanka. These kings are said to have set aside, as an expression of Buddhist piety, parks in which hunting was forbidden. Whatever the merits of the claim, the history of contemporary environmentalism in Sri Lanka, in which wildlife and nature conservation ('green environmentalism') remains a significant and dominant part, has more recent origins in the period of British colonialism.

The anthropologist Kay Milton distinguishes between the concept of culture, which she reserves for the ways in which particular groups or categories of people know and give meaning to the world, and "transcultural discourses", by which she means "areas of communication that cross cultural boundaries" (1996: 169). The point of this distinction is that it is 'groups of people' who create a shared culture: a way of knowing or interpreting and giving meaning to experience that is communicated in specific ways among specific groups of people and shaped by the particular circumstances of the time. Culture should be understood not as a thing or a set of traits but as a symbolic system, as a way of interpreting and apprehending the world. I note this because in much of the writings about globalization, typically by non-anthropologists, culture has been understood in the first sense, which has often led to the mistaken idea that the world is becoming culturally homogeneous. The presence of a McDonald's in Colombo does not mean that Sri Lankans are becoming Americanized; but the presence of an active and vocal environmentalist community in Sri Lanka does mean that some Sri Lankans, while remaining rooted in a cultural scheme of things that is territorially defined, are also partaking in one of Appadurai's 'global flows', in this case an environmentalist discourse that would be familiar to a member of the Sierra Club. This is what Milton refers to as a "transcultural discourse", in which systems of ideas and values, in this case about the necessity of protecting the environment from human-inflicted damage, are abstracted from the social context that initially produced them, to circulate globally. As Milton puts it, "it is in the character of discourse to flow across cultural boundaries. It goes wherever the channels of communication take it" (Milton, 1996: 169).

My argument in this chapter is that two distinct periods of globalization shaped an environmentalist ethos among a largely urban, 'middle-class' population in Sri Lanka. This ethos owes its origin to the transformations wrought by colonialism, and this social class was peculiarly located to receive and shape the discourse of environmentalism emerging in the West. They were anglicized, in some cases Christianized, fluent in English, and receptive to ideas originating in Europe and especially in Britain, where many of them were educated. The shared discourse of environmentalism was first transmitted to Sri Lanka and took root there in the period of British colonialism, through which and in the context of which, ideas about nature and wild places were introduced to this urban elite; these ideas underwent a second transformation and diversified under the pressure of a second stage of globalization taking place in the late twentieth century, a period of neo-liberal economic transformation. This period also saw a significant expansion of this bourgeois class to include large segments of the non-anglicized population.

Ramachandra Guha and Madhav Gadgil identify seven different varieties of environmentalism in India, which emphasize issues of either ecology or of equity (see Guha and Gadgil, 1995). Nature conservation for recreational or scientific reasons (exemplified by wildlife conservation) and for religious reasons, as well as a focus on scientifically based managerial regimes for more efficient resource extraction, are the three varieties that focus on ecology. In India, however, the dominant strand of environmentalism is what these authors call "the environmentalism of the poor" and they focus on issues of equity; the well-known Chipko movement in the Himalaya is a good example. Guha and Gadgil characterize the equity-focused strands of Indian environmentalism in the following terms:

> The first emphasizes the moral imperative of checking overuse and doing justice to the poor, and largely include Gandhians. The second emphasizes the need to dismantle the unjust social order through struggle, and primarily attracts Marxists. The third and fourth strands emphasize reconstruction, employing technologies appropriate to the context and the times. (Guha and Gadgil, 1995: 98–9)

Unlike India, however, environmentalism in Sri Lanka has been dominated by the struggle to preserve wild spaces and wildlife, and the kinds of social justice issues that have been included under the rubric of environmentalism in other contexts are poorly developed. One possible exception to this is the Sarvodaya movement, which is not, however, usually represented in environmentalist terms; it falls outside the scope of this chapter.[1]

In Sri Lanka, as in India, wildlife conservation and the struggle to protect wild areas is the preserve of a middle class whose origins are in the colonial period. Sri Lanka has—for a small state of modest standing in the world—a quite enviable record of preserving its wildlife despite a rapidly expanding population in a compact land area, thanks to the struggles and activism of generations of wildlife enthusiasts for well over a hundred years. This activism has gone through three stages, each more or less correlated with shifts in a wider socio-political and economic context in which the activism is located. The object of the activism has also gone through three conceptual shifts which are related to these wider contexts: a focus on 'game' became broadened to include a wider category of 'wildlife and nature' which, by the end of the twentieth century has become transformed into a focus on 'biodiversity'. The essential difference among these concepts is that both game and wildlife carry the connotation of things or objects that must be preserved (i.e., prevented from disappearing or becoming extinct), while the notion of biodiversity has a sense of information (genetic information) that must not only be preserved, but that must be kept under local control in the context of a liberalizing economy. The idea of sovereignty, which informs any discussion of biodiversity, is of crucial significance here. While debates over the conservation of wildlife do not typically invoke the idea of sovereignty, debates over biodiversity conservation invariably do. Unlike in India, where biodiversity issues such as the attempt to patent procedures relating to the commercial exploitation of the neem tree (*Azadirachta indica*) mobilized farmers (including a demonstration by half a million farmers in Bangalore in 1993) against the General Agreement on Tariffs and Trade (GATT) (Shiva and Holla-Bhar, 1996), the issue of biodiversity in Sri Lanka, like the issue of wildlife, has mobilized only certain segments of the middle class—essentially, a small number of wildlife activists.

In the late nineteenth century, British planters, mostly in the tea estates in the highlands, began to lobby the government for game laws to stem 'poaching' and ensure an adequate supply of certain species for them to shoot. Their interest was not in the preservation of wildlife in general but in the preservation of those species—such as *sambhur*, spotted deer, elephant, and buffalo—the hunting of which was an important aspect of their identity and status. Notions of 'sportsmanship' that were in vogue at that time in the British Isles shaped the values and attitudes of these expatriate Britons towards hunting. These values represented a way for these men, many of whom were from the less-privileged and less-moneyed parts of the middle and ruling classes in Britain, both to make claims about their own standing in colonial society and to distinguish themselves from 'native' hunters.

In the early decades of the twentieth century, attitudes about the killing of game began to change in the West and a preservationist ethos began to take shape, given expression in Britain by the establishment of the Society for the Preservation of the Wild Fauna of the Empire (today known as Fauna and Flora International). Ideas regarding the general preservation of nature, of scenic beauty, and of wild species came into vogue in Britain in late Victorian times, with the establishment of such societies as the Commons Preservation Society, the Selborne Society, and others (Ranlett, 1983). These ideas were taken up in Sri Lanka both by Britons of the planter class, who had earlier instigated the efforts to preserve 'game', and by Sri Lankans, who were not particularly engaged in the discourse of sportsmanship but were thinking more about the preservation of wildlife in general, not just those species suitable or designated for the hunt. Thus, R.L. Spittel, the first Sri Lankan President of the Ceylon Game and Fauna Protection Society and one of the strongest voices in mid century for this new perspective, in making the case for a government department to protect wildlife wrote: "The term Conservation Department or Bureau of Wild Life is much better than the term Game Department because the latter connotes slaughter" (1942: 13).

Following the Donoughmore Commission's constitutional reforms of 1931, Sri Lankans took an increasingly greater responsibility in the affairs of the colony. D.S. Senanayake, the Minister of Agriculture and Lands (and thus responsible for both wildlife and forests, which came under the purview of his ministry) gave a great impetus to participation in an area of activism that had once been the almost exclusive preserve of a class of British expatriates. These Sri Lankans were drawn from the bourgeois class whose origins have been described by Jayawardena (2000). I will refer to them as the anglicized bourgeoisie for the sake of a convenient shorthand; they were bilingual, and often, especially in the pre-independence generation, more comfortable with English than they were with their native language. Their discourse for the most part was preservationist, and village people whose livelihoods brought them into conflict with wildlife were often portrayed as part of the problem that had to be resolved.

The focus on wildlife began to shift in the 1970s and activists began to take a broader view of what constituted environment. Some activists in Sri Lanka, such as Sarath Kotagama, have pointed to the impact of the United Nations Conference on the Human Environment in 1972 (popularly known as the Stockholm Conference); but one factor contributing to this shift was undoubtedly the problems of industrial pollution resulting from the rapid industrialization that took place after 1977, when the newly elected United National Party (UNP) government ushered in a period of structural reforms and economic liberalization that continues to this day. This latter phase of globalization (as well as the ready availability of funding from foreign governments and international NGOs for environmental work) also spawned a vast number of NGOs to compete with the handful of environmental organizations that had existed prior to the late 1970s. Many of these newcomers were not membership-based NGOs, but consisted essentially of a few activists operating from their homes.

This last period of activism is also characterized by a broadening of the social base of the activists; while many of the more prominent organizations, especially the more visible ones internationally, were founded by members of the old anglicized bourgeoisie or its descendants, monolingual Sinhala speakers of the urban middle classes, or people who spoke English very much as a second language, also participated actively in the new environmentalism.

In this chapter I examine the development of environmentalism in Sri Lanka by focusing on its principal strand, the sustained effort since the late nineteenth century to preserve the island's wildlife, the social classes or segments of the population most responsible for these efforts, and the global and local contexts in which they worked and which shaped their assumptions, values, and activities.

COLONIAL HUNTING AND THE PRESERVATION OF GAME

> *Nay, nay, Hurry, there's little manhood in killing a doe, and that, too, out of season.*
>
> –James Fenimore Cooper, *The Deerslayer*

The Britons who came out to Ceylon to plant first coffee and then, after the coffee blight of the late nineteenth century had destroyed those plantations, tea, and also coconut and rubber, were drawn from a great variety of social backgrounds, but were, for the most part, of lower middle-class and urban origin, leavened by a sprinkling of the younger sons of the nobility, such as J.R. Gordon Cumming, a younger son of the Laird of Altyre. The European pioneers of coffee cultivation lived lives largely isolated from the company of other Europeans, supervising the clearing and planting of virgin montane forest land. One of the few sources of recreation and amusement in these circumstances was hunting; forests were abundant and game plentiful for much of the nineteenth century, but both were in decline by the century's close for a variety of reasons which I shall discuss in the following. The energy devoted for game protection by these hunters, who were drawn mainly from this planting milieu, was a response to this decline, and their primary motive was to ensure the survival of adequate numbers of game animals for 'sport'.

G.M. Henry, well known to generations of Sri Lankan bird-watchers as the author of the first comprehensive field guide to the island's avifauna and himself born and raised on a tea plantation in the highlands of Nuwara Eliya, writes of the planter class during the early part of the last century:

> At this time the European element in a population of five or six million Sinhalese and Tamils, never numbered more than 8000. A large proportion in government service or the mercantile community was stationed in Colombo, with a few hundred missionaries, surveyors and professional men in Kandy, Jaffna and Galle. The planting community was scattered about the tea and rubber growing districts, mostly in the hill zones and they generally had little contact with the *Colombo wallah*s. Recruitment to their ranks was mostly from young men sent out from Britain by their parents, often because they showed no aptitude for anything else or sometimes to lose them until some shady affair had blown over. They would be apprenticed for a fee to an experienced planter and were known as *creepers*. If their *Peria Dorai* (big boss) was a man of character and particularly if he had a good and sympathetic wife, the creeper would turn out well, but in too many cases the youngster would be inducted, along with planting techniques and Tamil learning, into whisky drinking and debauchery. By the time he had learnt sufficient to become a *Sunna Dorai* (little boss) he would be shunted off to take charge of a section of the estate, with his own small bungalow and running his own ménage with a servant or two. (Henry, 2000: 26)

Even though their social origins were not, for the most part, from the landed aristocracy, for whom hunting and fishing were defining attributes of status, these Britons came from a late nineteenth-century milieu in which hunting had been defined as an integral aspect of the manliness so necessary for the business of empire (see MacKenzie, 1988: 25–53). It was during this period that the notions of sport and sportsmanship (terms almost synonymous with hunting) were developed and refined, serving to distinguish the elite's preferred mode of killing wild animals from those pursued by the lower classes. While bear baiting and cockfighting were outlawed, a gentlemen's code of hunting was fully formulated by the end of the nineteenth century, and was worked into the ideology of empire. One aim of this code was to delegitimize the methods of hunting employed by the lower classes, whether they were to be found in the British Isles or among colonial subjects abroad. These values in turn, while originating among the upper classes, percolated downwards to other social strata, through the medium of (for example) popular literature aimed at boys and young men and movements such as Baden-Powell's boy scouts.

The concept of hunting carried with it the notion of adventure, excitement, and wild places; it was, in a word, manly, and thus a necessary aspect of the socialization of Britain's youth into the work of the empire. The glorification of hunting pervaded the mass literary culture of the period, and represented "adventure, travel, excitement" as well as a vehicle for moral instruction (MacKenzie, 1988: 43). Natural history, with an emphasis on collecting specimens, was made a compulsory subject in British schools after 1870; this not only encouraged boys to actively engage with the natural world, but it also helped reveal "to its practitioners the divine pattern of the moral as well as the physical universe" (ibid.: 42). It was an aspect in other words of what has been referred to as 'Muscular Christianity' (for instance, see Van der Veer, 2001): one discovers the complexity and diversity of God's creation by collecting and classifying it, which can only be accomplished by engaging with it and immersing oneself in it. To do this successfully required knowledge of hunting and killing. Authors of that period who facilitated the percolation of these elite values to the middle classes of British society included Kipling, P.C. Wren, Rider Haggard, and R.M. Ballantyne, to name a few who are still read today. For G.A. Henty, author of what was at the time a vastly popular literature for boys, "hunting lay at the centre of the imperial experience, and he had a horror of lads who shrank from shedding blood" (MacKenzie, 1988: 44). The essential aspects of sportsmanship were elaborated on in these books and in the magazines published for boys. MacKenzie sums up the basic features of this popular literature in the following terms:

> Youth and age, guileless, noble, self-reliant, killing to survive and to spread civilization, illustrating at every turn the mastery that was wrought by technical advance, environmental knowledge and moral worth: these were the images conveyed by a host of works written for children in the late 19th century. (MacKenzie, 1988: 45)

These values were notably expressed in Baden-Powell's *Scouting for Boys*, whose avowed aim was to inculcate in the youth of the empire the values needed to make them worthy servants of their King and Country. Baden-Powell's ideal, taught to generations of schoolboys in Britain and its possessions, and still taught to boy scouts today (albeit in a modified form more suited to the times), was the frontiersman, who, a master of scout craft, could survive and find his way in the jungle using the smallest clues that nature had to offer and who was "strong and plucky, and ready to face any danger" (Baden-Powell, 1908: 5).

Hunting in the nineteenth century was also about status. There was immortality to be achieved through discovering new species (which were shot and the skins provided to museums) and having them named after oneself. Successful hunters like Selous, Richard Meinertzhagen, and others gained entrée into elite aristocratic and scientific circles through their prowess as hunters (MacKenzie, 1988: 38). The connection between hunting and empire—that the search for wild game drew Englishmen to the areas they subsequently colonized—was often made by hunters themselves in the nineteenth century and echoed in popular literature (ibid.: 37). In colonial Sri Lanka, hunting was a way for the planter class not only to mark their status and their difference from the 'natives' around them, but also to claim a higher status in the context of colonial society itself, as measured by the values of the metropolis. Those who so jealously guarded their privileges in India and Sri Lanka could not have afforded to hunt at home in Britain (Bennett, 1984: 76). In India, where hunting (*shikar*) was dominated by the army and colonial officials, who comprised a large and important part of the European presence on the subcontinent, access to hunting was controlled through invitations (or the lack thereof) to join tent clubs or hunting expeditions, and restrictions on the issue of licenses; Bennett writes, "Other Ranks in the [Indian] Army were often forbidden from shooting wild game, on the grounds that such people would not understand how to hunt, would undoubtedly kill too many animals, and would generally spoil the outings of their superiors" (1984: 76). In Sri Lanka, on the other hand, the planters, despite the inferior class status of many of them, formed a large and well-organized part of the European presence on the island and such restrictions did not apply. The Planters Association of Ceylon was an influential organization with representatives (two of whom were Presidents of the Ceylon Game Protection Society) in the Legislative Council, which, prior to the constitutional reforms of 1931 advised the Governor on the Colony's affairs (Uragoda, 1994: 126). The status and prestige associated with hunting according to the norms of 'sportsmanship' did apply, however, and this ideology was helped by the fact that what motivated most of these men was the thrill of the chase rather than the need for subsistence. Samuel Baker summed up the essence of the idea of sportsmanship when he contrasted the values of the English hunter with his French counterpart, who, I need hardly add, were represented as having no sense of good sportsmanship whatsoever: "they take every advantage, while we give every advantage; they delight in the certainty of killing, while our pleasure consists in the chance of the animal escaping" (Baker, 1970: viii). To understand hunting by Britons in nineteenth-century Ceylon then, we must keep this context in mind. Planters were informed to varying degrees by this value system and the circumstances of their lives left hunting and engagement with the natural world around them one of the few sources of recreation available.

Sri Lanka in the early nineteenth century was a sparsely populated country covered in vast forests teeming with wild elephants and game animals, and in the first half of the century there were untrammelled opportunities for slaughter on a vast scale. Major Rogers, for example, who was the judge and military commandant in Badulla in the 1840s, is credited with shooting at least 1,300 elephants (the point at which he stopped counting; the real number is higher) during his time in Ceylon, and to shoot a hundred or more during one's sojourn in the island was apparently not uncommon (Gordon-Cumming, 1892: 219). Later sentiment among conservationists has been unfriendly to these early hunters as the following suggests: "The vogue for 'sport' which often meant shooting as many animals as possible in the shortest possible time was another formidable hazard the wildlife population had to face" (De Alwis, 1965: 173). Others, however, have tried to place these hunters in a more sympathetic context. Thilo Hoffman, an expatriate Swiss national who became one of the most important figures in wildlife and nature conservation in Sri Lanka during the 1970s and 1980s through his long tenure as President of the Wildlife and Nature Protection Society of Sri Lanka, writes magnanimously about these early hunters:

> They had their sport when conditions allowed for such sport, and even the much maligned elephant killers on a large scale, such as Rogers, Skinner, Baker, etc, [sic] killed from a multitude, a surplus, and thought they were doing the cultivator and the country a service, whilst enjoying a dangerous and strenuous pastime. (Hoffman, 1969: 335)

This situation changed by the end of the nineteenth century for a number of reasons, among which the large-scale slaughter of the large mammals by British officers and planters is only one. First, the immense tracts of forests were reduced, most dramatically in the highlands, by the expansion of the plantations. Second, the numbers and quality of guns in the islands increased during this period. Alfred Clark, a former Conservator of Forests and an early proponent for game laws to control and restrict hunting (by the natives, naturally), writing in 1901, estimated that there were 14,844 guns in jungle villages, or "more than one gun for every square mile of forest" (Clark, 1971: 99). The ancient and unreliable muzzle-loaders that village hunters had relied on began to be replaced with modern rifles, which had come into widespread use in the island by the 1870s. These facts, coupled to the demand for meat, horns, and hide for local consumption and export and the impossibility of getting village headmen to enforce the game laws meant that wildlife were slaughtered in greater numbers than before. All these factors were compounded by the dry season in the low country and the scarcity of water sources for wild animals. This lack of water, and the reliance of wild animals on the relatively small numbers of waterholes made it easier for "the natives" to "exercise their destructive method of shooting", that is, by lying in wait at the waterhole on moonlit nights to shoot animals that came to drink, without regard to sex and age. This was considered by the English to be thoroughly unsportsmanlike (Clark, 1971: 101). A good sportsman shot only the male of the species, and even then an older male was preferable to a younger one. The phenomenal decrease in game animals during the last decades of the nineteenth century led to the introduction of game laws; these, however, were enforced patchily. These game laws must be understood as a way in which a certain segment of society asserted its claim to a common resource, the country's wildlife. It was about the definition of rights, but it was also an articulation of a concept of civilization, through which the practices of the natives were defined as both illegal and uncivilized.

The elaboration of a code of hunting behaviour was developed as game declined in number during the closing decades of the nineteenth century. Some of the rules, such as the illegitimacy of killing the females of any species were, as Bennett points out (1984: 79) sensible, for they helped to preserve the species for the future. The value of others, such as not using lights to hunt at night, were more questionable, and debates raged "in club, newspaper and memoir" over these aspects of the code of sportsmanship (ibid.). Thus, British hunters were by no means always in agreement.

EARLY LEGISLATION

The earliest effort at game preservation was recorded in 1872, when an ordinance was introduced to protect deer, buffalo, and peafowl (Uragoda, 1994: 3). In 1891, an ordinance was introduced "to prevent the wanton destruction of Elephants, Buffaloes and other Game", followed by another in 1893 to prevent a similar fate for "Birds, Beasts and Fishes not indigenous to this colony" (ibid.: 4). Between 1902 and 1906, a Game Preservation Ordinance, a Fisheries (Dynamite) ordinance, and a Wild Bird Protection ordinance were introduced. In 1909, a comprehensive ordinance (No 1 of 1909) was introduced covering all these subjects, and the earlier legislation was repealed.

The decline in game was a matter of concern to the hunting fraternity in the plantations and on 23 May 1894, 26 expatriate Britons, including planters and military officers, met at the Bristol Hotel in Colombo to found the Game Protection Society of Ceylon (GPSC) (Uragoda, 1994: 5–6). At that meeting, they passed the following resolution:

> That H.E. the Governor be asked to prohibit the export of hides and horns of spotted deer and sambhur for at least 3 years, provided only that government reserves to itself the right of purchasing . . . horns and hides that are the property of genuine villagers. . . . The outcome of this meeting was the prohibition of the export of hides of sambhur and spotted deer for a period of 5 years as from January 1st, 1895. (Uragoda, 1994: 6)

The GPSC was a pressure group, lobbying the government for legislation to address the decline in game. Their focus during this time was not on wildlife protection but on creating the conditions that would allow for the continuation of hunting as a leisure activity for themselves—which required that hunting by other people in other ways be curtailed. They were successful in persuading the government to create an exclusive hunting preserve in Yala for local sportsmen; this was established in 1899 and later became Block 1 of the Ruhuna National Park (Uragoda, 1994: 15). The society, true to its aim of promoting the interests of hunting, attempted unsuccessfully to introduce exotic game animals to Sri Lanka, including *chukar* pheasants (released in Horton Plains in 1897), black buck from India (into Trincomalee), and European partridges into Uda Pussellawa (Tutein-Nolthenius, 1937).

One of the first actions of the new society was to prevail upon the government to prohibit hunting at elevations above 4,000 feet by any means other than the use of hounds, thus effectively ensuring that deer and especially *sambhur* at those elevations would be exclusively theirs. Forests above 5,000 feet were protected in 1879 to mitigate the disastrous environmental consequences of the clearing of land for plantations in the hills (Webb, 2002: 141), and they constituted some of the last remaining habitats for game animals in the highlands. The Tamil labourers, who worked the plantations, as well as Kandyan villagers, hunted deer for meat using shotguns. Hunting deer with hounds was a favourite sport of the planters, and was based more or less on foxhunting. The dogs used were mostly foxhounds, leavened (at least in Samuel Baker's pack on the Horton Plains) with greyhounds and deerhounds. The dogs would bring the stag to bay to be finished off by the hunter with a spear (Baker, 1970: 100–17). Hunting with the hounds in the highlands was a variation of the dangerous sport of pig sticking that was so eminently a mark of manliness in British society in colonial India (Bennett, 1984: 74–5).

The GPSC also lobbied successfully against hunting at night. The following extract regarding hunting in the Vanni from John Still's *Jungle Tide* suggests that legislation against hunting at night using spotlights was directed at Englishmen who strayed from the path of good sportsmanship as much as it was directed against natives ignorant of that code. It also summarizes the key elements of the code of sportsmanship:

> Men who are not sportsmen sometimes motor along its lonely roads by night, armed with rifle and spotlight, and shoot from their safe cars at dazzled animals staring from the edge of the black forest. ... No man worth calling such would fire at an animal unless prepared to track it down if wounded, even at some peril of his own skin, and, since night-shooting from a car precludes this act of much mercy and some courage, the cowardly practice should entitle its followers to be expelled from any club used by gentlemen, for some misdemeanours are punished more fitly in this manner than by law. (Still, 1971: 95)

The thrust of Still's criticism is clearly aimed at errant Britons. The 1909 legislation addressed this issue by imposing a blanket prohibition on shooting game between sunset and sunrise, and this prohibition remains in force today as a provision of the Fauna and Flora Protection Ordinance.

Hunting by (usually wealthy and titled) foreign visitors was also a source of irritation to the local hunting fraternity, for these foreigners were given privileges by the government that resident Europeans could not hope for. In 1907, for example, when the Grand Duke of Saxe-Weimar came to Hambantota on a shooting trip, the Resident Sportsmen's Reserve at Yala was closed, much to the outrage of the local British hunters, so that he could hunt there (Uragoda, 1994: 15). Another member of Europe's nobility who hunted in Ceylon was Archduke Franz Ferdinand, heir to the throne of Austria-Hungary, who shot an elephant in Kalawewa (Uragoda, 1994: 16). The solution proposed by the GPSC was to ask that license fees for hunting be vastly increased for such people. This was done in the 1909 ordinance, where, for instance, the resident's fee for a license to kill an elephant was Rs 100, while for non-residents it was Rs 300. The ordinance was shaped and informed by the ideology of British hunters on the island, and served their interests as they sought to affirm their status and their privileges with regard to both 'native' hunters and the privileged Europeans who visited the island from time to time to shoot.

FROM THE PROTECTION OF GAME TO THE CONSERVATION OF WILDLIFE

Game preservation was from its inception an almost exclusively white activity and the GPSC was an exclusively European club. One had to be proposed and seconded to join, and Sri Lankans interested in hunting or in wildlife were either not interested in joining or not invited to join. The first breach in the wall came when Dr Richard Spittel, a well-known Colombo surgeon of Dutch Burgher descent with a clientele among the Europeans resident on the island (including the Governor), was invited by a European planter friend to join the GPSC. Spittel, however, had given up hunting, stricken with remorse, according to Christine Wilson, his daughter and biographer, at having shot a doe in his youth, and had little sympathy for the aims of the GPSC. She writes,

> Those early Game Protection Society members found to their dismay that in Richard Spittel they had caught a tiger by the tail. Into their happy hunting clique they had introduced a rebel. They had not realized when they invited Spittel, the jungle lover and writer about the

forests into their midst, how he would change the very nature of their concept. (Wilson, 1975: 133)

Richard Spittel sought tirelessly, over many years and much acrimonious debate, to move the society towards a position favourable to the general preservation of wildlife and away from a narrow focus on hunting and game. Spittel advocated a holistic approach to protection; not simply a curb on hunting generally, but also policies (for example) to minimize the likelihood that elephants would come into conflict with human beings as their territories were encroached on through land development. In particular, he advocated protection for non-game animals such as bears, in which the general membership of the society at that period was not much interested. He served as President of the GPSC twice, in 1934–37, when he was a chief architect of the Fauna and Flora Protection Ordinance (Uragoda, 1994: 137), and again in 1957–58. In 1930, reflecting the trends in conservation both nationally and internationally, the GPSC changed its name to the Ceylon Game and Fauna Protection Society, signalling that it was no longer merely a club for hunters but had broader interests in conservation. In 1955 the society finally broke with its origins, changing its name to the Wildlife Protection Society of Ceylon. Spittel advocated the change; W.W.A. Phillips, one of the many English tea planters who had remained behind in the island after its independence, and who was one of the country's most important naturalists, opposed it (Uragoda, 1994: 24).

It is not surprising that Spittel should have been the thin edge of the wedge in transforming ideas and practices about wildlife conservation. He was first of all a Burgher, a small community (less than 1 per cent of the population) descended from Europeans who had settled in the island during the Portuguese and Dutch periods, and one that had benefited most from British colonialism in terms of status. English-speaking, Christian, and highly anglicized with claims to European heritage, they were of immense value to the British in staffing the lower echelons of the administrative apparatus. They saw themselves as modernizers and, writes Jayawardena, they were "aware of the currents of liberal thinking in Britain" (2000: 235--6). Sentiments in Britain were shifting away from the wildlife policies advocated by the old planting elite (hunting was finally abandoned as one of the objectives of the society in 1966, albeit despite strenuous objection). In 1903, the Society for the Preservation of the Wild Fauna of the Empire (now known as Fauna and Flora

International) was founded by a group of "penitent butchers" (ex-hunters of big game) who had become alarmed by the decline in the numbers of wild animals in the overseas territories ruled by Britain (Fitter and Morris, 1993). Furthermore, as a surgeon (and one with an exceptional reputation), Spittel came into contact with members of the planter class who sought out his professional services, and it was those ties that brought him into the GPSC. He was thus able to play an important role in 'Ceylonizing' the Game Protection Society, which began to recruit increasing numbers of members from the native-born elite.

THE ACTIVISM OF THE BOURGEOISIE

Kumari Jayawardena (2000) describes the emergence of this new elite out of the socio-economic transformations wrought by colonialism. It was a class drawn from all of the communities in the island that took advantage of new economic opportunities created during British rule. They included those who had acquired privileged status as minor functionaries and intermediaries under British rule (the Mudaliyars) and who were given land and titles by the British. Examples of these 'old rich' include the Bandaranaike and Obeyesekere families. Another component of this class, however, were those of modest origin who took advantage of opportunities for commerce, to acquire wealth (primarily through the lucrative trade in distilling and selling arrack), which they invested in landed property. The Senanayakes, who made their fortune mining graphite, were quintessential representatives of this second strand (Jayawardena, 2000: 191–2):

> Being in origin collaborative and imitative, members of the bourgeoisie transformed themselves culturally into Victorian ladies and gentlemen and adopted the language, religion and lifestyles of the British upper classes. They educated their sons and daughters in English, and where possible, sent them to British or Indian universities, thereby creating a group of professionals and bureaucrats who reinforced the new class. (Jayawardena, 2000: xix)

This class had the language skills, the inclination, and the opportunities (being educated in schools modelled on the British public school and its curriculum as well as in British universities) for some of its members to absorb the transcultural discourse of environmentalism. An exposure to British ideas of sportsmanship and wilderness was a part of the curriculum, for John Still's *The Jungle Tide* was required reading in the schools of Colombo (Webb, 2002: 165). Furthermore, an examination of what these members of the anglicized bourgeoisie with an interest in wildlife were reading is instructive. E.B. Wikramanayake, a prominent member of this class who served as President of the Wildlife Protection Society (as the Game Protection Society became known) in the 1960s, had a vast range of books on natural history and related subjects in his library. Apart from field guides and technical manuals of natural history, he had books on wild animal collecting, on *shikari* adventures, such as the books by Samuel Baker, accounts of jungle Ceylon by authors such as D.J.G. Henessey, Douglas Raffle, R.L. Spittel, and others, the *Bombay Natural History Society Journal*, the *Fauna of British India*, A.O. Hume's *Stray Feathers*, the works of Gerald Durrell, an indefatigable spokesman for the cause of conservation, and many others. His was an exceptionally large library, consonant with his resources and position, but the books he had probably represent what wildlife enthusiasts were reading at that period in the post-independence years.

Spittel was a tireless advocate of conservation and one of his lectures in the Town Hall in Colombo was attended by D.S. Senanayake, the Minister of Agriculture in the State Council created after the reforms of 1931. Senanayake, a product of the bourgeoisie created by the social and economic transformations of the colonial era, was also an enthusiast for wildlife. Wilson writes that "after the lecture, he and Spittel talked late into the evening" (1975: 135). From this contact and the discussions it generated grew the Fauna and Flora Protection Ordinance (FFPO), which marked a departure from the rationale of the game laws that it repealed and replaced, with the emphasis placed on a policy of preserving wildlife in general. Senanayake, who later became the first Prime Minister of independent Sri Lanka, is an important figure in wildlife conservation in the island, and the FFPO is in large part the product of his enthusiasm and energy, as well as that of Spittel. Sir Thomas Comyn-Platt, who visited Ceylon en route to Malaya to carry out a survey on the preservation of fauna in these two colonies for the Society for the Preservation of the Wild Fauna of the Empire, writes of his meeting with Senanayake:

> On arriving in Colombo I called upon Mr. Senanayake and told him of His Majesty The King's interest in my Mission and thanked

> him, on behalf of the Society, for his help, influence and support. He replied that not only was he a keen Preservationist, and would do all in his power to further our aims and objects, but that he realized fully the financial advantages of Wild Life in the development of Ceylon, how necessary were the present Reserves and sanctuaries, and hoped that there might yet be more. At the conclusion of our interview he told me he was about to propose further and more far reaching Wild Life Legislation; that he felt sure he could carry it through. (Comyn-Platt, n.d.)

Apart from the FFPO, the other signal achievement of the society was the creation of the Department of Wildlife in 1949,[2] following Sri Lanka's independence from Britain. The society had long felt that the protection of wildlife should not be entrusted to the Forest Department, which had been given the responsibility for enforcing the provisions of the FFPO, but should have its own independent agency. This position was linked to the belief that the most effective way to preserve wild animals was to create national parks and reserves that could be closely monitored and protected; such a solution required a specialized agency devoted to that task. The society eventually succeeded through incessant lobbying; D.S. Senanayake was by then the Prime Minister and his son, Dudley, had inherited his father's position as Minister of Agriculture and Lands, which, no doubt, helped.

The Department of Wildlife Conservation (DWLC) thus owes its existence to the sustained activism of the Ceylon Game and Fauna Protection Society over a period of decades. Despite criticisms from time to time, the society's relations with the department were cordial and collaborative. In the years after independence, however, the administrative service in Sri Lanka became increasingly politicized, culminating in the abolition of the Ceylon Civil Service (CCS) and its replacement in the early 1970s by the Sri Lanka Administrative Service, an institution rather more vulnerable to political pressure than its predecessor had been; the reasons are beyond the scope of this chapter. While no member of the CCS had ever been Director of the DWLC, a number of well-qualified individuals, well trained and familiar with the conservation of wildlife in the island, had served in this post. They included the first Warden (as the office was initially known), C.W. Nicholas, a Burgher who had served in the army in World War I and who, besides being an exceptional naturalist, was also a historian, and Lyn de Alwis, a Sinhalese who served as

Director of Wildlife in the late 1960s and again from 1977 to 1983. Most of the rangers recruited by Nicholas were ex-servicemen; this changed as time went by. The early years of wildlife conservation in Sri Lanka are thought of, by the subordinates of Nicholas and de Alwis and wildlife activists, as a golden age, a period during which the department was efficiently run, effective, and morale among its personnel high.

The years immediately before and after World War II were a period of transition in both the affairs and membership of the now-renamed GPSC. Spittel played an increasingly prominent role in the society's affairs, culminating in his election as President. He was able to bring increasing numbers of Sri Lankans into the membership, a process that accelerated in the post-war years. Both the aims of the society and the interests of the members changed, a fact reflected in the pages of *Loris*, the society's journal that Spittel had founded in 1936 and edited for 27 years. While the early issues are replete with articles of interest to sportsmen, on guns, hunting techniques, and accounts of hunting expeditions, these topics suffered a decline throughout the 1950s and finally, like old soldiers, simply faded away in the 1960s. The society was transformed from a small elite club of hunters, wish-ing mostly to preserve their way of life, into the major conservation organization in Sri Lanka until the early 1980s when others rose to challenge its position. Its effectiveness was a function of its access to power (in the person of politicians with an enthusiasm for wildlife) and its ability to lobby them. E.B. Wikramanayake for example was both President of the society and Minister of Justice in the mid-1950s. The heyday for this type of activism was the period from the 1930s to the 1960s.

The influence of the society began to wane for a number of reasons. Among them was the fact that the social context in which it was operating was changing while the society itself remained relatively unchanged in its social composition. 1956 marked the end of the hegemony of the anglicized bourgeoisie in Sri Lanka's affairs. While this was and remains a powerful and influential class, other social groups not grounded in anglicized values and more representative of the country's Sinhala—and Tamil-speaking—and educated majority, were moving to centre stage. This transformation also reshaped the political class, including those elected to the country's legislative bodies, who could no longer be counted on to share the social background or values of society activists. The society was slow to respond to this changing situation. Its publications were in English and its public discourse continued to be in that language. In belated recognition of this fact, the society introduced in 1976 a Sinhala-language magazine, *Warana*, to complement its flagship journal *Loris*, but it remained essentially an organization of the anglicized class. A telling indication of this is that unlike *Loris*, *Warana* was not automatically circulated to members, and until 1989 depended on a standing order for 3,000 copies from the Ministry of Educational Services to keep publishing. When the Ministry order was terminated, the print run had to be reduced to 1,000 copies heavily subsidized by the society and was reduced from two issues annually to one. It is mainly distributed to school nature clubs (Uragoda, 1994: 42–3).

THE MAGIC OF THE MARKET: CONSERVATION IN AN AGE OF GLOBALIZATION

The national and international context in which wildlife conservation was pursued changed after 1977, when the United National Party won a sweeping victory on the promise of liberalizing the economy, making it friendly to foreign investment, removing barriers to trade, and dismantling the dominant role of the state in economic life. These structural reforms reversed the quasi-socialist policies of previous governments and integrated Sri Lanka more firmly into the global economy; the International Monetary Fund (IMF) and bilateral institutions like the Asian Development Bank (ADB) played increasingly important roles in setting economic policy, and the role of the Finance Ministry and Central Bank were strengthened vis-à-vis other sectors of the state, particularly those vested in the welfare policies that had characterized state policy since independence. More opportunities for business were created and the once moribund private sector played an increasingly important role in economic life. The stringent restrictions on foreign travel, including education abroad, that had characterized the previous seven years were lifted, and increasing numbers of Sri Lankans began to travel abroad and seek higher education outside the island. Most importantly for environmental activism, large sums of money became available from international NGOs and foreign governments for environmental causes of various kinds, and in response to this ready supply, environmental NGOs of one kind or another blossomed and flourished. Globalization thus expanded the depth and range of contacts between Sri Lankan NGOs and their counterparts abroad while simultaneously making available large sums of money for their activities. In addition, private enterprise and the pursuit of profit acquired a respectability they had not enjoyed earlier, and these factors shaped the course that environment activism would take.

The most significant of the new organizations was Environmental Foundation Limited (EFL), founded in 1981 by nine students (many of them studying law) and a veteran environmentalist, Iranganie Serasinghe. It owed its genesis to a number of factors, principally *(a)* the frustration felt by a younger generation of activists towards the Wildlife and Nature Protection Society (or WNPS, as GPSC was now known), which had become moribund and ineffective through a period of internal power struggles and the declining effectiveness of its favoured method of lobbying; and *(b)* the realization on the part of law students that Sri Lanka possessed a well-developed framework of environmental laws that were ineffectively implemented and which could be used as a lever to promote environmental action. The model for EFL was the Natural Resources Defence Council (NRDC) in the United States. EFL was set up and incorporated as a public interest law firm, to use the courts to compel the state and its agents to carry out their statutory responsibilities towards the environment. It was the most effective and best-known environmental organization in Sri Lanka during the 1980s and 1990s and continues to be an important force today.

The social background of the nine male students who founded it was indistinguishable from that of members of the Wildlife and Nature Protection Society; indeed, all of them were or had been members of that organization.[3] All had been educated at the two most elite schools in the island, Royal College and St. Thomas' College—the same two schools, modelled on British public schools, which had produced a disproportionate number of the emerging bourgeoisie of the colonial period. All were comfortably bilingual in Sinhala or Tamil and English. Eight of them were Sinhalese and one a Muslim. Mrs Serasinghe, a generation older, was from the same social class.

The expanded understanding of what constituted environment is suggested by the cases that EFL filed or intervened in during the first 20 years of its existence, between 1981 and 2001. There were 64 cases in all (Patirana and Patirana, c. 2001) and they can be loosely categorized as follows:

- Cases brought against the Director of Wildlife Conservation 4
- Other cases involving protection of natural areas 2
- Cases under the fundamental rights clause of the constitution 3
- Cases involving industrial pollution and the abatement of minor nuisances 38
- Cases concerning the dumping of garbage 5
- Cases with significant impact on policy concerning environmentand development 6
- Miscellaneous 6

The first case filed by EFL came two years after it had been incorporated and was significant for the openly critical approach it took to relations with the Director of Wildlife Conservation.

In the last couple of decades, the leadership of the DWLC has been characterized by a series of poor appointments, often of people with little knowledge of conservation or wildlife, or with little administrative skill, contributing to deterioration in the relationship between the department's leadership and activists for wildlife conservation. Criticisms levelled at the department by EFL have been particularly scathing. EFL's first case in 1984 (SC No. 40/84) sought a stay order against the Director of Wildlife to prevent him ordering the withdrawal of 51 cases that had been filed by wildlife officers in Moneragala against squatters, who, backed by a powerful local politician, had encroached on 208 acres of the Gal Oya National Park. The court found for EFL. Another case concerned a private zoo, established in violation of the provisions of the FFPO but with the concurrence of the Director, DWLC. In both cases, political pressure had been brought to bear on the Director to act against both the spirit and the letter of the FFPO. The editor of EFL's newsletter, *Biosphere*, commented caustically,

> If the Department of Wildlife Conservation is to play a meaningful role in the Wildlife conservation in this country then it must change its attitude at once and work as a responsible body along with the non-governmental organisations involved in the conservation effort, and not be manoeuvered by disinterested [sic] politicians.[4] (Ladduwahetty, c. 1984: 2)

Three cases filed by EFL under the provisions of the constitution's guarantee of fundamental rights have served to win the confidence of the rank-and-file officers who represent DWLC in the field. All three involve officers of the Forest Department and the Department of Wildlife Conservation who had been detained and assaulted by other agents of the state (police, politicians, and army officers) while in the exercise of their duty.[5] Mohamad Faiz, a forest officer, had been assaulted by local politicians when he arrested some of their followers for illegally felling timber, and had then been detained by the police and subjected to further assault by the same politicians while in police custody. Weragama, a wildlife ranger, was assaulted by police officers when he warned them against hunting illegally, while I.D. Jayaweera, a wildlife ranger in the Uda Walawe National Park, had been detained by an army officer who had illegally shot an elephant. EFL appeared for the petitioners in all these cases, and prevailed in all of them. What is significant in these cases is that all of these officers, despite being agents of the state, had to have recourse to an NGO and public interest law firm to protect themselves and their rights against other agents of the state; their respective departments were unable to do so. One of the consequences of EFL's good relations with the rank and file of the department is that it is able to get information on egregious violations of the FFPO as they occur, a typical example being encroachment on national park lands at the instigation of local politicians.

The bulk of the cases, however, concern issues of industrial pollution and nuisance, as well as questions of administrative procedure. In many of these cases, EFL simply provided expert advice to the police or local administrative bodies, in others it appeared on behalf of local people who were fighting a nuisance, as in the case of two rubber factories that were polluting local wells. Several of the cases brought by EFL, however, have had more far-reaching consequences for environmental conservation in Sri Lanka. Two significant such cases during the 1990s include the Kandalama Hotel case and the Eppawela case.

The changing nature of the struggles over environment and nature and the continuing pivotal role of middle-class activists are illustrated by these two major struggles of the 1990s. The first involved the development of a luxury hotel by one of Sri Lanka's largest companies in Dambulla, on the banks of the Kandalama tank (an irrigation reservoir). Construction was strongly opposed by local villagers, who feared that the hotel's requirements for water would threaten their livelihood as rice cultivators, by the priest of the rock temple at

Dambulla, as well as by broad segments of the general public. This was a struggle in which a number of urban, middle-class environmental organizations, among them EFL, became involved. EFL sought to halt the project on the grounds that the procedure laid out in the State Lands Ordinance for the leasing of state land had not been followed (Guneratne, 1996: 122). The court agreed, and stayed the fulfillment of the lease until the procedure was followed. Guneratne writes: "However, the Land Commissioner, having complied with the order of the court and with the procedure, granted the lease in spite of a significant number of objections which he had received" (ibid.). While the struggle could not prevent the hotel from being built in 1994, it did force the hotel to make significant modifications to the design, enabling it to tout itself thereafter as an 'eco-friendly hotel'.[6] EFL chose not to pursue the struggle further to avoid compromising the cabinet's approval of the draft Environmental Impact Assessment regulations (EIA) which represented a significant advance in the field of environmental conservation in Sri Lanka.

The other significant case that EFL took on was against a proposed phosphate mine of enormous proportions in the North Central Province, in the vicinity of the small town of Eppawela. The Eppawela case is a landmark case in Sri Lankan environmental law. It began when the Sri Lankan government agreed to lease a large area in the North Central Province, centring on Eppawela, to a consortium led by IMC-Agro, whose parent company is Freeport McMoran. The project would have affected an area of 800 square kilometres extending up to the outskirts of Anuradhapura and displacing about 12,000 people from their homes. It would also have damaged a number of archaeological sites. Despite considerable public opposition, including the National Academy of Sciences and the National Science Foundation, thousands of villagers from the affected area, Buddhist monks, and activists, the government was determined to go ahead with the project, even though no proper studies had been done of the extent and quality of the phosphate deposits, and despite the lack of a proper environmental impact assessment. Eventually, seven individuals from the area, including the chief priest of the Eppawela temple, filed a case in the Supreme Court of Sri Lanka with the support of EFL, alleging that their fundamental rights to residence and livelihood guaranteed in Articles 12(1), 14(1)(g) and (h) of the constitution were threatened by the mine.[7] The mine had been approved in violation of laws that require both public participation in the decision-making process and an environmental impact assessment. The judges ruled in favour of the plaintiffs, ordering the government to carry out comprehensive studies first, and prohibiting the government from engaging in any project outside the national environmental laws, including judgments of the court. This is an important case because Sri Lankan courts had, in the past, been reluctant to rule on environment- or development-related issues. The resolution of the issue came not from the government's giving in to the sustained and broad-based public opposition, but through a decision of the Supreme Court in response to a case filed by EFL. While both these struggles—Kandalama and Eppawela—had elements of the broad-based mass participation found in India, especially in the Eppawela case, in both cases, the crucial difference was made by the middle-class organizations.

THE ASIAN DEVELOPMENT BANK PROJECT

Both the Kandalama and the Eppawela cases represent in different ways the impact of globalization—in the Kandalama case, the rapid expansion of tourism and the need to develop new sites (Kandalama is close to the Cultural Triangle, the development of the archaeological sites in the north-central plain for tourism), and in the Eppawela case, resource extraction by a major multinational corporation. The chronic fiscal crisis of the Sri Lankan state, in part due to the pressures of a decades-long civil war, has made almost any project likely to generate some revenue attractive to the government. The state however does not speak with one voice. Different agencies and agents of the state have different priorities and agendas, and compete with each other to achieve them. Economic globalization necessarily affects the balance among these various actors (Sassen, 1999). In the context of Sri Lanka's fiscal crisis, state agencies associated with the raising of revenue or in promoting trade have interests that are opposed to other agencies with different sets of priorities. Wildlife (or rather biodiversity, a concept that came into use in the late 1990s) represents a resource that, like other resources, can be exploited for commercial gain. The last environmental controversy I shall consider here draws attention to the struggle among different sectors of civil society and the state to both control a resource and define its meaning.

In December 2000 the government of Sri Lanka and the ADB signed an agreement under which the ADB agreed to arrange a loan of US$34.7 million to help the Sri Lankan government to conserve its biodiversity, in particular by upgrading the capacity of the DWLC to manage and administer protected areas, promote ecotourism, and enable community participation in the management of those areas, which cover about 15 per cent of the total land area. The DWLC has responsibility for about 85 per cent of all protected areas; the Forest Department for the remainder. In addition to a loan of US$2 million dollars provided by the ADB under concessionary terms, the Global Environmental Facility would provide a grant of US$9 million, and the government of the Netherlands a grant of US$4 million. The Dutch grant was earmarked for the creation of a Trust Fund to finance community-based biodiversity conservation efforts in villages on the periphery of Protected Areas (PAs). The Sri Lankan government's share of the total cost was US$7.7 million.

The ADB project became controversial for a number of reasons. First, it was negotiated and signed in secret. By the time the environmental community in Sri Lanka became aware of it, it was a *fait accompli*. Second, it was quite sweeping in its scope: no less than seven of Sri Lanka's protected areas, many of particular significance as reservoirs of biodiversity, were included. Third, the ADB was pushing for extensive amendments to the FFPO, and for its eventual replacement with a Biodiversity and Rainforest Conservation Act, the effect of which would have been to weaken the ability of the DWLC to regulate traffic in plants and wildlife (this, so far, has not come to fruition). A position paper for the cabinet on this proposed legislation, leaked to environmental activists, noted that "While biodiversity should be conserved because of its heritage value to the people of Sri Lanka, it also offers great opportunities as an employment-intensive value-added sector of growing importance, e.g. with regard to realizing the potential of medicinal plants and nature-based tourism".[8] Fourth, the project was quite explicit about facilitating bio-prospecting,[9] which led environmentalist critics to believe that what was intended was the wholesale exploitation of Sri Lanka's genetic resources for the benefit of foreign commercial interests, which would have taken place in the absence of an adequate framework of local laws governing intellectual property rights. Nor were they reassured in their concerns by the ADB's insistence that a major role in the project should be given to (unspecified) international NGOs.

Fifth, the ADB wished to set up a fund to finance popular participation in conservation and development activities among communities adjacent to protected areas that would be beyond the supervisory control of the Government of Sri Lanka and exempt from taxation; this was denounced by activists as an infringement on the country's sovereignty.[10] Finally, the project sought eventually to subordinate the DWLC to a Biodiversity Authority, one of whose central aims would be to "facilitate ... the sustainable use of biodiversity in a manner consistent with national development objectives".[11] In order to justify this agenda, the ADB depicted the DWLC as lacking the capacity to manage protected areas and implement conservation strategies, even as it systematically ignored one of the central reasons for that situation, the extensive political interference in the department's affairs.

Even though the project aroused a storm of controversy, that storm raged almost entirely in the English-language press and among the English-educated urban wildlife activists. This act of globalization brought to the fore the varied interests of this category of people, all sharing more or less the same class background. Indeed, like their ancestors a generation and more ago, they were almost all educated in the elite boys' schools of St. Thomas', Royal, and Trinity, and in girls' schools such as Ladies College. The DWLC was hostile to the project, whose (intended) effect was to weaken it as an institution, and the controversy was characterized by a steady stream of supposedly confidential documents that were leaked to wildlife activists, making it impossible for the ADB to keep the project details confidential.

The project was supported mainly by those wildlife enthusiasts who, coincidentally, had something to gain by its implementation. Its stress on ecotourism as a source of revenue for conservation, for example, would benefit the expanding ecotourism sector in Sri Lanka, which has become a profitable component of the hotel industry. Some of these wildlife enthusiasts have invested heavily in this sector. The ADB's insistence on replacing the FFPO with a Biodiversity Act that would loosen the control the Director of Wildlife Conservation has over the export of fauna and flora has the support of some Sri Lankan environmentalists and others who (often illegally, when they fail to obtain a permit) export the same. And there are environmentalists who see the ADB as promoting an equity-based approach to conservation and support it for that reason. The ADB has been able to weave the language of equity into its proposals, although a careful reading suggests that the real benefits would accrue to urban-based business and political elites, with a few symbolic crumbs going to villagers living adjacent to protected areas. A weakness of the position of wildlife activists in Sri Lanka (certainly the ones most opposed to the ADB project) is that they have little vision of what an equity-based approach to nature conservation might look like, and have never made a sustained argument for one. This is very different from the situation in both India, where equity-based approaches are the dominant strand in environmentalism, and the African continent, where equity-based approaches have been integrated into wildlife conservation (Adams and McShane, 1992). In India, equity-based approaches are developed in the grassroots, not by outside elites. In Sri Lanka, people detrimentally impacted by national parks and wildlife have organized no social movement to make their voices heard and to affect policy.

When lobbying, writing to the papers, and other methods of middle-class protest had failed, a group of wildlife activists resorted to the court of appeal, on the grounds that the very existence of the project violates the provisions of the FFPO, which continues to be in force. The lawyer who filed the case—the same one who appeared for the plaintiffs in the Eppawela case—notes that "for the Government to enter into a project that is contrary to the law on the mere promise to amend the law is *ultra vires* and a usurpation of the powers of Parliament and the People" (Ruana Rajapakse, personal communication). The case was ultimately settled in favour of the plaintiffs. Most significantly, the government agreed that the project would not be applied to any protected area other than the ones mentioned in the original agreement and that it would terminate on 30 June 2007. The authority of the Director-General of the DWLC was reaffirmed and many of the more controversial provisions of the original agreement were annulled, substantially modified, or made to conform with the provisions of the FFPO, and the plaintiffs were granted representation on the steering committee for the project.[12] It was a major victory.

CONCLUSION

Environmentalism in Sri Lanka has been transformed over the years from a narrow focus on game and the regulation of hunting, whose ultimate beneficiaries were a small colonial hunting elite, to an activism based on the elaboration of the concepts of wildlife and nature by the successors to that colonial elite, the anglicized bourgeoisie that emerged in the colonial era, and dominated Sri Lankan public life for a good part of the twentieth century. While this chapter has focused on the role of the anglicized middle class in this activism, and while I argue that for much of the twentieth century this class was the principal actor in environmental struggles, the class basis of environmentalism in modern Sri Lanka is much broader today. There are hundreds, maybe thousands, of small environmental NGOs in rural and small-town Sri Lanka, but the major players are located in Colombo and draw their membership and support from the urban middle class, both those comfortably bilingual as well as those whose primary competence is in either Sinhala or Tamil. Environmentalism as a concept broader than simply the conservation of wildlife and the preservation of nature did not emerge until the last decades of the twentieth century. It was spurred on both by a global discourse on the environment to which many activists were exposed and in which they came to be engaged, and by the impact of economic globalization on Sri Lankan society. This new environmentalism was exemplified not only by the public nuisance cases which EFL instigated, but by responses to more sweeping threats to the livelihood and well-being of rural as well as urban people, such as the Eppawela Phosphate Mine project.

While the concept of 'game' no longer has relevance in Sri Lanka, the concept of 'wildlife' is beginning to be displaced in environmentalist discourse by that of 'biodiversity'. These concepts have fundamentally different meanings. 'Wildlife' encompasses the idea of species to be protected for their own sakes, for both aesthetic and moral reasons. The notion of 'wildlife' (as well as 'nature', which includes non-mammalian and avian species, and the habitats in which they are to be found) concerns things to be preserved. Biodiversity, on the other hand, is about genetic information and data, and contextualized not in terms of wildlife treaties such as the Convention on International Trade in Endangered Species (CITES), but of trade conventions such as Trade Related Intellectual Property Rights (TRIPS). This, in fact, is how many Sri Lankan environmental activists understand it, and is the basis of their sharp and polemical critique of the ADB project. This perspective is clearly articulated by Jagath Gunawardene, perhaps the leading environmental lawyer in Sri Lanka:

> Crop wild relatives [i.e. wild relatives of crop plants] are increasingly being subjected to bio-piracy, by corporate interests, research institutes and universities in developed countries. It is vital to place safeguards to protect our rights over these plants. (Gunawardene, 2002)

Until the 1970s environmentalism in Sri Lanka had a fairly restricted meaning, both conceptually and in the way it informed activism. Environment was not in fact the concept deployed. The activists involved were a relatively small group, drawn more or less from the same social background, and to a great extent sharing the same values and orientation to the task at hand. In the decades since all this has changed. Not only are social backgrounds more diverse, there is no longer a consensus on what the problem is or how it should be addressed. This is illustrated very well in the controversy over the ADB project, in which a broad range of people, all with impeccable credentials as environmentalists, staked out contradictory and opposing positions. This can (and has) been attributed both to honest conviction and to the desire to take advantage of the opportunities for advancement created by globalization.

To sum up, environmentalism in Sri Lanka passed through three principal stages, each associated with a certain social category and with a particular socio-economic and political context. Colonial society gave rise to the first stage of activism, the preservation of game pursued by expatriate hunters, for whom hunting was a form of identity and status affirmation as much as it was a form of recreation. Over the course of the colonial period, and shaped by a conservation discourse and ethic originating beyond the colony's borders, this social group came to be replaced by an indigenous elite with little interest in hunting, but which shared the expatriate's desire to preserve the jungle for recreation and which sought to limit the other uses to which the jungle and its wildlife might be put by other segments of Sri Lankan society. Those who participated in both these stages shared a more or less unified ideology—facilitated by the smallness of their numbers and the limited range of options for alternative uses for wildlife, they could agree on the nature of the task at hand and how it was to be achieved. This aspect is evident from the hegemonic status in environmental activism enjoyed by the Wildlife and Nature Protection Society (known originally, as we have seen, as the Ceylon Game Protection Society) during this period. This consensus and the social cohesion which engendered it broke down with the contemporary era of globalization, which, while involving a great many more actors of diverse social backgrounds, also created splits among the ranks of the traditional activists (many of whom were members of the WNPS) with respect to what conservation meant, the uses to which wildlife (or biodiversity) could be put, and the legitimacy of exploiting wildlife for private commercial gain. Environmental activism is more broad-based and democratic in the range of perspectives offered than it used to be, but it remains a form of activism that disproportionately attracts the urban middle class.

NOTES

1. The Sarvodaya movement, inspired by Gandhian ideals, focuses on social justice and community development, and is one of the oldest NGOs in Sri Lanka. See Bond (2004) and Goulet (1981).
2. It was renamed the Department of Wildlife Conservation (DWLC) in 1970.
3. I was one of the founding members of EFL but left the country to study abroad shortly after it was created and played no role in its later development.
4. The author means politicians with no interest in wildlife conservation.
5. *Mohamad Faiz* vs. *A.G. and Six Others*, SC No 89/91, *Weragama* vs. *Indran and Others*, SC No. 396/93 and *I.D.Jayaweera* vs. *Col. A.L.R. Wijetunga and Others*, SC No. 42/97/FR). The Eppawela case (discussed in the following) is also a fundamental rights case, but I treat it separately in this chapter as its significance for environmental activism is much broader.
6. One guest at Kandalama wrote in an online review, "There were eco friendly soaps and shower gels. Eco friendly writing paper could be found in the bedroom. Guests were advised that their rubbish was sorted and that the money raised paid for two full time employees to do the recycling". (Available at http://www.epinions.com/content_142942834308#, accessed on 27 May 2005).
7. *Tikiri Banda Bulankulama and Others* vs. *Director of Geological Survey & Mines Bureau and Others*, SC No. 884/99/FR.
8. Memorandum to the cabinet entitled 'Biodiversity and Rainforest Conservation Act'. Mimeo.
9. 'Report and Recommendation of the President to the Board of Directors on a Proposed Loan to the Democratic Socialist Republic of Sri Lanka for the Protected Area Management and Wildlife Conservation Project', September 2000, p. 29.
10. 'World Bank and Asian Development Bank Memorandum of Understanding of the Joint Pre-Appraisal Mission for the Protected Area Management and Wildlife Conservation Project', 3 May 2000; letter from Selvam Canagaratne, one of the plaintiffs in the Court of Appeal Application No. 1357/2002, to the Director, Department of Wildlife Conservation, dated 6 June 2002. Canagaratne's letter is an excellent and detailed analysis of specific provisions in the ADB's original 'Report and Recommendation of the President' cited in note 7. This document, originally an internal paper for the

ADB, was eventually made publicly available by the bank in response to the pressure brought to bear on it by activists in Sri Lanka, and became the defining document for the whole project.

11. 'Biodiversity and Rainforest Conservation Act' cited in note 8.
12. 'Final Terms of Settlement of Court of Appeal Application No. 1357/2002', 28 September 2005.

REFERENCES

Adams, Jonathan S. and Thomas O. McShane. 1992. *The Myth of Wild Africa: Conservation without Illusion*. New York: W. W. Norton and Company.

Baden-Powell of Gilwell, R.S.S. 1908. *Scouting for Boys: Part I*. London: Horace Cox.

Baker, Samuel. 1970 (1853). *The Rifle and the Hound in Ceylon*. Dehiwela, Sri Lanka: Tisara Prakasakayo.

Bennett, Scott. 1984. 'Shikar and the Raj', *South Asia*, 7(2): 72–88.

Bond, George D. 2004. *Buddhism at Work: Community Development, Social Empowerment and the Sarvodaya Movement*. Bloomfield, CT: Kumarian Press.

Clark, Alfred. 1971 (1901). *Sport in the Low-Country of Ceylon*. Dehiwela, Sri Lanka: Tisara Prakasakayo.

Comyn-Platt, Sir Thomas. n.d. (c. 1936). 'A Report on Fauna Preservation in Ceylon', National Archives, Kew, England, CO 54/937/1.

De Alwis, Percy. 1965. 'National Parks: Their Growth and Importance', *Loris*, 10(3): 172–5.

Fitter, Richard and Jacqui Morris. 1993. 'The Fauna and Flora Preservation Society – Conserving Wildlife for 90 Years', *Journal of Biological Education*, 27(2): 103. Academic Search Premier, EBSCOhost (accessed on 16 December 2008).

Gordon-Cumming, C.F. 1892. *Two Happy Years in Ceylon* (2 vols). London: William Blackwood and Sons.

Goulet, D. 1981. *Survival with Integrity: Sarvodaya at the Crossroads*. Colombo: Marga Institute.

Guha, Ramachandra and Madhav Gadgil. 1995. *Ecology and Equity: The Use and Abuse of Nature in Contemporary India*. London and New York: Routledge.

Gunawardene, Jagath. 2002. 'Crop Wild Relatives and Legal Protection', *The Island*, 15 May 2002.

Guneratne, Camena. 1996. 'Country Report: Sri Lanka', *Asia Pacific Journal of Environmental Law*, 1(1 and 2): 114–24.

Henry, G.M. 2000. *Pearls to Painting: A Naturalist in Ceylon*. Colombo: WHT Publications.

Hoffman, T.W. 1969. 'The Wildlife Protection Society of Ceylon: Some Historical Reflections on the Occasion of its 75th Anniversary', *Loris*, 11(6): 333–45.

Jayawardena, Kumari. 2000. *Nobodies to Somebodies: The Rise of the Colonial Bourgeoisie in Sri Lanka*. Colombo: Social Scientists' Association and Sanjiva Books.

Ladduwahetty, Nalin. c. 1984. 'Wildlife Dept: A Change of Attitude Needed', *Biosphere*, 1(3): 2.

MacKenzie, John M. 1988. *The Empire of Nature*. Manchester and New York: Manchester University Press.

Milton, Kay. 1996. *Environmentalism and Cultural Theory: Exploring the Role of Anthropology in Environmental Discourse*. London and New York: Routledge.

Patirana, Chandi and Wathsala Patirana. c. 2001. 'The Journey from Gal Oya to Eppawela', Colombo, Environmental Foundation Limited. Available at www.efl.lk/pdf/efl cases/galoya.pdf (accessed on 25 May 2005).

Ranlett, John. 1983. '"Checking Nature's Desecration": Late-Victorian Environmental Organization', *Victorian Studies*, 26(2): 197–222.

Sassen, Saskia. 1999. 'Embedding the Global in the National: Implications for the Role of the State', *Macalester International*, 7: 31–44.

Shiva, Vandana and Radha Holla-Bhar. 1996. 'Piracy by Patent: The Case of the Neem Tree', in Jerry Mander and Edward Goldsmith (eds), *The Case Against the Global Economy and for a Turn to the Local*, pp. 146–59. San Francisco: Sierra Club Books.

Spittel, R.L. 1942. 'The Creatures of our Jungles', *Loris*, 3(4): 11–17.

Still, John. 1971 [1930]. *The Jungle Tide*. Colombo: Hansa Publishers Ltd.

Tutein-Nolthenius, A.C. 1937. *37 Years of Game Protection in Ceylon: A Short History of the Ceylon Game and Fauna Protection Society, 1894 to 1931*. Colombo: Times of Ceylon.

Uragoda, C.A. 1994. *Wildlife Conservation in Sri Lanka*. Colombo: Wildlife and Nature Protection Society of Sri Lanka.

Van der Veer, P. 2001. *Imperial Encounters: Religion and Modernity in India and Britain*. Princeton and Oxford: Princeton University Press.

Webb, James L.A. 2002. *Tropical Pioneers: Human Agency and Ecological Change in the Highlands of Sri Lanka, 1800–1900*. Athens, Ohio: Ohio University Press.

Wilson, Christine Spittel. 1975. *Surgeon of the Wilderness: The Biography of Richard Spittel*. Colombo: Lake House Investments Ltd.

Chapter 10

Civil Society and its Fragments

WILLIAM F. FISHER

This chapter reflects on the interconnections among a series of research projects I have conducted over the past 20 years on activism in South Asia.[1] It argues that civil society is best understood as a fragmented and politically contested realm where the challenge is to understand how the fluid and changing local, regional, national, and transnational processes and connections can both potentially support and suppress an insurrection of subjugated knowledge.

I began this reflection by considering the set of questions on activists and civil society that David N. Gellner identified as underlying the conference in which these papers where first presented: Do activists form a class? Do particular types of activists tend to come from specific communal, regional, class, or educational backgrounds? Are there radical differences between ethnic and other types of activists? Does activism arrive at particular historical junctures? Are government attempts to encourage inclusiveness and democracy undermined by the forms used to propagate these values? These are straightforward and intuitive questions. But they also forced me to recognize that my own research had led me to focus much more on processes, and less on activists themselves. The dilemma I found myself reflecting upon was, 'How is it that questions about ethnic activism in Nepal and anti-dam activism in India had eventually led me to places like South Africa, Brazil, and Vietnam?' That is, what does activism in South Asia have to do with activism elsewhere in the world? While my research questions remained focused on the efforts of activists to influence lives lived locally, why is it that I had become increasingly drawn to wider processes and frequently to translocal activism? Activists as individuals came and went; they often moved on to other efforts, started new movements, and sometimes joined governments, bureaucracies, or mainstream non-governmental organizations (NGOs), etc., but the processes they initiated continued to evolve. While pursuing the kind of multi-sited research that George Marcus has exhorted us to do in the contemporary world, I had come to focus less on activists and more on we might call 'following the activism'. It was this investigative pursuit that led me from the Narmada valley in western India, to Washington DC, and then Japan. And then later as the same activism (and some of the same activists) expanded into an effort to create a World Commission on Dams (WCD), it led me to follow the activism loosely organized under the rubric of the International Committee on Dams, Rivers, and People (ICDRP) and their activities in Sao Paulo, Capetown, Cairo, Hanoi, Bangkok, and Prague, as well as to the International Meetings of Dam Affected Peoples in Brazil and Thailand. It is significant, however, that while the activism spread ever more transnationally, the focus and concerns of the South Asian activists never wandered far from the needs of people in valleys like the Narmada.

What quickly became clear was that the different agendas and interests within complex local conflicts did not all originate there nor were they all played out there. It was important then to analyse the ability of locally based groups and activists to reach beyond local boundaries (and often beyond the boundaries of the state) and to join translocally with other individuals, groups, and movements in order to influence the actions and policies of other groups, international organizations, and their home states. What we might call the 'globalization' of activism both emerges from and impacts upon global flows of people, technology, money, influence, and ideas. In focusing on subsets of these flows, my research questions how our ethnographies of local activism can take into account transnational activism and the advocacy networks along which communication and values move freely across national borders. At stake is an understanding of the relationships among local lives, local social movements, and global processes. The attempt to contribute to this understanding raises questions about how studies of activists and their transnational connections, flows, and alliances can contribute to contemporary understandings of the interrelatedness of processes of globalization and lives lived locally. The attempt to analytically approach the relationship between complex global processes and local lives highlights the need to reconceive both the 'global' and the 'local'.

CATEGORIZING AND CORRALLING CIVIL SOCIETY

Many analysts have commented on the associational revolution that has swept the world since the late 1980s. Miklos Marshall (2004), for example, called the 1990s "the decade of civil society" and the first decade of the twenty-first century has seen continued growth in civil society organizations. There has been great speculation about its transformational potential and a recasting of academic and activist discourse in terms of civil society. Academics and practitioners now openly discuss the role of civil society in development, how to build vibrant civil societies, the relationship between civil society and the state, the role of civil society groups in transnational connections, the emergence of a global civil society, the ability of civil society to empower people and to contribute to processes of democratization (see, for example, Fisher, 1997; Lewis and Kanji, 2009). But despite all this enthusiasm, we still have a great deal of difficulty in making useful connections between the abstraction of civil society and the hard realities of our research experiences.

Elsewhere I have expressed considerable scepticism about the analytic utility of terms like civil society that are used in many different ways to mean whatever anyone seems to want them to mean (Fisher, 1993, 1997; Fisher and Ponniah, 2003b). Too frequently terms like civil society and NGO are used as if they carry some analytic meaning when in fact they carry very little. Resisting Humpty Dumpty approach to analytic categories, I am inclined more to the cautious approach of Wittgenstein who saw the terms as utilitarian but in a limited way. Recognizing the need to categorize and the constraints categorization places on understanding, Wittgenstein noted that he used his propositions like tools, more specifically as ladders to climb up to a new level of understanding and once there he threw them away.[2]

So what do we mean when we talk about civil society? What is it we are trying to understand by repackaging or reframing the world or our worlds with such references? How is it that so-called civil society groups have come to be seen as central to widely different analytic perspectives and to very different policy and political agendas?

In fact it often seems that analysts who refer to civil society are not all talking about the same set of associations. In truth they are not: divorced from ethnographic particulars, abstract debates hinge on several essentialized categories—civil society, NGOs, social movements, and globalization—used in different ways by different theorists. What we call things and how we define them has a tremendous impact on what we understand. The definitions of all the key terms in the debate about social movements and activists—civil society, global civil society, and globalization—are so contested that they need to be critically interrogated.

Though the term civil society has come to be widely embraced, it is often used as an essentialized category employed in different ways by different theorists. The idea has always been rife with ambiguity and the term is "as contested as the social and political institutions it purports to describe" (Hunt, 1999: 11). Civil society, when it is not used as a synonym for society in general, is used to refer to "that segment of society that interacts with the state, influences the state and yet is distinct from the state" (Chazan, 1992: 281). Some contemporary writers have enthusiastically embraced civil society in a simplistic teleological framework that emerges from the conventional wisdom about the transformation of Eastern Europe in the late 1980s. In this view, civil society organizations are celebrated as representing the beginning of the democratization process. Some recent re-conceptions by South Asian scholars have tried to define civil society such that it includes institutions of the state (and other exploitative bourgeois institutions) and distinguish it from 'political society' defined as a more inchoate, informal realm of subalterns. Though this creates enormous terminological confusion, it does help to expose the pitfalls that open up when the term is used in simplistic normative contexts. And it serves to expose the gaps that do exist between those groups that operate to manage society and those that attempt to resist or alter the form of this management. What remain under-theorized are the relationships among various civil society groups and processes and the institutions of the state. Not surprisingly, South Asian governments have often seen civil society groups as undermining state power and legitimacy and have attempted to bring these groups under control through government agencies set up to service them. We have only to contrast the Indian state and the Nepalese state, or, alternatively, the different constraints and opportunities provided by the Nepalese state at different points in its history (during, for instance, the Panchayat period, the early post-1990 democratic state, or the post-insurgency state) to recognize how the nature of the state can dramatically alter the opportunities and constraints facing civil society groups.

Many analysts have tried to define civil society in terms of its constituent institutions and actors: NGOs, activists, social movements, etc. But this compounds the ambiguity as the categories of 'NGO' and 'social movement' are also applied in varying and problematic ways. 'NGO', for example, is employed to refer to a wide range of formal and informal associations: community-based organizations (CBOs), grassroots organizations (GROs), government-organized NGOs (GONGOs), international non-governmental organizations (INGOs), etc. There is little agreement about what NGOs and social movements are and perhaps even less about what they should be called. The generalizations about the NGO sector obscure the tremendous diversity found within it. Indeed, the category is so heterogeneous that it is hard to generalize accurately (see Fisher, 1997). It includes community-based or grassroots organizations; membership-based, locally autonomous groups; and groups of urban intellectuals working in issue areas. Some of these are autonomous from the state and the market; while others are linked in varying ways and in varying degrees to governments, international organizations, INGOs, and the private sector.

So-called global civil society is a concept of more recent and vaguer usage than globalization. It implies a world-wide social interaction analogous to the form and function of civil societies we find grounded within nation-states, yet for some authors it refers to no more than NGOs flocking together at ad hoc conferences like UNCED (the 1992 UN Conference on Environment and Development in Rio) or to social movements gathering at the annual and regional meetings of the World Social Forum.

The increasing interest in civil society arises simultaneously with the interest in globalization and concern about how a global civil society can interact with the major actors and process of globalization. But globalization is probably the most overused term in the contemporary political and social science lexicons. The contemporary discussion about globalization has emphasized the intensification of trans-border interactions in the contemporary world. Hannerz calls globalization "a matter of increasing long-distance interconnectedness" (1996: 17). Appadurai notes that it "entails a radical acceleration of the flows of images, people, money, technologies across the face of the globe" (1990).

There is a widespread sense that globalization weakens states and strengthens civil society in many countries. This view is too simplistic and the effects of globalizing processes are too complex to be so easily generalized. I use 'globalization' to refer to social, economic, cultural, and demographic processes that transcend nations, such that attention limited to local processes, identities, and units of analysis yields incomplete understanding of the local.[3] 'Transnationalism' entails a more limited range: global processes are decentred from national territories and take place in a deterritorialized global space, whereas transnational processes are anchored in but transcend one or more states.

One thing needed to flesh out our understanding of the complexities of civil society in South Asia is more nuanced and empirically based studies of the relationship among various actors like those between NGOs and social movements. Analysts generally contrast the bureaucratization or institutionalization characteristic of some NGOs with the more fluid and fragmented nature of social movements. But the relationship is much more complex than this dichotomy would suggest. NGOs often initiate or sustain social movements (Lehman, 1990) or are the institutional vehicles that articulate protest and collective action (Diani, 1992). As Clarke (1993) demonstrated for a case in the Philippines, some social movements are composed to a significant extent of NGO coalitions. More closely integrating the separate literatures that have developed around social movements and NGOs would help illuminate their complex interrelationships and also encourage us to see how these processes of association change over time.

FOCUSING ON PROCESS

One productive way to think about civil society is not as a sector that either contests or supports the aims of governments but as a "vector of agonistic contentions over governmental relations" (Gordon, 1991: 23). This emphasis on the way civil society grows through a fueling of ongoing contentions, rather than merely through the multiplication and differentiation of structures, refocuses our attention on the processes and not merely the institutions of civil society. The expansion in the numbers of and connections among associations in South Asia in the past two decades and the struggle for new linkages support Adam Ferguson's processual view of society as an entity that repeatedly tears itself apart and endlessly remakes itself (Ferguson, 1995; see also Gordon, 1991).

Foucault's view of modern civil society as "the concrete ensemble within which ... economic men need to be positioned in order to be adequately manageable" also emphasizes the constraints that micro-level practices place upon the individual, and the shape they give to macro-level governmental rationalities (quoted in Gordon, 1991: 23).

Change rests on the ability of individuals and associations to challenge the terms of 'truths' and struggle to change the limits of what is 'thinkable'. Activists elsewhere have long been alert to this fundamental necessity for change: "Change the way people think," argued Steven Biko, "and things will never be the same".

The real challenge for analysts of civil society is to break down the 'black box' categories of NGO, social movement, and civil society and to examine the ways organizations so designated operate within and across local, regional, national, and transnational contexts. As noted earlier, associations designated as NGOs, for example, differ from one another in functions; the levels at which they operate; and their organizational structures, goals, and membership.[4]

Amid their wide range of translocal connections, all NGO practices remain discursively constructed through reference to the 'local'. Yet while a notion of the local remains centrally important to the legitimacy of NGOs, it is frustratingly elusive (Forbes, 1995; Peters, 1996; Ribot, 1996). Studies of civil society processes, that both alert us to the complexities of local sites and direct our attention from local sites to larger contexts, are both in and of the world systems.[5] Unpacking the micropolitics of these processes is dependent upon understanding these associations within larger contexts, and thus seeing them not as local wholes subsumed within larger national and global political contexts but as fragmented sites that have multiple connections nationally and transnationally (Marcus, 1995). In the past two decades, resistance to particular development projects, like the Sardar Sarovar dam on the Narmada River, for example, has often been conducted with the assistance of national coalitions and transnational issue networks of individuals and INGOs, even when the agendas of these disparate players are not wholly consistent (Baviskar, 1995; Fisher, 1995; Khagram, 2004).

It is critical to recognize that civil society, however we conceive of it, is not free from power struggles, nor is it an open space for rational argument and apolitical decision-making. This is perhaps easiest to see when we examine the debate surrounding civil society processes like the World Social Forum (WSF).

The WSF is the latest and fullest manifestation of the transnational connections I've been following for the past 20 years. The founders of the WSF have described it in the WSF Charter of Principles as

> an open meeting place for reflective thinking, democratic debate of ideas, formulation of proposals, free exchange of experiences and linking up for effective action, by groups and movements of civil society that are opposed to neo-liberalism and to domination of the world by capital and any form of imperialism, and are committed to building a global society of fruitful relationships among human beings and between humans and the Earth. (cited in Fisher and Ponniah, 2003a: 354)

In interviews, participants have acknowledged this aspect of the WSF and go on to emphasize its importance in facilitating the building of networks and alliances, the exchange of ideas, strategies, and tactics, and, perhaps most importantly for many activists who come from isolated areas, demonstrating that they are not 'bowling alone'.

For me, the 2004 WSF held in Mumbai, India, served as an interesting point of convergence for the interconnected series of research projects on activists I have undertaken during the past 20 years. It was the first place where the ethnic and human rights activists I knew from Nepal and the Narmada activists I knew from India, as well as a large set of their colleagues from other parts of the world, came together to exchange views and to discuss strategies. Without moving from my perch along the main avenue of the conference grounds, I encountered old acquaintances from the Janajati and Dalit movements in Nepal, current and former Narmada Bachao Andolan activists, academics/activists from Mumbai and Delhi, and members of the ICDRP.[6]

Each day from the 16th to the 21st of January 2004, over 80,000 people descended on the NESCO grounds off the Western Express Highway in the Goregaon neighbourhood of Mumbai to attend the 4th annual WSF. The WSF in Mumbai brought together a wide collection of political and social activists including leaders of local struggles, trade unions, farmer organizations, Dalits, ethnic activists, environmental activists, academics, and religious leaders. Among the attendees were Zapatistas, Tibetan monks, Nepali Dalits; in total, there were representatives of more than 2,660 organizations from 132 countries. Among those facilitating the WSF were over 800 volunteers and 180 translators using 13 languages. The meetings attracted 3,200 journalists. All of these individuals converged on the NESCO grounds for a wide array of panels, roundtable discussions, conferences, public meetings, and impromptu gatherings and street demonstrations. Panels organized by attending groups like Attac, the National Alliance of People's Movements, NACDOR, DAWN, SAPI,[7] and Forum for the Global South, covered topics ranging from 'Land, Water and Food Security' to 'Militarization' to 'Combat Against a Common Enemy'. They included sessions on 'Problems faced by Domestic Workers', 'Dalit Oppression and the Struggle for Assertion', 'Forming a Directory of Social Movements', 'How to Resist the World Bank', 'Defeat Bush 2004', 'NGOs, Social Movements, and the University', and 'The Evolution of Civil Society and Educational Alternatives in India'. Perhaps even more striking than the wide array of forum topics was the relentless and non-stop energy of dawn-to-dark street performances, marches, and spontaneous demonstrations that filled the air with rhythmic chants, drumbeats, and dust.

The 2004 WSF was a raw and dramatic demonstration of civil society energy in South Asia. It followed upon the successful Asian Social Forum held in Hyderabad in January 2003 and served as a catalyst to a number of regional forums in South Asia. The expanding set of WSF-like forums has been widely celebrated by activists in triumphant tones. Since the first WSF in 2001 the process has generated a wide range of regional and thematic forums.[8] This convergence in Mumbai encouraged me to think more explicitly about the various connections among the groups of activists I had come to know in South Asia.

Speyer (2003) has described the WSF as a civil society "Mercado — a marketplace where goods, services, and ideas from all over the planet were mixed and matched to create one of the most powerful political gatherings ever held on this planet". The WSF has also been described as carnival, jazz, religion, and as an arena, a political actor, a logo, and a brand. It is, in fact, all of these things. While the WSF presents itself as an open space, many social and political groups have attacked it as a co-opted imperialist tool. During the 2004 WSF in Mumbai, groups which saw themselves as opposing the WSF set up an alternative meeting called Mumbai Resistance 2004 (MR2004). MR2004 was a political project set up in criticism of, opposition to, and competition with the WSF that was variously described by its organizers as a 'genuine', 'anti-imperialist', 'class', 'activist', 'socialist', and 'revolutionary' forum. At issue were several key principles. One was the tendency of the WSF to accept funding from mainstream NGOs in the global north. A second was the statement in the WSF charter of principles that declared the forum open to all except those organizations that seek to take people's lives as a method of political action. Within the discourse of MR2004, NGOs clearly occupied the position of extreme evil: NGOs were seen as agents of imperialism that serve to confuse, corrupt, and mislead the masses, who would otherwise be in mass organizations, led by vanguard parties and carrying out a socialist revolution. Ironically perhaps, for some participants there was no real boundary between the meetings of the WSF or WR2004; they moved easily back and forth making contacts, sharing information, and discussing strategies without regard for what they saw as artificially imposed bureaucratic or ideological boundaries.

The debate demonstrates one of the ways in which civil society is a hotly contested political arena in which power is in flux (see also Schechter, 1999: 81). There are clear breaks among those civil society groups that wish to be part of the governance process, those who wish to remain autonomous from it, and those that wish to replace the current governance with new structures. There are also clear breaks in the strategies activists are willing to embrace to achieve their ends.

The active engagement in global or transnational arenas reflects a desire of many civil society groups to be part of a global governance process rather than simply fighting or protesting it. Though, to be sure, for some groups I have studied, like the ICDRP, for example, this is a fine line. Within the open space of the WSF, the desire of groups to be a part of the governance structure is regarded very suspiciously.[9]

There are two significantly different ways to think about civil society. The first model conceives of civil society as a means by which citizens are disciplined or brought under control, a process Foucault refers to as governmentality. The second conceives of civil society as a space where counter-hegemonic discourses become possible. Seen in this dual sense, civil society is simultaneously dangerous and full of promise; it is most certainly imperfect and yet evolves as a terrain within which various groups compete. Some civil society groups thus appear to be cooperative, accommodating, and assimilationist, seeking to sit at the table with other decision-makers; whereas, others are non-cooperative, struggling to remain independent of dominant power structures. We might then compare and contrast the strategies and aims of recent examples in the global arena, juxtaposing 'conference-goers', those civil society groups who actively engage in global or transnational gatherings seeking to be part of the governance process, with 'meeting-stalkers', those groups who follow and protest the meetings of global institutions in Seattle, Washington DC, Prague, or Bangkok. Groups like the ICDRP and forums like the WSF may present an alternative to the strategies engaged in by conference-goers and meeting-stalkers, providing a middle path of cautious, occasional, and conditional cooperation. In the World Commission on Dams case, for example, groups engaged with (rather than protested the actions of) governments, the private sector, and international institutions under very specific circumstances to achieve limited ends that could then be used to further ongoing political efforts.

Until recently, many of the groups that anthropologists study have not seen themselves within the realm of civil society, though, when participating within processes like the WSF, this is beginning to change. There remains a tension between the way academics categorize these groups and they way they would categorize themselves. This is a tension that reflects the different goals of activists and academics, between categories that best aid understanding and those that generate greater political agency. Both within national and transnational contexts there is a great deal at stake in the claim to be a legitimate voice of 'civil society'. Effectiveness may rest in part on access to arenas of decision-making, while legitimacy derives from a plausible claim to represent the interests of a genuine local constituency. In their own discussions, ICDRP participants highlighted distinctions among civil society groups and placed high value on the ability to channel the interests of project-affected peoples. At the same time, they also recognized the dangers of both co-option that might result from excessive cooperation and marginalization that stems from complete non-cooperation. For many of the participants of ICDRP, desires to be part of the governance structure are regarded very suspiciously and they recognize the fine line between their own strategies and those of 'conference-goers'.

The political space for the emergence of transnationally connected civil societies, a space where interactions and common discourses can evolve that are understood by individuals coming out of different cultures, may well be represented by the processes of the ICDRP, the WCD, and the WSF. However, our understanding of these processes is not aided by quickly labelling it and lauding it as civil society, especially as it is clear that this emergent process is far from the kind of civil societies found grounded in nation-states. These differences can be best clarified through the analysis of empirical cases.

Studies can avoid simple generalizations and reveal the rich ideological and functional diversity of civil society processes if they *(a)* focus on civil society as an arena composed of uneven and fragmented space within which battles from society at large are internalized rather than as a set of entities, and *(b)* focus on fluid and changing local, regional, national, and international processes and connections, which both potentially support and suppress an insurrection of subjugated knowledges. Placing the emphasis on a fluid web of relationships reveals the connections of actions to numerous levels and fields and draws our attention to the flows of funding, knowledge, ideas, and people that move through these levels, sites, and associations. These multiple relationships include those among intermediaries, governments, constituencies, communities, leaders, elites, municipalities, state institutions, other local, national, and INGOs, social movements, and NGO coalitions. This kind of transnationalized but fragmented civil society presents both opportunities and considerable risks, and negotiating its shoals requires both skill and luck, assets whose unequal availability still favours northern groups over southern.

The Janajati, Narmada, WCD, ICDRP, and WSF processes raise questions about the engagement of transnational alliances with the disparate voices of a widely varied civil society. How and why do some local voices come to be amplified while others fail to find an effective outlet through the practices of NGO advocacy alliances? The amplification of voices is imperfect and selective—for every group brought into an alliance there are several others which are ignored. This was true in the alliance against the Narmada and complaints of this nature have already been heard among those groups feeling increasingly isolated from the discussions and negotiations concerning the WCD.

There are both intentional and unintentional constraints on this process of selection and interactions among activists and the possibility for effectively participating vary depending upon two sets of factors. One of these is the nature of domestic political context within which local groups operate: some institutions and states are more open to leverage than others and we expect that activist groups from democratic states will be more integrated into transnational alliances. Second, among these groups, those whose values and principled ideas fit or can be made to be consistent with INGO campaign goals and those whose members have demonstrated highly developed 'multi-focal' framing skills are more prominent and influential in these alliances.

NEW IMAGINED COMMUNITIES

Civil society networks may be usefully seen as imagined or invented communities. This tendency has a great deal of support: Calhoun (1991), for instance, has argued that there can be a great many different kinds of imagined communities. But whose imagined community is this? At best, this is a fragmented world of cross-cutting communities where different sets of actors define different realms of interaction and fields of trust based on differently perceived goals, values, and strategies. Gupta and Ferguson (1992: 9) have suggested that there are new forms of imagining community and that "any strictly bounded sense of community or locality [is] obsolete". Hannerz (1996: 20), too, has commented on the tendency of analysts to find new forms of imagining community "all over the place". But to refit the trope of community to span the spatially discontiguous connections and solidarity that characterize civil society activist networks we need to ask what these new kinds of imagining, specifically, the imagining of an activist community, entails.

Like the national collectivities to which Benedict Anderson applied the term "imagined communities", these transnational collectivities are distinguished by "the style in which they are imagined".[10] While the shifting construction of space and time, which results from endless capitalist adaptation, creates for many individuals severe problems of identity, and weakens allegiances to a local community, city, region, or nation, it also creates an opportunity for greater identification with transnational issue networks, epistemic communities,[11] or interest groups.[12] The social practice of transnational advocacy networks creates a social space within which new forms of community are possible.[13]

Many of the civil society networks in South Asia are unbounded and fluid and thus differ in significant ways from the imagined communities of nationalism: the values, allegiances, and global flows among translocal activist networks crosscut national, regional, and local collectivities. The communities of activists they engender, while spatially diffuse, nevertheless share values and a sense of belonging. Networks like those which gave rise to the alliance involved in the opposition to the Sardar Sarovar Project, for example, or many of those which interact through the WSF forums are organized around shared discourses and shared values, or at least the presumption of shared values.[14] Gupta and Ferguson (1992: 9) have argued that

> something like a transnational public sphere has certainly rendered any strictly bounded sense of community or locality obsolete. At the same time it has enabled the creation of forms of solidarity and identity that do not rest on an appropriation of space where contiguity and face-to face contact are paramount.

This notion of community was explicitly invoked by activists within the ICDRP and WSF who, in interviews with me, frequently described themselves as members of an activist community, a social justice community, an NGO community, or a human rights community.[15]

Yet, despite the sense of belonging and shared goals, emerging communities like the WSF are also marked by an element of heterogeneity, fragmentation, and transformation. The networks within which the WSF arose are part of an emerging transnational civil society which is "an arena of struggle, a fragmented and contested area" (Keck and Sikkink, 1998: 33–4) and where politics focus on different groups jostling for position and recognition—both by government and by other groups.

The transformative potential of the civil society processes may emerge less from ordered and controlled participation than from relatively chaotic sets of multiple opportunities and interdependencies. Thus, 'empowerment' may not be achieved best by institution building or perpetuating existent associations, and may even be undermined by the bureaucratization of once-radical activist organizations. In assessing the success or failure of activist groups, it may be more appropriate to look at the permanence of the process of activism rather than the survival of particular social or political activist groups. Civil society groups may come and go, but the space created in their passing may contribute to new activism that builds up after them and continues their efforts.

The growing interconnectedness of a multi-centric world and the often trans-local activities of growing numbers of non-state actors have had significant impacts on the sites and communities of South Asia that have been the focus of anthropological research. While our initial attention to activists may focus on community-based organizations, the networks and alliances they increasingly have come to form open up new possibilities and call for innovative research methodologies.

New work by anthropologists in South Asia, as amply demonstrated by the results presented in this volume, needs not only to contribute to our knowledge of what activists are doing, but also to provide insights into the fluidity of local and trans-local networks. The challenge is to consider the practice of activist groups as one specific possible form of collective action and human community and to undertake comparative analysis of the different configurations these forms of collective action have taken and are taking in a complexly woven field of trans-local connections.

NOTES

1. My research on civil society activism over the past 15 years has focused on several distinct multi-stakeholder processes, including: the Janajati movement in Nepal (Fisher, 2001a), the resistance to the damming of the Narmada River (Fisher, 1995, 2000), the involvement of the International Committee on Dams, Rivers, and People (ICDRP) with the World Commission on Dams (Fisher, 2001b, 2009), and the World Social Forum (Fisher and Ponniah, 2003a, b).
2. "I don't know what you mean by 'glory'", Alice said.
   Humpty Dumpty smiled contemptuously, "Of course you don't—till I tell you. I meant 'there's a nice knock down argument for you!"
   "But glory doesn't mean 'a nice knock-down argument", Alice objected.
   "When I use a word", Humpty Dumpty said in a rather scornful tone, 'it means just what I choose it to mean—neither more nor less".
   "The question is", said Alice, 'whether you *can* make words mean so many different things".
3. My distinction between the terms 'globalization' and 'transnationalism' builds upon Hannerz (1996), Basch et al. (1994), Kearney (1995), Giddens (1990), and Glick Schiller et al. (1992).
4. In an attempt to conceptually organize such diverse groups, analysts have distinguished among associations according to various sets of criteria, littering the literature with acronyms. Designations like CBOs (community-based organizations), GROs (grassroots organizations, or POs (people's organizations) distinguish membership-based, locally autonomous groups from groups of urban intellectuals working in relatively impoverished settings as intermediary

support organizations (ISOs), which are sometimes varyingly designated as MSOs (membership support organizations) or GSOs or GRSOs (grassroots support organizations) (see, in particular, Carroll, 1992; Fisher, 1993; Korten, 1987, 1990).

5. See, for example, Marcus (1995). One such study is Baviskar's insightful study (1995) of *adivasis* along the Narmada River.
6. The International Committee on Dams, Rivers, and People, a transnational coalition that had attending members and colleagues from India, Nepal, Pakistan, and Sri Lanka as well as Brazil, Switzerland, Japan, Thailand, and the United States.
7. Attac is an anti-globalization network; the National Alliance of People's Movements brings together social movements in India; NACDOR is the National Conference of Dalit Organisations [of India]; DAWN is Development Alternatives for Women for a New Era, SAPI stands for South Asian Peoples' Initiatives, a joint platform for marginalized people's social movements set up for the Mumbai meeting.
8. Speyer (2003) summarizes most of these through the end of 2004.
9. For more on the ICDRP, see Fisher (2009).
10. Anderson (1991: 6). With respect to imagined global communities, see also the discussion by Lash and Urry (1994: 314–16), who contrast two understandings of the global—one in which the universal triumphs over the particular, and a second, more fragmented model, built around notions like Heidegger's "being-in-the-world" or Bourdieu's "habitus", a model which provides both the political space for new communities and is at the same time "the world of racism and ethnic hate" (ibid.: 315). Lash and Urry place global communities in between Heidegger's "being-in-the world" and Anderson's "quintessentially modern" imagined communities, characterizing them as "invented communities"—communities into which we are not so much thrown as communities into which we throw ourselves (ibid.: 316). A full response to the valuable discussion by Lash and Urry is not appropriate here, but my use of the term 'invented communities' for global networks is not meant to align them with the imagined communities of nationalism but to contrast them with both these and with the 'worlded' rather than global character of many social movements.
11. Haas (1992) and Keck and Sikkink (1998: 1, 30) usefully distinguish epistemic communities (based on shared causal ideas and professional ties) from other activist groups. As described by Haas, epistemic communities are transnational networks of experts characterized by a shared command of potentially instrumental technical knowledge, common values, agreed ways of testing truth, and a shared understanding of causality. Epistemic communities are generally limited to groups of scientists and exclude activists.
12. Robert Keohane (1995: 184) has argued that the number of committed individuals who think and act transnationally is the critical component in globalization. Some of these actions are driven by different ideas and motivations—some by shared principled ideas, others by shared causal ideas, and others by shared understandings about the possibilities for action. The alliances involved in the ICDRP and the WSF derive primarily from a set of shared principled ideas—ideas that specify criteria for determining whether actions are right or wrong and whether outcomes are just or unjust. To the extent that the actions of these

networks challenge sovereignty, they also draw on ideas about the possibilities for action. See also Sikkink (1993).

13. Scholars are beginning to note the important role played by the internet in the building of these communities. For early discussions of this, see Linda Harasim's (1993) discussion of computer networks as social space.
14. And yet, at the same time, values are often contested within as well as by means of these networks.
15. This kind of open acknowledgement of community was far more common for actors located in developed than in developing countries. Note, however, that country of origin is not the only factor that might account for this difference. My interview subjects in the global north were also invariably urban based, while those in South Asia were often closely tied to rural locales and deeply invested in developing community ties among rural residents with whom they worked.

REFERENCES

Anderson, Benedict. 1991. *Imagined Communities: Reflections on the Origin and Spread of Nationalism*. London: Verso.

Appadurai, Arjun. 1990. 'Disjuncture and Difference in the Global Cultural Economy', *Public Culture*, 2(2): 1–24.

Basch, Linda, Nina Glick-Schiller, and Christina Szanton Blanc. 1994. *Nations Unbound: Transnational Projects, Postcolonial Predicaments, and Deterritorialized Nation-States*. Basel: Gordon and Breach.

Baviskar, A. 1995. *In the Belly of the River*. Oxford: Oxford University Press.

Calhoun, C. 1991. 'Indirect Relationships and Imagined Communities', in P. Bourdieu and J.S. Coleman (eds), *Social Theory for a Changing Society*, pp. 95–121. Boulder, CO: Westview.

Carroll, T.F. 1992. *Intermediary NGOs: The Supporting Link in Grassroots Development*. West Hartford, CT: Kumarian.

Chazan. N. 1992. 'Africa's Democratic Challenge', *World Policy Journal*, 9(2): 279–307.

Clarke, G. 1993. 'People Power? Non-governmental Organizations and Philippine Politics since 1986', *Philippine Quarterly of Culture and Society*, 21(3): 231–56.

Diani, M. 1992. 'The Concept of a Social Movement', *The Sociological Review*, 40(1): 1–25.

Ferguson, Adam. 1995 (1767). *An Essay on the History of Civil Society*. Cambridge: Cambridge University Press.

Fisher, W.F. 1993. *The Road from Rio: Sustainable Development and the Nongovernmental Movement in the Third World*. Westport, CT: Praeger.

Fisher, William F. (ed.). 1995. *Toward Sustainable Development? Struggling over India's Narmada River*. Armonk, NY: ME Sharpe.

———. 1997. 'Doing Good? The Politics and Antipolitics of NGO Practices', *Annual Review of Anthropology*, 26: 439–64.

———. 2000. 'Sacred Rivers, Sacred Dams: Competing Visions of Social Justice and Sustainable Development along the Narmada', in C.K. Chapple and M.E.

Tucker (eds), *Hinduism and Ecology*. Cambridge, MA: Harvard University Press, pp. 401–30.

———. 2001a. 'Grands barrages, flux mondiaux, et petites gens', *Critique International*, 13(October): 123–38.

———. 2001b. *Fluid Boundaries: Forming and Transforming Identity in Nepal*. New York: Columbia University Press.

———. 2009. 'Local Displacement, Global Activism', in A. Oliver-Smith (ed.), *Development and Dispossession: The Crisis of Forced Displacement and Resettlement*, pp. 163–80. Santa Fe: School for Advanced Research Press.

Fisher, William F. and Thomas Ponniah (eds). 2003a. *Another World is Possible*. London and New York: Zed.

———. 2003b. 'Under a Tree in Porto Alegre: Reflections on the World Social Forum', OpenDemocracy. Available at www.opendemocracy.com

Forbes, Ann. 1995. 'The Importance of Being Local: Villagers, NGOs, and the World Bank in the Arun Valley', paper presented at AAA Annual Meeting, Washington DC, November 19–23.

Giddens, Anthony. 1990. *The Consequences of Modernity*. Cambridge: Polity.

Glick Schiller, Nina, Linda Basch, and Christina Blanc-Szanton. 1992. 'Transnationalism: A New Analytical Framework for Understanding Migration', in Nina Glick Schiller, Linda Basch, and Christina Blanc-Szanton (eds), *Towards a Transnational Perspective on Migration: Race, Class, Ethnicity, and Nationalism Reconsidered*, pp. 1–24. New York: New York Academy of Sciences.

Gordon, C. 1991. 'Governmental Rationality', in G. Burchell, C. Gordon, and P. Miller (eds), *The Foucault Effect*, pp. 1–52. Chicago: Chicago University Press.

Gupta, A. and J. Ferguson. 1992. 'Beyond "Culture": Space, Identity, and the Politics of Difference', *Cultural Anthropology*, 7: 222–37.

Haas, P.M. 1992. 'Epistemic Communities and International Policy Coordination', *International Organizations*, 46(1): 1–36.

Hannerz, Ulf. 1996. *Transnational Connections: Culture, People, Places*. London and New York: Routledge.

Harasim, Linda. 1993. 'Global Networks', in L. Harasim (ed.), *Global Networks: Computers and International Communication*. Cambridge, MA: MIT Press.

Hunt, Louis D. 1999. 'Civil Society and the Idea of a Commercial Republic', in M. Shechter (ed.), *The Revival of Civil Society*, pp. 11–37. New York: St. Martin's Press.

Kearney, M. 1995. 'The Local and the Global: The Anthropology of Globalization and Transnationalism', *Annual Review of Anthropology*, 24: 547–65.

Keck, Margaret E. and Kathryn Sikkink. 1998. *Activists beyond Borders: Advocacy Networks in International Politics*. Ithaca and London: Cornell University Press.

Keohane, Robert. 1995. *Power and Governance in a Partially Globalized World*. London and New York: Routledge.

Khagram, S. 2004. *Dams and Development: Transnational Struggles for Water and Power*. New Delhi: Oxford University Press.

Korten, D.C. 1987. 'Third Generation NGO Strategies: A Key to People-centered Development', *World Development*, 15(suppl): 145–60.

———. 1990. *Getting to the 21st Century: Voluntary Action and the Global Agenda*. West Hartford, CT: Kumarian.

Lash, S. and J. Urry. 1994. *Economies of Signs and Space*. New York: Sage Publications.

Lehman, D. 1990. *Democracy and Development in Latin America: Economics, Politics, and Religion in the Postwar Period*. London: Polity.

Lewis, David and Nazneen Kanji. 2009. *Nongovernmental Organisations and Development*. London and New York: Routledge.

Marcus, George. 1995. 'Ethnography in/of the World System: The Emergence of Multi-sited Ethnography', *Annual Review of Anthropology*, 24: 95–117.

Marshall, Miklos. 2004. 'What's Next for Civil Society: More Powerful than Ever', *Elections Today* 12(2). Available at www.ciaonet.org/olj/et/et_v12n2/et_v12n2b.pdf (accessed on 17 August 2009).

Peters, Pauline. 1996. 'Who's Local Here? The Politics of Participation in Development', *Cultural Survival Quarterly*, 20(3): 22–60.

Ribot, Jesse. 1996. 'Participation without Representation', *Cultural Survival Quarterly*, 20(3): 40–4.

Schechter, Michael (ed.). 1999. *The Revival of Civil Society: Global and Comparative Perspectives*. New York: St. Martin's Press.

Sikkink, K. 1993. 'Human Rights, Principled Issue Networks, and Sovereignty in Latin America', *International Organization*, 47(3): 411–41.

Speyer, Anne Marie. 2003. 'The World Social Forum: Overview of an Ongoing Process', *Convergence* 36(3–4): 19–36.

Glossary and Abbreviations

ADAB	Association of Development Agencies in Bangladesh founded in 1974
ADB	Asian Development Bank
Awami League	mainstream secular political party in Bangladesh founded by Sheikh Mujibur Rahman, now led by his daughter Sheikh Hasina
Bahun	*see* Brahman
BC	*see* OBC
BDC	Block Development Committee (India): elected body at the level of the block, i.e. above the village and below the *jilla*
BDO	Block Development Officer (India): civil servant tasked with assisting elected representatives at the block level
BJP	Bharatiya Janata Party, founded in 1980 as a successor to the Bharatiya Sangh Party; the BJP led coalition governments and provided the Indian Prime Minister from 1998 to 2004
Block	Indian local government unit or tier larger than a village and smaller than a district; several villages make a block
BNP	Bangladesh Nationalist Party, mainstream political party founded by General Ziaur Rahman in 1978; his widow, Khaleda Zia, led a four-party government from 2001 to 2006
Brahman	highest of the four *varna*s, the priestly caste; known as 'Bahun' in Nepal, where they make up approximately 13 per cent of the population
CBO	Community-based Organization
CDO	Chief District Officer
Chhetri (Chetri)	the Nepali spelling of *ksatriya*, the second, warrior-ruler *varna*; in Nepal it refers in particular to the largest of the Parbatiya castes,

	comprising approximately 16 per cent of the total Nepali population, who are in many Nepali villages the socially and politically dominant caste
CO	central office
Congress	oldest Indian political party; for Nepal, see NC
CPN	Communist Party of Nepal, founded in 1949, it first split in 1962
CPN-M	Communist Party of Nepal (Maoist), the name adopted in 1995 by one of the two factions into which the Communist Party of Nepal (Unity Centre) had split the previous year; it launched its 'People's War' in February 1996; following the Second People's Movement of April 2006, it entered mainstream politics and won the largest number of votes (nearly 30 per cent) in the elections of April 2008
CPN-ML	Communist Party of Nepal (Marxist-Leninist): communist grouping founded in 1978 in east Nepal by those who had been active in the Jhapa uprising; it later was one of the main elements that formed the CPN-UML in 1991
CPN-UML	Communist Party of Nepal (Unified Marxist-Leninist), the main parliamentary opposition party in Nepal between 1991 and 2002, which formed a minority government on its own for nine months from 1994 to 1995 and was later a partner in coalitions; despite the name and the communist history and affiliation, it is essentially a social democratic party; came third in the elections of April 2008
Dalit	modern term for ex-Untouchables, the lowest category in the caste system, outside and below the four *varnas*; literally 'the oppressed'
Damai	tailor caste (Dalits) in the Nepalese hills
DFID	the UK's Department (Ministry) for International Development
DWLC	the Department of Wildlife Conservation, Sri Lanka, set up in 1949, then called the Department of Wildlife (renamed in 1970)

EFL	Environmental Foundation Limited, a non-profit public interest law foundation set up in Sri Lanka in 1981 to monitor the enforcement of environmental laws
FFPO	Fauna and Flora Protection Ordinance, passed in Ceylon in 1937 and amended several times thereafter
FNB	Federation of NGOs in Bangladesh, founded at government behest in 2003
FO	field office (of a development organization)
GATT	the General Agreement on Tariffs and Trade, set up in 1947 to negotiate reductions in trade tariffs; replaced by the World Trade Organization in 1994
GO	governmental organization
GONGOs	government-organized NGOs
GPSC	Game Protection Society of Ceylon, founded 1894; it changed its name to the Ceylon Game and Fauna Protection Society in 1930 and later to the Wildlife and Nature Protection Society (WNPS)
gram panchayat	village council, the lowest level of local government, with elected members and an elected chair (*sarpanch* or *pradhan*) (India)
gram sabha	village assembly, attended by all adult members of the village, which meets twice yearly or more regularly to check on the actions of the council (India)
ICDRP	International Committee on Dams, Rivers, and People founded in 1997
INGO	international non-governmental organization
Janajati	originally Hindi neologism coined to translate 'tribe' in the 1930s, it was adopted in Nepali at the very end of the 1980s and gained currency after 1990 to refer to tribal groups in Nepal; often translated as 'ethnic group' in English, the preferred translation of NEFIN is 'indigenous nationality'
Janajati Mahasangh	*see* NEFIN
jati (in Nepal usually *jat*)	caste; literally 'birth' or species

JVP	Janatha Vimukthi Peramuna, a violent insurgent movement in southern Sri Lanka (1971–73), later political party representing rural Sinhala nationalists
Kham Magar	sub-section of the Magars, speaking their own language, Kham, consisting of approximately 50,000 people in over a hundred settlements spread across 25 VDCs
khas	land reclaimed from rivers/sea earmarked by government for redistribution to the landless (Bangladesh); in Nepal the word is an old term for Chhetri
LTTE	Liberation Tigers of Tamil Eelam: founded in 1976 it became the dominant armed group fighting for an independent Tamil homeland in the north and east of Sri Lanka until its military defeat by the Sri Lankan army in May 2009
Madhesi	literally 'an inhabitant of Madhes/Madhyades', it has become a highly contested new ethnic category within Nepal for inhabitants of the Nepalese Tarai who share language and cultural heritage with Indians on the other side of the border, principally castes such as Yadavs, Rajputs, and Brahmans. Other groups, such as Tharus, Muslims and have been listed as Madhesis by the Nepalese state and are claimed as Madhesis by Madhesi political parties and activists, but their own activists organized vociferously during 2009 to insist that they should be considered indigenous Tarai-dwellers and a religious minority respectively instead of Madhesis
Magar	largest of the Janajati groups in Nepal with a population of 1,622,399 (7.2 per cent) according to the 2001 census
Magarant Autonomous Region	an ethnically defined political region set up by the Maoists in 2004–06, with its headquarters in the village of Thabang

Mahila Mandal	women's circles (India), encouraged by local development agencies
mandal	circle, club, association
MLA	Member of Legislative Assembly, i.e. an elected representative to a state assembly in India
mukhiya	old Nepali term for the headman of a village
NC	Nepali Congress, founded 1947; won landslide election victory in 1959; banned 1960–90; the largest Nepali political party, 1990–2002; came second to Maoists in 2008
NEFIN	Nepal Federation of Indigenous Nationalities (Nepal Janajati Adivasi Mahasangh), a federal body with one representative organization for each Janajati group in Nepal (*see* nefin.org.np) (previously known as NEFEN, the Nepal Federation of Nationalities, the term 'indigenous' was added in 2003)
Newar	ethnic group in Nepal, who are included in the Janajati category, despite being concentrated in the Kathmandu Valley and sub-divided by caste. According to the 2001 census they numbered 1,245,232 (5.5 per cent)
NGO	non-governmental organization
Nijera Kori	Bangladeshi NGO founded in 1980 by activists opposed to the dependency created by 'service-delivery NGOs'; the name means 'We do it ourselves'
NPC	National Planning Commission
OBC	Other Backward Classes (Indian official term for those low castes who are neither Scheduled Castes nor Scheduled Tribes but are classified as educationally and economically 'backward')
Panchayat	*(a)* literally and originally 'rule of five [elders]', i.e. supposedly 'traditional' local or caste councils widely found across South Asia; hence the name was adopted for *(b)* democratically elected local councils, the new institutions of local self-government in India after independence; it was also

	adopted as *(c)* the name both of specific local (village, district) and national councils and the national legislature in the period of 'partyless democracy' (1960–90) in Nepal; hence *(d)* it is also used as the name of the regime and period in Nepal of that time
panchayati raj	literally 'rule by panchayats', it is the Indian term used for local government with elected bodies (panchayats) at the levels of village (*gram*), block (*kshetra*), and district (*zilla*)
People's Movement	(*jan andolan*), the commonly accepted name for the revolution of 1990 that overthrew the Panchayat regime; the revolution of 2006 is known as People's Movement II
People's War	(*jan yuddha*) the name given by the Maoists to their insurgency, begun in Nepal in 1996
PRA	Participatory Rural Appraisal, techniques for involving rural people in assessing their own situation, popularized by Robert Chambers
Pradhan Panch	village head (Nepal) during the Panchayat era (1962–90)
pradhan	head of a village council in India (also called *sarpanch*)
Proshika	founded in 1975, Proshika is one of the largest Bangladeshi NGOs; it claims to have brought a million people out of poverty, to have made over a million literate, and to have planted over a billion trees; the name comes from the first syllables of the Bengali words meaning training, education, and action
purdah	literally 'curtain' or 'covering'; refers to rules of female modesty (including wearing the veil), and restrictions on women's movement, especially in north India and Pakistan
Rana	surname assumed by the family (previously named Kunwar) who provided the hereditary prime ministers of Nepal from 1846 to 1951; hence the name of the period of Nepalese history when the Shah kings were reduced to figureheads without real power

RPP	Rashtriya Prajatantra Party a.k.a. Nepal Democratic Party (post 1990 Nepal): rightist party led by prominent politicians who had participated in the Panchayat regime
Sadbhavana Party	regionalist party based in the Nepalese Tarai
samiti	committee
SC	Scheduled Castes, official Indian term for those formerly untouchable castes placed 'on the schedule' and entitled to 'reservations', i.e. positive discrimination
seva	'service', particularly selfless social work on behalf of others
SLFP	Sri Lanka Freedom Party, founded in 1951, generally considered more left-wing and more nationalist than the UNP
SSNCC	Social Service National Coordination Council, Nepal, set up in 1977
suruwal	Nepali trousers that are baggy at the top and tight around the shins
swabhasha	literally 'own language', used for education in Sinhala or Tamil in Sri Lanka
SWC	Social Welfare Council, Nepal, the body with which NGOs are obliged to register in order to receive funds from foreign sources
Tarai (Terai)	strip of Gangetic plains territory belonging to Nepal and bordering India, now home to half the Nepali population
Thakuri	royal sub-caste, considered superior to ordinary Chhetris, in Nepal; equivalent to Rajput in India
Thangmi	small Janajati group numbering around 35,000 in Nepal and in the Indian states of West Bengal (Darjeeling district) and Sikkim
Tharu	large ethnic group found throughout the Nepalese Tarai and the neighbouring states of India; in Nepal it is classed as a Janajati group and is the second largest among such groups, counting 1,533,879 people (6.7 per cent) according to the 2001 census

UML	*see* CPN-UML
UNP	United National Party, Sri Lanka, founded in 1946, generally considered more right-wing and pro-Western than the SLFP
UPF	United People's Front (Samyukta Jan Morcha), the political wing and electoral vehicle of the Unity Centre, a communist group which split in 1994; one of the factions subsequently became the CPN-M Nepal
VDC	Village Development Committee, the smallest political unit in Nepal; renamed from 'Village Panchayat' after the fall of the Panchayat regime in 1990
WCD	World Commission on Dams, founded in 1997 and wound up in 2001 with the release of the report *Dams and Development: A New Framework for Decision-making*
WNPS	Wildlife and Nature Protection Society (Sri Lanka): *see* GPSC
WSF	World Social Forum, annual meetings of 'civil society' or 'third way' organizations and movements, started with Porto Alegre in Brazil in 2001, and held in Mumbai in 2004, with the aim of producing more democratic alternatives to the Davos World Economic Forum
zilla parishad	district councils (India)

About the Editor and Contributors

EDITOR

David N. Gellner is Professor of Anthropology at the University of Oxford and a Fellow of All Souls. He is the author of *Monk, Householder, and Tantric Priest* (1992) and *The Anthropology of Buddhism and Hinduism: Weberian Themes* (2001), and the co-author (with Sarah LeVine) of *Rebuilding Buddhism: The Theravada Movement in Twentieth-Century Nepal* (2005). Among his other edited volumes are *Contested Hierarchies: A Collaborative Ethnography of Caste among the Newars of the Kathmandu Valley, Nepal* (with D. Quigley, 1995), *Nationalism and Ethnicity in a Hindu Kingdom* (with J. Pfaff-Czarnecka and J. Whelpton, Harwood, 1997; 2nd edition, 2008), *Resistance and the State: Nepalese Experiences* (2003; Berghahn, 2007), *Nepalis Inside and Outside Nepal* and *Political and Social Transformations in North India and Nepal* (both with H. Ishii and K. Nawa, 2007), *Local Democracy in South Asia* (with K. Hachhethu, 2008), and *Ethnic Activism and Civil Society in South Asia* (2009).

CONTRIBUTORS

William F. Fisher is Associate Professor and Director of IDCE (International Development, Community and Environment Programs) at Clark University, USA, Research Professor at the Marsh Institute at Clark University, and Visiting Associate Professor of Social Studies at Harvard University. He received a PhD in anthropology and MIA in international affairs from Columbia University. He is the editor of *Toward Sustainable Development: Struggling over India's Narmada River* and the author of *Fluid Boundaries: Forming and Transforming Identity in Nepal* (2001).

Arjun Guneratne is Professor of Anthropology at Macalester College in Saint Paul, Minnesota, USA, and Editor of *Himalaya*, the *Journal of the Association for Nepal and Himalayan Studies*. He is a Director of the American Institute for Sri Lankan Studies. He received his PhD in 1994 for a study of ethnic identity formation among the Tharu of Nepal, which formed the basis for a book, *Many Tongues, One People: The Making of Tharu Identity in Nepal* (2002); he has edited a second book, *Culture and Environment in the Himalaya*, published in 2010. He is currently working on a study of the development of environmental sensibility in Sri Lanka and the role played in it by Sri Lanka's urban middle class.

Siripala Hettige is Professor of Sociology at the University of Colombo, Sri Lanka and is the Sri Lankan director of the MIDEA project. He is also the honorary Director, Social Policy Analysis and Research Centre (SPARC) at the same university. He had his undergraduate education in sociology from the University of Colombo, while his PhD is from Monash University Australia. He has published over ten books and edited volumes and numerous research articles on a range of themes such as social inequality, urban informal sector, migration, education, health policy, social development, and poverty. Prof. Hettige currently chairs the Social Science Research Committee of the National Science Foundation of Sri Lanka.

Mrigendra Bahadur Karki is Lecturer in Sociology at Tribhuvan University, Nepal, and a member of the Centre for Nepal and Asian Studies. He was part of the project 'The Impact of Activism in Nepal: An Anthropological and Historical Study', directed by David N. Gellner and Krishna Hachhethu, from 2003 to 2006. His paper, co-authored with David N. Gellner, on 'The Sociology of Activism in Nepal: Some Preliminary Considerations' will appear in 2007 in H. Ishii, D.N. Gellner, and K. Nawa (eds), *Political and Social Transformations in North India and Nepal: Social Dynamics in Northern South Asia, Vol 2*. He is currently preparing his PhD for Kwansei Gakuin University on the topic of 'Motivation, Networking and the Recruitment Processes among Activists in Nepal'.

David Lewis is Professor of Social Policy and Development at the London School of Economics and Political Science. An anthropologist by training, he has carried out research in Bangladesh since the mid-1980s. His books include *Technologies and Transactions: Interaction* *between New Technology and Agrarian Structure in Bangladesh* (1991), *Anthropology, Development and the Postmodern Challenge* (1996, co-authored with K. Gardner), and *The Management of Non-governmental Development Organisations* (2001 and 2007). His recent edited volumes include *Exploring Civil Society: Political and Cultural Contexts* (2004, co-edited with M. Glasius and H. Seckinelgin), and *The Aid Effect: Giving and Governing in International Development* (2005) and *Development Brokers and Translators: The Ethnography of Aid and Agencies* (2006), both co-edited with David Mosse.

Anne de Sales is 'Chargée de Recherches' at the CNRS and member of the 'Laboratoire d'Ethnologie et de Sociologie Comparative' of the University of Nanterre-Paris X (France). She has published widely on the Kham Magars, including the monograph, *Je Suis Né de vos Jeux de Tambours: La Religion Chamanique des Magar du Nord* (1991).

Sara Shneiderman is a Research Fellow in Anthropology at St Catharine's College, University of Cambridge. Her research explores the relationships between political discourse, ritual practice, cultural performance, and cross-border migration in producing identities in the Himalayas. She has conducted fieldwork in Nepal, India, and China's Tibetan Autonomous Region, and holds a PhD from Cornell University, USA. Recent articles include 'Reservations, Federalism and the Politics of Recognition in Nepal', *Economic and Political Weekly*, 43(19); 'Revisiting Ethnography, Recognizing a Forgotten People: The Thangmi of Nepal and India', *Studies in Nepali History and Society*, 11(1); 'Agency and Resistance in the Thangmi-Newar Ritual Relationship: An Analysis of Devikot-Khadga Jatra in Dolakha, Nepal', *The European Bulletin of Himalayan Research*, 28; and 'The Path to Janasarkar in Dolakha District: Towards an Ethnography of the Maoist Movement', in M. Hutt (ed.), *Himalayan People's War: Nepal's Maoist Rebellion*.

Celayne Heaton Shrestha is a Visiting Research Fellow in the Anthropology Department at the University of Sussex, the UK. She is currently working on a research project exploring the effects of the insurgency on non-governmental public action in Nepal, under the ESRC-funded NGPA research programme. Articles and chapters published on Nepal's NGO sector include:

'The Ambiguities of Practising *jat* in 1990s Nepal: Elites, Caste and Everyday Life in Development NGOs', *South Asia*, 27(1): 39–85; 'NGOs as *Thekadar* or *Sevak*: Identity Crisis in Nepal's Non-governmental Sector', *European Bulletin of Himalayan Research*, 22: 5–36; 'Representing INGO-NGO Relations in Nepal: Are we being Donor-centric?' *Studies in Nepali History and Society*, 11(1): 65–96; and '"They can't mix like we can": Bracketing Differences and the Professionalisation of NGOs in Nepal', in D. Mosse and D. Lewis (eds), *Development Brokers and Translators: The Ethnography of Aid and Agencies*, Bloomfield: Kumarian, pp. 195–216.

Stefanie Strulik is Lecturer in Social Anthropology at the University of Zurich, Switzerland. From 2001 to 2005 she was Lecturer in the Department of Sociology, Sociology of Development Research Centre, University of Bielefeld, Germany. She has been working on India for many years with different research projects. For the last few years she has been researching gender and local democracy.

Name Index

Subject Index